Free Online Resource

A six-month subscription to ABA-PC3 for one student is included with the purchase of this book. In order to access this software you will need the registration number printed on inside front cover.

Simply email your name and the registration number to:

Support@abapc3.com and you will receive a registration package, 50 page user manual, and additional information.

What's Next for YOUR ABA Program?

ABA-PC3 Software Provides Online Curriculum Development Environment for ABA Teams

Behavior Analysts and Special Education Professionals providing intensive ABA services to students with autism or related disabilities have a powerful online resource called ABA Program Companion 3.0 (ABA-PC3). This is the newest version of a curriculum development tool specifically designed for ABA programs that helps with just about every phase of the program creation process from selecting individual target performances to writing detailed step-by-step procedures to generating data sheets, entering data, and producing graphs. There's also a program review module that structures the process of revising procedures based on observation and student performance measures.

Developed by a behavior analyst consulting to ABA programs for over 20 years, versions of this flexible and comprehensive software have been used by dozens of professional teams in schools and private programs since 2006. Users say they don't know how they ever got along without it.

The unique software has a built-in library of 650 programs and over 4000 individual learning targets, all fully customizable by the user for their particular circumstances. Users can quickly search the library using keywords and select appropriate programs or write their own, rapidly building a comprehensive set of student programs. The set can be implemented or used to quickly create multi-step *sequences* of programs for a variety of settings and instructional purposes.

The software helps focus and streamline the process of building an individualized comprehensive curriculum for students in an ABA program and provides a common workspace to enhance collaboration among different service providers on the special education team. In addition to the program library and learning targets, a variety of easy to use tools are included that help accomplish essential ABA implementation tasks including:

- Automatically-generated data sheets customized for each student

- Simple data entry screens for skill acquisition and behavior reduction programs

- 2-click graphing that automatically labels changing conditions

- Reports of active and mastered programs

- A structured workspace to assemble clear and well-defined prompt hierarchies and error correction strategies

- A centralized area to organize the goal performance specifications and individual targets, record mastery dates, flag targets for implementers, and construct subsets of the comprehensive target list (condition sets) for presentation to the student

- Clinical review and progress determination area that allows a user to enter information from observations and provides summary statistics on the progress of individuals or groups of students

ABA-PC3 software provides a one-stop, flexible system of tools that is available from anywhere to help teams collaborate, document, organize, and manage the highly technical process of intensive service delivery. It's a common environment for creatively implementing the team's vision and staying on-track. It's simple to use and understand and reduces training costs by applying consistent formats and common structure to everyday instructional tasks like following a prompt hierarchy, producing and filling out data sheets, data entry, and graphing. When the program is adopted by everyone on the special education team, it provides an unbelievable boost to collaboration when all team members are following the same program format and have access to all data from all programs, all the time; multiple implementations of common goals throughout the programming day become commonplace and generalization and incorporation of mastered skills enhance the progress of the student in ways that are almost impossible otherwise.

> **ABA-PC3 is a unique curriculum design and implementation environment for ABA programs that want to manage their implementations more effectively and augment their collaboration and creativity.**

The *New* ABA Program Companion

What's Next for YOUR ABA Program?

J. Tyler Fovel, M.A.,

Board Certified Behavior Analyst™

Edited by Meghan Fovel Danielski

The *New* ABA Program Companion

What's Next for YOUR ABA Program?

with The ABA Program Companion 3.0 Curriculum Development Software

Copyright © 2013 J. Tyler Fovel, M.A., BCBA™

Published by: DRL Books, Inc.
                     37 East 18th Street, 10th Floor
                     New York, New York 10003
                     Phone: (212) 604-9637
                     Fax: (212) 206-9329
                     www.drlbooks.com

All rights reserved. No part of the material protected by this copyright notice may be reproduced or used in any form or by any means, electronic or mechanical, including photocopying and recording or by any information storage and retrieval system without prior written permission by the copyright owner.

NOTICE: J. Tyler Fovel grants permission to the user of this manual to photocopy the forms printed in the Appendix and Chapter 9. Reproduction for resale is not permitted.

Library of Congress Control Number: 2013943746
ISBN Number: 978-0-983-62268-0

Printed in the United States of America

To my daughter and son, Meghan and Scott, who taught me everything I know about *not* knowing everything

Table of Contents

Preface	11
Acknowledgements	17

Chapter 1: Attributes of an Effective ABA Program — 19

Common Misunderstandings about Effective ABA Programs	20
Systems of ABA Service Delivery	22
Nine Characteristics of Highly Successful ABA Programs	22
Is an ABA Program Just for Students with Severe Special Needs?	23
What Kind of a Team?	25
What is Defined and Intensive?	28
Defined In Order to be Intensive	29
Where do the *Other* Components of an ABA Program Come From?	35
What's Next? Put this Chapter to Work	37

Chapter 2: Introduction to Instructional Program Writing — 39

Extreme Program Writing - ABA Edition	39
Are you Qualified?	41
Is Extreme Programming for You?	41
The Need for Detailed Program Plans	42
How Detailed Should a Program Be?	44
Guidance from a Research-Based Tradition	45
Program Format	46
Program Procedure Content	47
Seven Strategies of Effective Program Writing	49
What's Next? Put this Chapter to Work	50

Chapter 3: Managing the Setting and Materials — 51

General Environment, Location, Setting	52
The Environment Dictates the Curriculum	53
Organizing Curriculum to Address Environmental Requirements	54
Including the General Environment, Location and Setting in Written Programs	54
Managing the Physical Elements of Environments	56
The Setting of Discrete Trials	56
Seating Configurations for Discrete Trial Instruction	58
Arrangement of Task Materials	59
Tasks and Fields of Stimuli	59

Section Summary   61
Suggested Competencies for Implementers   63
What's Next? Put this Chapter to Work   66

Chapter 4: Attention and Engagement   67
Attention as a Response to the Environment   68
The Behavior of Attending   70
Stimulus Saliency   71
Directed Sensing Behavior   72
Problems in Attention and Engagement   76
Increasing Attention and Engagement   77
Sample Program to Shape Early Joint Attention   82
Attention and Engagement Prompts   83
Summary of Strategies   85
Case Study   90
Training Competencies for Attention and Engagement   92
What's Next? Put This Chapter to Work   94

Chapter 5: Prompts and Prompt Hierarchies   95
Errorless Teaching and Avoiding Errors   96
Types of Instructor-Based and Environmentally-Based Prompts   97
Prompt Hierarchies, Fading Prompts and Following Prompting Criteria   98
Documenting Prompts with Discrete Trial Instruction   105
Task Analyzing a Performance into Steps   108
Training Competencies for Prompts and Prompt Hierarchies   115
What's Next? Put this Chapter to Work   117

Chapter 6: Developing a Solid Reinforcement Strategy   119
The Past as Present: Effects of a "History" of Reinforcement   120
Characteristics of Stimuli that Act as Reinforcement   120
Satiation, Deprivation, and Programming for Variety   123
Preference Assessment   124
Preference Assessment Protocols   127
Sample Protocol   128
Is a Preferred Stimulus Also a Reinforcing Stimulus   129
An Expectancy of Reinforcement – Establishing Effective Contingencies   131
Intermittent Reinforcement   133
Token Reinforcement   136
Token Training Procedures   138
Competition of Concurrent Schedules and "The Matching Law"   141

The Role of Discriminative Stimuli in Successful Contingencies	144
Arranging Discriminative Stimuli to Facilitate Strong Instructional Contingencies	146
Towards a Long-Term Reinforcement Strategy	149
Complex Visual Systems of Motivation	151
Super Hero Cards Motivation System	152
What's Next? Put this Chapter to Work	160

Chapter 7: Errors and Error Correction — 163

What to Do About Errors? Contingencies Applied to Errors	164
Error Correction Studies	165
Table of Error Correction Steps	168
Discussion of Contingent Error Correction Procedures	170
Errorless Design Principles – Revisited	172
The Initial Response Requirement	173
Intermediate Responses and Transfer of Stimulus Control	174
Avoiding Coercive Prompts	177
Issues with Antecedent-Focused Procedures	178
Using Error Correction	180
What's Next? Put this Chapter to Work	182

Chapter 8: Generalization and Incorporation — 183

Promoting Transference of Skills to New Environments and Conditions	185
Task Analysis of Natural Environment Activities	186
Sample Kindergarten Observation	187
Connecting with a Standards-Based Curriculum	202
Defining Specific Target Performances	203
Generalization	205
Sample Intervention	209
Incorporation of Programs – Sequences	212
Function of Sequence Components	213
Strategies to Facilitate Generalization of Performances	214
Combining Programs to Establish General Routines	216
Combination of Skills to Create an Outcome or Product	217
Low-P followed by High-P	219
High-P followed by Low-P	220
Sample Sequences	225
Chapter Appendix: Common Kindergarten Worksheet Instructions	235
What's Next? Put this Chapter to Work	238

Chapter 9: Data-Based Decision Making — 241
Creation of Measurable Instructional Objectives — 242
Observing and Describing Behavior — 243
Characteristics of Behavior — 245
Behavioral Definitions and Objectives — 245
Learning Sets — 247
Management of Learning Sets — 251
Initial Measurement — 252
Condition Sets — 255
Data Collection — 260
Compilation of Data — 266
Graphing — 269
Analysis of Data — 274
The Data-Based Revision Process — 281
Decision Rules — 282
Pinpointing Instructional Barriers — 283
Observation of Students — 290
Classification of Learning Barriers — 294
What's Next? Put this Chapter to Work — 298

Chapter 10: The Big Picture: ABA Project Management — 299
The Concept of Workflow Applied to Instruction - Processes and Products — 300
Products and Control Structures — 300
Some Workflow Questions to Consider about Implementation — 301
The Analysis of Workflow — 302
Measuring Workflow — 303
The Standardization-Individualization Continuum — 306
Recommendations for Control Structures, Processes, and Products — 308
What's Next? Put this Chapter to Work — 317

Appendix — 319
Clinical Activity Log
Consultation Plan
Inclusion Plan
Project Management Grid
Program Audit
MSWO Preference Assessment Data Sheet
Instructor Observation and Feedback Form

References and Bibliography — 343

Preface

What's Next for Your ABA Program?
Instructional Development Practices to *Take It to the Next Level*

Since 2002, when the first volume of the ABA Program Companion was published, instructional programming based on the science of Applied Behavior Analysis for children with autism and related developmental disabilities has evolved in many ways. Expanding knowledge and acceptance of ABA methodologies has fueled the demand for services like never before. Programs in schools, centers, and homes, have grown substantially as a result, in turn creating an enormous demand for qualified practitioners, ready and able to deliver on the promise of success fostered by a vibrant, rapidly developing science and technology of behavior change.

In some ways, the times are remarkably similar to my early days in ABA, 37 years ago. Way back before Cooper, Heron and Heward, (2007) and most other published resources existed, while working in a state-supported residential facility for adults and children with mental retardation, we awaited each new issue of the *Journal of Applied Behavior Analysis* or *Behavior Modification* as if it were the next installment of a mystery novel, pouring over each article for ideas to help us improve our programs[1]. These were exciting times, when a new applied science made dramatic contributions to the lives of people and new developments emerged practically every day.

So it continues to be in the world of Applied Behavior Analysis. If anything, the pace has quickened. New concepts, techniques, and methodologies in ABA are proliferating. I believe that a large reason for this technical growth is our dual role as "scientist-practitioners." Whether we are behavior analysts, special education teachers, or fulfill

---

[1] I distinctly recall Repp and Deitz's articles on DRO and DRI and Stokes and Baer's work on generalization as having an extremely short latency – about one day – between their appearance in print and incorporation into my programs.

another leadership and development role within the educational team, in ABA, we are *all* teachers and we are *all* scientists. As such, we employ the best available evidence-based practices to teach needed skills. We understand the importance of careful selection of methodologies and consistent implementation. Yet, we are not mere consumers of research-based technology. As professionals who work each day with students, we are in the best position possible, on the proverbial cutting edge, to understand the unique needs of students. Therefore, as scientifically-oriented behavior *analysts,* we use conceptually systematic principles and appropriate applied technology to analyze the behavior of our students in order to arrive at our own solutions to critical questions and problems. Commendably, within the professional community of ABA, practitioners are expected and encouraged to share problems as well as solutions and, thus, a dynamic and ever-growing body of research mounts.

The *New* ABA Program Companion is completely new – only 20 pages were used from the original book. It's an up-to-date manual and online software package for practitioners who need to solve educational problems through analysis and creation of technically powerful solutions. It offers important information and ideas on how to design, document, implement, evaluate, and optimize the best skill acquisition programs you can create for your students. Although there is no substitute for extensive experience and a large, ready repertoire of programming procedures (and we all would like to have plenty of both), there is also no substitute for individual analysis and customization of procedures. Besides, most good teachers have plenty of their own ideas and excellent insights into their students that provide a solid basis for programming. This book is intended to be your partner, not your father or mother. It respects the idiosyncratic nature of educational programming for individuals and your knowledge of the student. It avoids presenting "canned" programs that preempt you from thinking, and supports you in your responsibility to make the proper decisions concerning each phase of the design and implementation process. Managing a complex, multi-dimensional task like an ABA program involves vision, teamwork, and infinite coordination. Wherever you may be in the process, this book is to help you choose and attain your next steps.

For program designers and supervisors, truly, the devil is in the details. This book is simply organized to address the most important practical elements of program development from establishment of team structures through evaluation of effectiveness:

Chapter 1: Attributes of an Effective ABA Program
- *Nine attributes of an effective ABA program*
- *Transdisciplinary teams*
- *Intensive and defined programming*

Chapter 2: Introduction to Instructional Program Writing
- *Become an "extreme" program writer*

Chapter 3: Managing the Setting and Materials
- *Control the physical environment of instruction*

Chapter 4: Attention and Engagement
- *Facilitating perception of and response to discriminative stimuli*

Chapter 5: Prompts and Prompt Hierarchies
- *Errorless teaching*
- *Stimulus control*

Chapter 6: Developing a Solid Reinforcement Strategy
- *Preference assessment, novelty and variety, conditioned reinforcement*

Chapter 7: Errors and Error Correction
- *The nature of error correction*
- *Error correction vs. errorless teaching*

Chapter 8: Generalization and Incorporation
- *Establish functionally competent behavior in the natural environment*
- *Inclusion*

Chapter 9: Data-based Decision Making
- *Defining and measuring behavior*
- *Graphing and evaluation*
- *Observations, procedural integrity, and instructional barriers*
- *Data driven revisions*

Chapter 10: The Big Picture: ABA Project Management
- *Workflow and project control structures*
- *Standardization vs. Individualization: protocols, training, and procedural integrity*

Each chapter begins with a thorough discussion of basic (and not-so-basic) concepts with relevant underlying research and then weaves in considerable practical advice on using the information in your programs with frequent illustrations and sample procedures. Each chapter also contains a detailed "What's Next?" summary of specific application points extracted from the material and a bibliography of references for further reading. An appendix of useful forms for ABA project management follows the last chapter.

ABA Program Companion 3.0 Curriculum Development Software

Don't forget to take advantage of the free six-month subscription to the on-line curriculum development software, ABA Program Companion 3.0, which is included for one student with the purchase of this manual. The software helps focus and streamline the process of building an individualized comprehensive curriculum for students in an ABA program and provides a common online and secure workspace to enhance collaboration among different service providers on the special education team. In addition to a program library of 650 fully customizable programs and over 4000 learning targets, a variety of easy to use tools are included that help accomplish essential ABA implementation tasks including:

- Automatically generated data sheets customized for each student

- Simple data entry screens for skill acquisition and behavior reduction programs

- 2-click graphing that automatically labels changing conditions

- Reports of active and mastered programs

- A structured workspace to assemble clear and well defined prompt hierarchies and error correction strategies

- A centralized area to organize the goal performance specifications and individual targets with the capacity to record mastery dates, flag targets with specialized designations for implementers, and construct unlimited subsets of the comprehensive target list (condition sets) for presentation to the student

- Clinical review and progress determination area that allows a user to enter information from observations and provides summary statistics on the progress of individual or groups of students

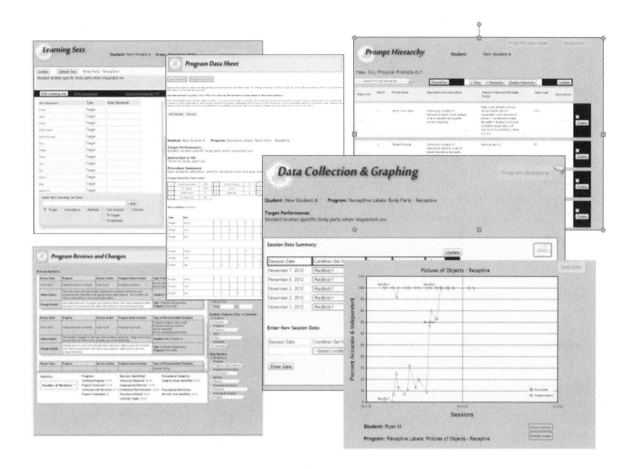

So, what's next for YOUR ABA program?

ABA programs are more established than ever before, offering exciting educational possibilities for students. As practitioners, therefore, it is up to us to create the very best programs possible, incorporating the latest and most appropriate technology and to reject any complacency that may have crept into our thinking and push forward to identify each source of inefficiency, insufficiency, or error – any impediment to efficacy at all – that exists in our programs: a formidable but eminently worthy task for a teacher and one which will concern us throughout the following chapters.

Acknowledgements

This manual owes its existence to many dedicated special education professionals who cared enough about their students to ask deep, probing questions and collaborate with me to find workable answers to daily problems. I have watched with admiration as they found incredibly creative practical applications for our conceptual discussions and proved over and over that *analysis* is the most important activity in Applied Behavior Analysis. I would especially like to thank Michelle Gada, Rachel Mastronunzio, Katie Cameron, Rebecca Giammatti, Courtney Rinaldi, Sarah Craley, Jennifer Smith, Elisa Brown, Liana Lilburn, Holli Spalding, and Anton Yurack for their active participation in the development and application of many ideas elaborated on in the book. Publisher Julie Azuma of DRL Books has been an encouraging partner for over ten years and helped me to communicate my "take" on ABA instructional practices to a far wider audience than I ever thought possible.

This book and the corresponding software has been a family project. Whether it was a meeting of the "board," a long telephone conversation, or just listening attentively as I talked on, my daughter, son, and wife contributed more than they will ever know. Their love, enthusiasm, and genuine nurturing spirits sustained me during the long creation effort and I am profoundly thankful. Of course, my daughter, Meghan Danielski, scrupulously edited every page with amazing understanding for what I was trying to communicate. She contributed to both the software and manuscript with intelligence and needed objectivity. This book is immeasurably better because of her hard work. My wife Jan continues to inspire me with her insight, creativity, and constant regard for others. As a master teacher she knows what to be, not just what to teach. Our nightly conversations about education are woven into every page of this book.

Finally, I want to thank the readers of the first ABA Program Companion. Your warm reception and continued support inspired me to continue asking, "What's next?" throughout the seven years that I worked on this material. I sincerely hope we never stop asking the same question about our students.

Chapter 1

Attributes of an Effective ABA Program

*E*ducational programs for students with autism and related disabilities based on the principles of Applied Behavior Analysis vary considerably but, like good educational programs in general, they have certain characteristics that form the core of everything they do. These core characteristics are the subject of this chapter. Effective ABA programs implement their defining characteristics explicitly and systematically, often far more than other program models, with a firm commitment to objective, data-driven analysis of behavior and teaching strategies.

In 1994, Catherine Maurice vividly described her struggle to find help for her children with autism. "Let Me Hear Your Voice" brought Applied Behavior Analysis to the attention of thousands of parents looking for an effective therapy for their children. Educational programs based on the science of Applied Behavior Analysis are shown to be the most effective educational alternatives available for students with autism and related disabilities. They benefit from an active and dynamic science with thousands of scientist-practitioners contributing to support both basic research and the technology of application. Nevertheless, for some time there have been questions and concerns about the characteristics of service delivery and the rigor of implementation that entitle a program to legitimately call itself an "ABA Program." This is a vital question that ultimately concerns the potential effectiveness of a program service delivery system. Certainly, not all "ABA" programs are alike. In comparisons of "intensive" programs implemented within public school settings, clear differences were found in effectiveness (Eikeseth, Jahr, & Eldevik, 2002; Howard, Sparkman, Cohen, Green Stanislaw, 2005). Understanding *how* ABA programs are fundamentally constituted to deliver high quality ABA services is a primary need for today's educational community and consumers of ABA services.

In his milestone paper describing the Young Autism Project, O. Ivar Lovaas (1987) reported phenomenal growth in student ability and progress surpassing that of other documented methodologies. The reaction of the autism community to this and subsequent papers (e.g., McEachin, Smith, & Lovaas, 1993; Eikeseth Smith, Eldevik, 2002) was such that the work continues to be routinely cited in justifications of the use of "ABA therapy" (Matson et al, 1996, NY State Department of Health, 1999, Aubrey, 2005,). However, the evolving research presently supporting the use of ABA methodologies is far from a complete and definitive "how to" manual. As the popularity of programs based in ABA has skyrocketed, curricula and manuals on dozens of topics have appeared, many firmly grounded in evidence-based practices. Still, no certification process or comprehensive agreement on essential practices has been widely adopted in the field. This void has led to unfortunate inconsistencies and some problematic program implementations, especially in settings where experienced practitioners were not available or where proper resources were not allocated.

Common Misunderstandings about Effective ABA Programs

Inevitably, with the rapid proliferation of new methods, there are misunderstandings and misapplications of the technology, leading to less desirable outcomes (Bibby, Eikeseth, Marin, Mudford & Reeves, 2001). According to Leaf and McEachin (2009), who worked with Lovaas on the Young Autism Project, a number of common misimpressions have led to departures in implementation from the original research within some ABA settings. For example:

- While an average of 40 program hours per week was delivered, the actual amounts varied, according to student, between 20 and 50. Only actual hours of direct teaching were counted in the figure (i.e., not lunch, snack or recess). Students with more severe needs received more hours

- Even though one therapist at a time worked directly with each student, a second therapist was also available to take data, give assistance when needed, or train. This was called "double therapy"

- Staff providing services were specially selected for their abilities to deliver intensive treatment, received one to two months of prior training and received daily and weekly supervision from highly qualified professionals

- Extensive use of natural setting teaching was employed and 1:1 intervention was faded as quickly as possible

Problems in implementation sometimes arise from insufficient familiarity with the technology. For example, overuse of a single teaching format – discrete trials – led to a widely held misimpression that Applied Behavioral Analysis and discrete trials are synonymous, and, consequently, that ABA methodologies are limited to isolated, repetitive, individual sessions. In fact, while important, discrete-trial methodology is most often implemented together with other formats such as incidental teaching, play and social skills training, and, if appropriate, work in groups. All settings are amenable to task analysis and methodologies such as reinforcement, prompting, error correction, and attention/ engagement strategies. Indeed, there is no "ABA time" during the day if the whole day is analyzed and programmed with a balanced set of educational experiences – all recognized as part of the ABA program.

A widespread and rather grievous error exhibited in some programs has occurred when inadequate attention is paid to providing sufficient frequency, quality, variety and novelty in reinforcement, producing or exacerbating resistance to programming and strong escape-induced problem behavior. Programs may fail to integrate the preferences and choices of students into instruction or they may present long sessions of uninterrupted, unreinforced trials.

In an effort to bring some necessary accountability to the field, the Association for Behavior Analysis International (ABAI) created a certification process for professionals. Likewise, the Special Interest Group for Autism of the ABAI published an extensive set of recommendations to consumers for evaluating the credentials of those calling themselves "Autism Consultants" (2007). While these developments have brought some regulation for individual practitioners, organizations providing ABA services are not scrutinized with an equivalent certification process. Some states, including New York, New Jersey, Connecticut, and California, and the United States Department of Defense have published "quality indicators" or "guidelines" for programs for students with autism focusing on general components and outcomes of service associated with quality service delivery. While not always specific to ABA programs, they discuss the nature of quality service delivery and set general expectations for providers in relevant areas.

Systems of ABA Service Delivery

Programs considered "ABA Programs" are responsible for knowing and meeting the highest current standards of practice. Such programs deliver ABA services constituting the majority of a student's educational experience and invoke association with the scientifically validated, highly successful methods of the published literature. Ethically, this requires active participation in the community of scientist-practitioners and exposure to developing ideas as well as thorough examination of the published literature. Decision makers contemplating the establishment of an ABA program are, therefore, well-advised to begin with a consideration of some general entry-level requirements for systems of service delivery. The following characteristics, derived from the existing research and experience, are proposed as a basic description:

Nine Characteristics of Highly Successful ABA Programs

An "ABA Program":

- Delivers highly *defined and intensive* education

- To students with *severe special needs*

- Who require *teams* of implementers and specialists to work together to deliver instruction

- The student is objectively evaluated in extensive detail

- Using a comprehensive and highly articulated curriculum

- Socially significant, functional and pivotal behaviors are taught and are generalized across a wide variety of life settings

- Programs of instruction use conceptually systematic principles and evidence-based methodologies from the science of Applied Behavior Analysis, individualized for each student

- Implementation of programs is highly organized and systematic

- Extensive data-based methods are employed to ensure program integrity and student progress

Highly effective programs are associated with the consistent implementation of **all nine characteristics** and can document their compliance as well as the effectiveness of their programs objectively. Each characteristic is a part of an interdependent system – each piece is a vital step in the process or, put another way, a piece of the foundation upon which progress is built. While these fundamental characteristics are somewhat general, systems of ABA service delivery create the necessary detailed control structures responsible for fully addressing each particular attribute.

Some additional exploration of the statements may help to clarify some parameters of their influence and guide those undertaking the creation of an ABA system—provided below in the form of answers to frequently asked questions.

FAQ 1: Is an ABA program just for students with severe special needs?

Behavior analysis has been incorporated into the educational programs of countless students. Structured individualized and group teaching, social skills programs, and behavior deceleration programs are just a few of the many educational areas using behavior analytic principles. The thoroughly researched methodologies of ABA may be of substantial benefit for many students regardless of their diagnosis. Most often, following the doctrine of least restrictive environment, programs are implemented in an environment as typical as possible. However, some students will require a substantially different level of services because they require:

- sustained and comprehensive education using these methods throughout *most of their day*, receiving many more learning opportunities than are usually available
- complex analysis, accommodation, and/or modification of the target learning performances from certified specialists in applied behavior analysis and other specialists
- strict and elaborate structuring and coordination of programming including specific methods to ensure program integrity such as inter-observer reliability, frequent observation and feedback to implementers, and detailed technical write-ups
- specific and careful generalization, maintenance, and incidental teaching programs

- structures to be in place for daily, data-based decision making such as daily data collection and review by specialists and frequent program adjustment or adaptation

Dedicated ABA programs are not casually created and do not pop into existence overnight. They require the development of structures and application of resources that address the complex needs of certain kinds of students. It is unwise to expect to apply the technology with such students successfully without addressing all of the characteristics enumerated above. Other students with less complex needs may not require the same structures or all aspects of the system. The decision to create an "ABA Program" implies that the program will imitate the characteristics (and, therefore, the success) of programs reported in the research and, therefore, fidelity to the models as described is the determining factor of authenticity.

It is also true that, in ABA programs, a continuity of services from most structured to least structured will be offered to students, based on their need. It is expected that in any ABA program, students will require varying levels of service depending on their baseline level of skills and the course of their progress. Good ABA programs are prepared to offer this continuity of service with flexibility in staffing, locations, settings, and teaching formats since actual program delivery will always depend on the needs of individual students. Regardless of whether many or even all students may presently need the highest degree of structured programming, ABA programs must maintain a *capability* to respond if needs or students change.

Rather than maintain extensive, unnecessary structures, programs serving students who do *not* meet all of the characteristics above may elect to forgo the designation of "ABA Program" while still incorporating some of the scientifically validated principles of ABA programs. Any attempt at a distinction should be commended as ethically responsible as well as pragmatic—undoubtedly, consumers will come to understand the true nature of programs including their limitations and hold service providers responsible for past promises, even implied ones. Ultimately, the designation "ABA Program" is meaningless if the terms do not connote specific qualifications that are well understood by consumers and some form of professional or even statutory regulation is probably the best future course of action.

FAQ 2: What Kind of a Team?

Meeting the challenge of providing intensive, high quality, effective services usually requires a team of highly knowledgeable but, most of all, highly coordinated individuals who work together to design, implement, and perfect the myriad of details that go into a successful implementation. As with the proliferation of any complex technology, competence of implementation and, in general, questions of program integrity must be central to the use of the technology. For ABA programs this means that team members are *actually* delivering services consistent with a highly successful approach. Board Certified Behavior Analysts (BCBAs) are professionals who study the specific principles and practices of the science of Applied Behavior Analysis. However, this certification is not specific to *any* particular technological application and, therefore, sub-specialties within the profession are recognized (although these distinctions are informal at present). Consequently, within the Association for Behavior Analysis International (ABAI) the Special Interest Group for Autism developed guidelines to guide consumers in choosing ABA professionals as lead consultants and program supervisors. In addition to holding a BCBA, these guidelines stipulate that supervisors of ABA programs possess a minimum of five years of supervised experience developing programs for individuals with autism as well as other important qualifications.

In some locations (e.g. public schools), non-ABA specialists as well as ABA professionals collaborate in the delivery of service. In addition to behavior analysts and trained ABA teachers, regular education teachers, special educators, occupational therapists, speech/language pathologists, physical therapists, school psychologists, social workers, and nurses may have a role. Regardless of team composition, effective service delivery requires an affirmative answer to the following question:

> *Can ABA programs incorporate services from a variety of team members and, at the same time, ensure program integrity consistent with the characteristics of highly successful programs?*

In the United States there seems to be common ground for multi-disciplinary collaboration:

1. Federal special education law requires a commitment to "scientifically based

instructional practices" and interventions "...*based on peer-reviewed research...*" in schools

2. Professional disciplines commonly providing special education services to children in school settings have made public commitments through their national organizations to providing evidence-based services

Yet the rhetoric of some professionals can lead one to believe otherwise. Despite endorsement by numerous federal and state agencies, ABA programs are still criticized as "mechanical" or "limited." For their part, some behavior analysts can be reluctant to collaborate. Asked whether he hired related service personnel in his program, one behavior analyst remarked, "Why would I hire someone I'm going to argue with every day?" In fact, competent professionals from many disciplines have a positive effect on ABA programs. Specialists such as speech therapists, reading specialists, or physical therapists concentrate on a particular subset of behavior and may become especially knowledgeable about that subset. Thus, they may be able to contribute unique information to the team, not available otherwise.

Implementation of ABA programs in a multi-disciplinary team is a fact of life in many settings but, while team collaboration is much sought after, it may not occur spontaneously. For many teams, the problem occurs because details of collaboration are not explicitly specified, rather than because of deep philosophical or methodological differences. Program supervisors should be prepared to understand the features and processes of collaborations that enhance, rather than compromise, the integrity of the program. Detailed analysis of the organization and implementation of service delivery from goal setting onwards is crucial to avoid underutilizing the resources of the team and compartmentalization of service delivery, leading to inadequate implementation plans. For example, a review of IEP objectives for twelve students in an ABA program was conducted by Fovel, Lilburn, Robertson, Carr, & Donowitz (2010). Among the problems noted were:

- Overlapping language objectives set by both the special educator and the speech and language pathologist but with learning sets (list of specific target performances) that were not coordinated and did not intersect

- Mastered performances in classroom activities that were not exhibited in therapy settings (and vice versa) and therapists and teachers who were not aware of specific student capabilities in other settings

- Prompting that was inconsistently performed by different implementers

- Error correction, attention/engagement, and reinforcement strategies that varied widely between implementers

Fovel et al. used a "structured collaboration" approach to unify service delivery in a middle school ABA program. Through guided discussions, team members of different educational backgrounds and experiences explored and eventually adopted specific common practices that formed a system of definition, documentation, and objective progress review for the team. Along the way, team members reviewed and ratified a "Statement of Commitment:"

STATEMENT OF COMMITMENT

We believe in and commit to evidence-based practices in all of our interventions. To that end we will ensure that all procedures implemented with students will adhere to the following principles:

Right to Effective Education and Treatment

All students have the right to receive services which are effective, beneficial, and consistent with their individual education plan. Service providers have a responsibility to provide effective services. Service providers are expected to be knowledgeable about current best practices and base individualized programs on scientifically established principles. They will engage in ongoing observation and evaluation using objective measures to monitor the student's progress towards established goals. Implementers will use objective data to revise procedures in a timely manner if progress is not evident or sufficient.

Technological

All target behaviors will be explicitly defined in observable and measurable terms. All procedures will be described in comprehensive detail so that others may carry out the procedure (with sufficient training).

Comprehensive, Developmentally Appropriate, Functional, and Pivotal

Student goals are set that address all educationally relevant skill deficits and for which the student exhibits the appropriate prerequisite skills. It is vital that goals focus on skills that are reinforced in the student's natural environment. Specific opportunities for the student to develop and practice new skills in a variety of settings are crucial. **To that end, all service providers will become competent in all aspects of a student's curriculum, including knowledge of learning targets and instructional procedures and be prepared to carry out service delivery in a manner consistent with the whole.**

Transdisciplinary

Through professional training, experience, and abilities, certain team members may be uniquely knowledgeable and capable of undertaking aspects of a student's program. This represents an important resource to the team. The nature and needs of special education students requires all team members to collaborate, participate, and contribute to all aspects of a student' program. We recognize that skill development takes place in a multitude of settings and that it is sometimes necessary to go beyond the boundaries of traditional roles to achieve progress.

As part of the process to improve consistency and coordination, Fovel et al. (2010) provided a detailed set of common practices including common program procedure formats, data sheets, and observation/feedback to individual team members based on progress with the overall system.

FAQ 3: What is Defined and Intensive?

Defined and *intensive* are terms that seem to capture the unique nature of ABA programs and their ability to produce results. The definition of "intensive" has received considerable discussion. According to the Connecticut Guidelines for Identification and Education of Children and Youth with Autism (Connecticut Department of Education, 2005), "Intensity...must be considered on many levels, including...the number of hours per day or week that services are provided; the number of weeks of educational intervention per year; the number and/or type of environments in which the teaching occurs..." With respect to specific student behavior, the Connecticut guidelines identify "engagement" as a key indicator:

> "Engagement, as a measure of intensity, refers to the amount of time a child is attending to and actively interacting with others. A key aspect of individualization for students with ASD involves approaches for supporting high rates of engagement. Engaged time can be provided at different levels of intensity and in a variety of settings using a range of strategies, including one-to-one instruction, independent work time, small-group instruction, and instruction in the general education environment. Thus, across all of these settings, the goal of intervention for the child with ASD is to increase the amount of time he or she is engaged throughout the day in order to achieve outcomes identified on the IEP."

Cohen-Alemeida (2007) suggests that "intensive" is most usefully defined as the number of opportunities to learn provided for the student per unit of time. Howard et al. (2005) defined "intensive" as 25-40 hours per week of 1:1 intervention for students with 50-100 learning opportunities per hour presented. In a clinic setting, instructors were evaluated on their ability to provide 25 learning opportunities per minute (Carbone, 2007).

Defined In Order to be Intensive

"Defined" refers to the detail in which procedures are specified. In order for an intervention to be delivered in a manner conforming to "intensive" as discussed above, it must be well defined. Well defined procedures are "technological" in the sense that they objectively specify all of the goals and specific methods they contain (Cooper et al. 2007). Defined also means that terms used to describe interventions are conceptually systematic—that is, that they only refer to objectively defined principles that are based on consistent scientific assumptions. Finally, *defined* requires the application of validation measures ensuring program integrity like inter-observer agreement for data collection and observation and feedback checklists for all implementers.

The process of structuring educational activities to provide highly defined learning opportunities can be illustrated with any common event that occurs in a classroom in which students participate. Recently the author observed a group activity with three young students with autism. A version of the notes taken is illustrated on the following page:

Observer's Notes

March 15, 2013, East Lawford, CT Mrs. Ward
9:15 Circle Time

3 students in circle facing group leader.   Two paras sitting directly behind. Teacher greets all students and leads them through greeting routine. She models with first student and each student repeats. Next calendar. Posted on the wall with days of month, days of week, and year. Teacher gives directions to put date on calendar, cound days up to today, locate/pronounce days of week, and recite rhyme containing days of week and recite rhyme containing days of week. Students get small white-boards and markers. Follow instruction in group to draw shapes and letters on white-boards. Put away - students identify number cards displayed to group and perform motor actions while counting from 1-10 (e.g. clap while reciting 1, 2, 3, etc.)

**Need goals and learning sets for: (1) greeting routine (2) movement songs, (3) calendar activities, (4) following instructions in a group (use white-board and marker), (5) name numbers (up to 10? 20?)

March 15, 2013, East Lawford, CT Mrs. Ward   P. 2
9:15 Circle Time

Learning Sets:	
Songs: Tap, Tap	Tap locations -
(Find 2 more songs)	Move in air, taphigh, tap on knees,
	in front, in back, tap fast, tap slow
Greetings:	Howdy Neightbor. Shake my hand, Welcome!
White Board Group	Draw circle, square, line, circle the ___, underline
Instructions	The __. Color in the __. Write letter __.
Name Numerals	Clap hands and count to 10
	Jump and count to 10
	Take turns naming numeral that's displayed
Calendar/Weather	Put date card in square of pocket calendar
	Count days - first to present date while pointing
	Identify the day, month, year; "Today is..."
Dismissal	Leave according to condition instruction (name,
	wearing a color, boy/girl)

Observation of the *Circle Time* activity led to enumeration of the required performances necessary for students to succeed. Each general performance is linked to specific mastery criteria, specific learning targets, a step-by-step procedure, and data collection procedures. Some of these details are apparent from the observation and narrative. Others need to be filled in. Step-by-step programs contain details of implementation for teachers or teaching assistants such as mastery criteria, prompting directions, error correction, reinforcement, and other important information for maintaining effective and consistent procedures.

Individual learning targets are specified for all of the programs which comprise the components of the *Circle Time* activity.

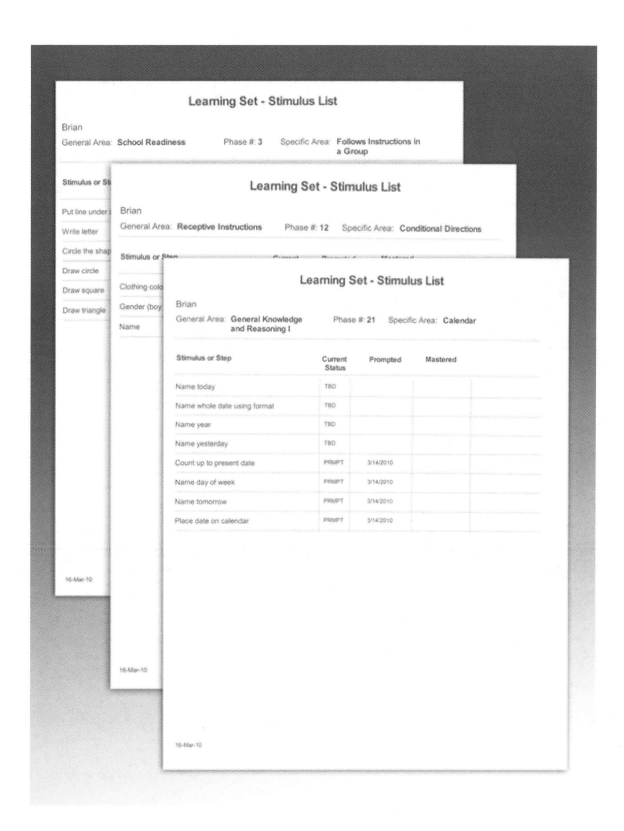

Objective measures of student performance are developed and recorded on data sheets.

The results of instruction are measured objectively and visually depicted over time on a graph to assess the pace and consistency of student performance within the program. Targets for progress are established and the data that is gathered is compared to the expectation for progress each week. Failure of the student to achieve the expected progress results in program review and revision according to defined "data-based decision making" rules.

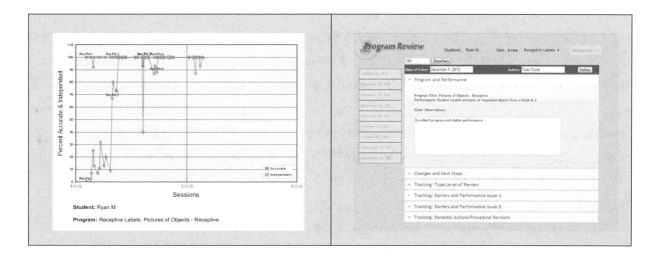

Each of the components aids in defining a consistent implementation and sets the occasion for intensive intervention/education. Such definition also allows inspection by various program supervision personnel and aids in the ongoing review and possible changes to programming. Without these materials and this level of detailed structure, coordination of implementation with more than one implementer and objective review of progress is difficult if not impossible.

FAQ 4: Where do the *other* components of an ABA Program come from?

In many respects, ABA programs are no different from other multi-component, multi-phase projects. Control structures like personnel systems (recruitment, hiring, administrative and clinical supervision), program development (defining populations served, entry/exit criteria, long-term assessment of program success), or training (professional development, fundamental ABA practices, training for instructors, physical management procedures) are developed and overlay the clinical/educational process. This includes the interface between ABA programs and administrative structures not directly involved in the delivery of ABA services (e.g., school district administration). Control structures and the application of Applied Behavior Analysis to the workflow of service delivery *itself* will be topics discussed in a later chapter.

Conclusion – ABA *is* Rocket Science

Of course, putting together a program that meets such stringent requirements as those discussed in this chapter is not easy. However, educators and behavior analysts tackle the challenge every day. The science of ABA provides a solid footing for understanding how humans learn and the methods likely to effect a change. Thousands of controlled studies have investigated many conditions of learning and teaching. The *technology* of implementation while lagging behind the science is moving forward. Over the course of the last 50 years, thousands of implementations have been conducted from the first small steps in residential institutions to home programs to public and private schools. Much more has yet to be done but much has been accomplished. Successful programs will find the means to steadfastly implement the nine core characteristics despite the inherent difficulties, whether through redesign of inadequate service delivery systems, addition of human and material resources, or through renewed vision and determined commitment to change. Each effort moves towards better consistency and effectiveness.

What's Next?

Put this chapter to work: **ATTRIBUTES OF AN EFFECTIVE ABA PROGRAM**

Assess your mission:

- Set up a meeting with decision makers to discuss the mission of your program and consider the answers to the questions below and their implications:
    - Do your students' needs necessitate an "ABA Program?"
    - Does your program identify itself as an "ABA Program" to consumers?
    - How would you assess your compliance with the "Nine Characteristics of Highly Successful ABA Programs?"
    - Which of the nine characteristics are not sufficiently addressed?

Assess your team:

- Organize a group meeting to facilitate "structured collaboration." Explore and adopt specific common practices that form a system of definition, documentation, and objective progress review for the team. Review and ratify a "Statement of Commitment" (see example on page 8)
- What are some other ways that you can encourage collaboration in your multi-disciplinary team?
- How are target performances practiced in multiple settings with multiple team members? How are mastered performances integrated into functional routines across implementers?

Assess your procedures:

- Evaluate the intensity of your program presentation. How many learning opportunities are offered for each student per unit of time in each major activity of their days?
- Do your procedures objectively specify all of the goals and specific methods they contain?
- Are all procedures only based on principles consistent with scientific evidence?

Assess your training:

- What measures are you using to ensure procedural integrity?

Assess your practices and protocols:

- Are all practices and protocols highly defined?
- Are all programs written?
- Are results documented for all target behaviors?
- Do protocols exist for managing student progress through the curriculum in all settings?
- Do protocols exist for routinely identifying lack of progress and barriers to learning?

Chapter 2

Introduction to Instructional Program Writing

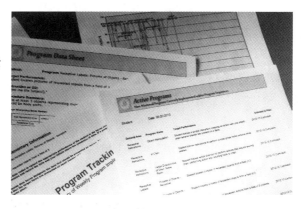

*T*his chapter will discuss the importance of being both passionate and practical about communicating instructional methodologies to help students with severe learning deficits. Passionate program writers take the time necessary to write good programs. A practical approach acknowledges that a procedure is only as good as its ability to establish accurate and consistent implementation of its methodology. The "test of necessary and sufficient" will be offered as a guiding principle for deciding how much detail to include in programs. Some lessons on ABA technical writing will be reviewed as well as advice on program format and content.

Extreme Program Writing – ABA Edition

I'm starting a movement called Extreme Program Writing. It's extreme because it's different, it works, and because I'm opinionated on the subject. I've been talking to ABA consultants and teachers for some time about writing skill acquisition programs and, frankly, I don't detect much enthusiasm. I don't understand this because I feel that developing effective programs for students is one of the most stimulating and creative things I do. I collected and distilled some of the sentiments expressed to me—they are like the evil twin of what the reality of program writing could be. Yet, there is a familiar ring to some of the comments and I must admit that I've shared the feelings at times.

> "Writing programs now is so different from graduate school. Before, we spent time thinking out and programming every detail, trying it out and using our creativity and skill to make it better. Now, it's just not as much fun."
>
> "I see all this superfluous detail in programs. I get lost in the words."
>
> "The written program becomes just a peripheral piece of the implementation that is there for show. You can't document all the things that really count. It took me years to learn to do what I do and that doesn't come through in a write-up."
>
> "Writing programs is difficult, time consuming, tedious, and boring—it's necessary but it's an unrewarding task which is often ignored anyway. Do it quickly, get it over with, and move on to more important things."
>
> "I just don't have time to write all of the programs the way I should."

In response to these real but disempowering sentiments I'd like to offer "The Extreme ABA Program Writer's Creed."

As an Extreme ABA Program Writer I believe that:

- Programs are never finished, you develop them over time

- Program development isn't about writing pretty sentences or even about "informing" implementers—it's about controlling the actions of instructors to deliver quality instruction

- A skill acquisition program must be at the center – not the periphery – of program implementation. It is a vital roadmap for implementers. It must communicate all essential details of the developer's vision

- ABA program development is a creative and fun process. Writing a good program is like solving a complex puzzle and creating a work of art at the same time

- As a competent, trained program developer, programs are my unique and valued contribution to the team

Want to take the pledge? I warn you that believing is not enough. To have a rewarding experience writing creative programs that solve the puzzles of student need and effectively control the actions of implementers, you must write great programs. So read on!

Are You Qualified?

If you want to be an extreme program writer, you might still wonder about your qualifications. We all feel a little insecure from time to time about our technical prowess and behavior analysis is nothing if not technical. There are so many research areas that impinge on program writing—it is tempting to leave it to others more "expert" than us. But the truth is that as a committed practitioner, your experience is invaluable. ABA has a long tradition of calling its adherents "scientist-practitioners." Likewise, the recent trend in education is towards data-driven decision making. The aim in both fields is on becoming analytical and experimental, immersed in the program creation process and, in effect, functioning as our own experts. Extreme programming strongly advocates a commitment to this scientifically oriented program development process rooted in data-based evaluation and revision based on results. Becoming proficient is a lifelong pursuit for all of us. From basic preparation to advanced study we all endeavor to better master the fundamentals and fine points because we are committed to improve our instruction.

Is Extreme Programming for You?

Don't just jump in. Consider your personal style and process:

- If you want or need an "expert" to tell you exactly what to do and do not intend to question, revise, or customize your programs, then this approach to skill acquisition programming is definitely NOT for you

- If you are too busy or unable to evaluate your programs and use the results to make them better, then you will not be interested in this approach

- However, if you think you know a good idea when you see one, if you "collect" novel techniques, waiting for a good time to use them, if you've already thought of and use a fair number of your own creative strategies…

- If you get a ton of ideas every time you watch a program being implemented…

- If you scour books and journals and attend workshops and conferences looking for new information and methods…

Then you just might be looking for an approach to program development that respects your creativity and dedication, encourages and facilitates a hands-on attitude, and tries to give you a consistent framework and tools for organizing an, admittedly, complex process.

The Need for Detailed Program Plans

The previous chapter pointed out that ABA projects like classrooms or home programs are complex endeavors because a *team* of professionals and paraprofessionals work together to implement an instructional program. When there is more than one instructor, consistency immediately becomes a critical issue and the need for program planning, training, supervision, documentation, coordination, and standardized evaluation is multiplied exponentially.

Experienced instructors may have developed excellent instincts about how to teach but improvised methods can quickly devolve into confusion, inconsistency, and error when a team of instructors is involved. This is when good program plans shine. Yet it is understandable that we sometimes resist expending the effort to actually write something. Teaching programs are necessarily complicated entities because students are complicated. Programs include information on a variety of topics:

1. The design of materials and instructional setting
2. Attention and engagement issues
3. Structuring the presentation of the skill program
4. Implementation of prompts and prompt-fading strategies
5. All-important issues related to motivation and reinforcement
6. Error correction
7. Generalization and incorporation of mastered skills

These are well known requirements, both from common professional experience and the scientific and technical literature. The Behavior Analyst Certification Board™ has published a task list enumerating all of these areas as essential areas of knowledge for competent behavior analysts (Behavior Analysis Certification Board, 2012). Daily experience in educational settings confirms a detailed structured plan is extremely useful. We see that:

- Advance planning allows us to be prepared for many foreseeable eventualities

- Writing our plans down allows us to communicate more effectively with others about our plan

- Arranging a plan in a conceptually systematic manner helps ensure that we have all our bases covered and that the plan is logical

- A conceptually systematic plan allows us to explicitly evaluate our methodology objectively and to revise it as needed, including whatever level of detail is necessary

- A conceptually systematic plan allows us to talk about our plans using a common vocabulary referring to empirically tested principles

This is not to say that instruction resulting from a systematic program development process need be devoid of creativity, flexibility, or even spontaneity. Novelty and variety are indispensable ingredients in all forms of teaching. On the other hand, we also must acknowledge that effective teaching, planned or spontaneous, has a structure and obeys the rules governing human learning and behavior change.

Questions to Think About:

1. Honestly (it's just us), do you think written program plans are necessary? A necessary evil or a good thing?

2. Do you feel that following a program plan interferes with your ability to teach the way you see fit at the moment?

3. Do you resist writing down program plans? If so, why?

4. What would comprise an ideal program plan?

5. What level of detail do you need to adequately run a program if you are unfamiliar with it?

How Detailed Should a Program Be?

A written program plan should be as detailed as it needs to be; the key requirement is that programs achieve "procedural integrity." Procedural integrity means that the written description of what should be done consistently matches what is *actually* done by all implementers. Procedural integrity is not achieved when the instructors are doing their own versions of a program. Procedural integrity is not achieved when instructors constantly change what they are doing. And, procedural integrity is not achieved when instructors are not adequately trained to implement the program or when program changes are not effectively communicated. Indeed, procedural integrity is the result of careful training, supervision, and effort by program supervisors and implementers, all based on the content of the written procedure.

Problems with procedural integrity will occur if a program has too much as well as too little detail. Breaking any task into 20 steps when four are sufficient runs the risk of allowing superfluous detail to interfere with the learning process for both students and implementers. Finding a balance between too little and too much is paramount. Experienced program writers subject the content of written programs to the "test of necessary and sufficient." That is, in order for material to be included in a written program, it must be both necessary and sufficient to successfully communicate the procedure to the instructor. Keep in mind that program integrity does not necessarily mean that the procedure results in learning or behavior change on the part of the student – only on the part of the instructor.

More Questions to Think About:

- Can you think of specific examples from your experience when too much or too little detail in written programs has contributed to problems in implementation?

- Read Strunk and White's *The Elements of Style*. They are well known advocates of the "less is more" style of writing

- How have you determined how much detail to include in your programs? Do you feel that you are getting it right?

- How would we know if the written program is at fault when an instructor doesn't implement a procedure correctly?

Guidance from a Research-Based Tradition

Writing programs filled with content that is necessary and sufficient to establish accurate and consistent instructor performance requires more than deciding how much detail to include – we must look closely at the terminology we use, how we organize our writing, and decide how to refer to the concepts and methods of teaching. What exactly should programs tell those who will teach students? What vocabulary, format, and information will effectively communicate to them? Essentially, the problem is one of stimulus control – the control of the written instructions over instructor behavior – and, considered as such, it is useful to look for inspiration at other writing concerned with effectively communicating methodology. Technical writing about behavior change procedures, as seen in professional journals such as the Journal of Applied Behavior Analysis (JABA) and the Journal of the Experimental Analysis of Behavior (JEAB) takes a well-established form. Detailed, written descriptions of carefully controlled procedures are provided:

- Target behaviors (the "dependent variables") are precisely and objectively defined and measured

- The setting, apparatus, and materials of the project are described in detail

- The actions of the experimenter (the "independent variables") are described for each condition of the experiment in a step-by-step fashion

Basically, experimentally-based research articles state exactly what was presented to the subject and the conditions under which it was presented. These well-established bodies of experimental and applied literature contribute conceptual as well as methodological language (terms, definitions, descriptions of principles, relationships, laws, etc.) relevant to communication of technical issues. For example, in stimulus control literature we find descriptions of:

- The design and presentation of instructional materials as prompts to facilitate errorless formation of conditional discriminations

- Analysis of student errors in the redesign of procedures

- Discussion of remediation procedures applied contingently on student errors

Taken together, the precise methodological descriptions of these thousands of applied research studies provide a fundamental (albeit evolving) and more or less standardized terminology that is readily available for use in program writing. It is to a program designer's great benefit to become acquainted with it.

Program Format

As discussed, the stimulus characteristics or form of an instructional methodology may be manipulated to enhance communication from the author to others. The effectiveness of the communication will be measured by the fidelity and consistency of its implementation. When preparing instructional procedures, programmers should choose appropriate presentation formats and arrange other details to communicate optimally. Most often procedures take a written rather than oral form but there is no reason why formats like slide presentations (e.g., PowerPoint) or video demonstrations could not be helpful in the process of communication – indeed, these may be extremely effective and use of these methods is growing rapidly. Nevertheless, the requirements of documentation and the relative ease of creation and distribution of text-based media causes them to continue to prevail as the primary format for program procedures, usually relegating other media to supplemental roles.

If a text-based program format is to work well as an effective communication medium, program writers must incorporate appropriate visual design principles into their write-ups. Use of headings, diagrams, tables, lists, and other visual elements like font size and white space on a page help communicate information quickly and succinctly. Use of examples and a clear, direct, and logical writing style also make the task of the reader easier. Remember, however, that, ultimately, the power of a write-up comes from the intelligence of its methodology; a sub-standard procedure that is clearly articulated and appealingly formatted remains sub-standard. Yet, a brilliant teaching strategy that is poorly understood by implementers will fail as well. It is only through concerted efforts to address both the needs of students *and* implementers that program authors will consistently succeed.

Recommendations on Program Format

In keeping with the preceding discussion, the following recommendations are presented for written programs, covering both writing style and content. Many sources of such advice exist already. *The Publication Manual* of the American Psychological Association (2009) provides excellent guidance for authors of formal publications readying their work for journals. It is considered a primary source for technical writing in the field and should not be overlooked in the quest to become an effective program writer. However, after 38 years of trying to write good programs, I would also offer a simple "Top Ten" list of critical points that are most often missed, based on experience as both a writer and reader of instructional programs:

General

- Establish a common outline/format for programs and stick with it
- Include headings and titles that quickly orient the reader
- Always include the student's name, author(s), and dates of creation and revision
- Pay close attention to the logical flow of ideas

Style

- Explain all technical terms
- Do not use abbreviations
- Do not be overly casual
- Whenever appropriate use step-by-step procedure sections; directly address the reader using directive language and active verbs
- Use diagrams and tables where helpful
- Don't crowd text together in dense paragraphs. Use numbered and bulleted lists, increase space between lines

Program Procedure Content

In this chapter we have discussed some specific practices of program authors that focus on the use of written language as an engine of implementer behavior change. The following chapters will be substantially devoted to the *content* of instructional programs, organized into topics roughly equivalent to the familiar outline of a lesson plan. Based on current research in ABA and clinical experience, each chapter will discuss concepts, principles, and practices related to its content area intended to foster new, productive directions in instructional design for program authors. Seven separate content areas are integrated into the chapter material as well as advice on ABA project management as a whole:

Seven Strategies of Effective Program Writing

Materials & Setting	**Structure the Physical Environment** Set up the classroom or learning area so that it propels students into learning and decreases the opportunities for off-task behavior. List necessary materials and describe their preparation; if relevant, include a description of the arrangement of the setting including the time, personnel, location, and overall context
Attention & Engagement	Explicitly describe a strategy for gaining the student's attention and engagement with instruction prior to delivering instruction
Prompts	**Teach Errorlessly** Analyze the skill into its component parts and develop a strategy to teach it a little at a time, starting with the simplest parts and minimizing errors. Objectively define the target performance, sometimes called the "terminal objective" including objective mastery criteria Enumerate component learning targets like a task analysis or list of items to be mastered Specify the procedures governing the use of prompts, both instructor-based and environmentally-based
Program Presentation	**Ensure Readiness** Make sure that the student has the prerequisite skills for accomplishing the tasks set before them and that the requirements are not too hard. Stipulate next steps for the program after mastery such as generalization to other settings and/or incorporation of the skill into more complex skills. List procedures and steps for presenting the instructional "trial" including procedures designed to elicit the target performance such as directions and/or presentation of materials, number of trials, etc.

Program Presentation (cont.)	**Keep the Student Busy** Keep instruction fast paced and moving. Reinforce appropriate alternative behaviors at a high rate.
	Allow the Student to Be Competent Plan the daily schedule so that students are spending a significant amount of time performing things that they CAN do
	Listen to the Student Describe progress evaluation methods The behavior of the student is the most reliable indicator of how things are going. Learn to analyze it carefully and objectively.
Error Correction	**Specify an error-correction strategy that is appropriate and beneficial**
Reinforcement	**Specify a reinforcement strategy that will adequately maintain the student's performance over the life of instruction** **Stack the Deck** Choose potent and varied reinforcers and have plenty available. **Maximize Choice and Individual Control** Build choice and preference into the curriculum. Recognize that too many rules and obvious controls can be counterproductive and provoke rebellion. Use preference assessments. **Eliminate the Competition** Make competing reinforcers and other distractions unavailable as much as possible.
Generalization and Incorporation	**Plan generalization strategies from the inception of instruction** Analyze and understand the target environment using ecological assessments Use incorporation and generalization strategies to create functional skills that survive in natural environments

What's Next?
***Put this chapter to work*: INTRODUCTION TO INSTRUCTIONAL PROGRAM WRITING**

How extreme are you?
- Talk with others about writing programs. What are their preferred formats? Are you committed to a scientifically oriented program development process rooted in data-based evaluation? How does that actually work out in your day to day workflow? Look for ways that you can become more proficient by reading journal articles, signing up for professional development, observing other ABA programs and/or attending an ABA conference. (And, yes, working through this manual counts!)

What's your style?
- Do your programs rely on improvised teaching methods? If so, try to analyze a session and look for the following inherent structure:
    - The design of materials and instructional setting
    - Attention and engagement issues
    - Structuring the presentation of the skill program
    - Implementation of prompts and prompt-fading strategies
    - Error correction
    - All-important issues related to motivation and reinforcement
- Consider how improvised sessions could benefit from the following:
    - Advanced planning
    - Writing plans down
    - Arranging a plan in a conceptually systematic manner
- Evaluate the details of your program write-ups:
    - Do you have too much or too little detail? Are the setting, apparatus, and materials sufficiently described?
    - Does the terminology reflect exactly what you want to say?
    - Is the writing organized? Would it benefit from categories or a format change?
    - Have you standardized and effectively communicated the concepts and methods of teaching?
    - Is each action described in a step-by-step fashion?
    - Does each section pass the "test of necessary and sufficient?"
- Review the chapter with other program personnel and draft a common program format for adoption by your agency

Chapter 3

Managing the Setting and Materials

Preparing the setting and managing the materials of instruction is a multi-faceted task that determines in advance how some or, perhaps, many aspects of the educational activity will occur. Will the activity flow smoothly or awkwardly? Will the student's performance be as error-free as possible or will learning opportunities be plagued with interruptions and distractions, delays, and unnecessary movements of materials that interfere with correct responding? The competent program designer understands the importance of good planning and strategically stacks the deck in favor of the student by engineering the environment before the student ever sits down. Once the session begins, a competent instructor confidently stage-manages educational materials with agility and deftness.

The present chapter presents terminology and concepts that fall under the general category of *stimulus control*. Stimulus control refers to the control of a student's performance by specific environmental stimuli and is concerned with the physical environment and its manipulation[1] to control behavior. Within this very large topic, six

---

[1] See later sections including "Attention and Engagement" and "Prompts and Prompt Hierarchies" for a discussion on the *instructor* as an environmental stimulus.

levels of organization will be discussed:

- General Environment
- Location
- Setting
- Setting Details
- Arrangement of Task Materials
- Stimulus Prompts

We will consider the instructional "environment" as more than a physical collection of objects and materials. The environment at any level of organization is defined by a complex array of relationships between objects, events, individuals, and their history of interaction. Arranging the physical environment optimally to enhance instruction and the acquisition of skills requires careful attention.

General Environment, Location, Setting

The term "general environment" can be used to refer to the highest level of environmental organization, characterized by a common set of culturally-consistent features that distinguishes it from other general environments. For the purposes of organizing and focusing instruction, general environments can be further divided along practical lines. Home, school, work, and community are four common subdivisions. Locations and settings further delineate the environment. For example, the school environment is divided into various locations such as the resource classroom, music room, and cafeteria. Within a resource classroom, various settings include the art center, group area, cubby area, and bathroom.

Differences in General Environments

An instructional environment is intertwined with its general environment. Thus, differences in general environments often lead to differences in instructional programming. For example, consider the potential variations in student instruction, between communities that vary markedly in the following attributes:

- Physical geographical features
- Dwellings and structures
- Transportation
- Preferred types of food, recreation, clothing, tools, furnishings
- Economic resources

Effects both large and small may follow from such divergences. One interesting example occurred when a student from Taiwan began an ABA program in the eastern United States and, despite repeated preference assessments, did not express a preference for any type of edible until shrimp flavored crackers from home were offered. To be sure, the influence of the general environment is pervasive. Virtually, every instructional target is significantly influenced by the general environment. In some respects, general environments determine the what, when, who, how, and why of target behavior. The role of teaching is to prepare students to function competently in such common, natural and "real" environments as defined by accepted cultural practices, traditions, and roles.

The Environment Dictates the Curriculum

"Managing" the environment begins by analyzing it to discover the practices, contingencies, and behavior relevant to "success" (obtaining reinforcement) and helping the student become competent in those behaviors. Analysis discovers what objects and people are present, what actions, processes, and interactions are necessary, and what potentially reinforcing events are available and desirable. The term "functional" has been used in behavior analysis and special education in a variety of ways but, here, we will use it to refer to behavior that produces a reinforcer that is intrinsic to a particular environment. For example, raising one's hand to volunteer an answer may be reinforced (and, therefore functional) in classroom groups. Discovering functional behavior within an environment is called "ecological assessment"[2] and is an essential activity for choosing goals and targets of instruction.

Environments are dynamic and complex entities which challenge analysts looking for consistency. The nature of functional behavior and the conditions under which it occurs may vary widely between environments. For example, behavior reinforced in a classroom could be very different from behavior reinforced in a neighborhood game of baseball. Differences exist between environments even in the ways one performs identical tasks. In one location or setting, bathrooms have automatic towel dispensers while others require manual cranking. Eating lunch at home is different than eating lunch at school or work. Contingencies between environments are not always consistent for the *same* behaviors. While one setting consistently rewards hard work another does not. Differential treatment often exists for self-initiation, courtesy, social interaction, or use of a particular vocabulary. Even within environmental settings that are ostensibly the same, the existence and operation of contingencies maintaining functional behavior can vary considerably.

Organizing Curriculum to Address Environmental Requirements

There is much that program planners can do to effectively prepare students for environmental realities. Once "real" (functional) behaviors and performance conditions required for success are clearly articulated they can be built into a "curriculum" by creating specialized goals and objectives with conditions and criteria that take into consideration the scope and fluency actually required of successful behavior to obtain intrinsic reinforcement built into each environment. The creation of skills necessary for successful inclusion is a prime example of the practice of complex environmental management and it will be discussed in detail within Chapter 8 – Generalization and Incorporation. However, manipulation of the environment to enhance generalization is extremely relevant to the present topic and some initial points will be introduced below.

Including the General Environment, Location and Setting in Written Programs

Program designers sometimes become concerned about the environment of an educational activity when it is time to expand into additional environments. However, since

---

[2] "Ecological assessment" (Cooper, Heron, & Heward, 2007) as applied to curriculum development will be further discussed in detail in Chapter 8.

all truly functional programs must eventually emerge into natural environments, planning from the start pays important dividends later on. Include generalization technology into programs as exemplified by the following recommendations:

- Establish common protocols for programs offered to students that address expansion of the program. Identify the target setting, include necessary pre-requisites, and devise standard phases of implementation relevant for each program. For example, create a rule for all imitation programs that a generalization component is completed for all programs prior to finally marking them "Mastered." Identify "hallway," "regular classroom," "groups," "gym," and "cafeteria" as the target locations and specify the conditions of performance for each (such as "imitates a one-step gross-motor movement when standing in a class group in the gym and modeled by the gym teacher from 20 feet")

- Whenever possible conduct programs in the target location and setting. For example, if the student has the minimum pre-requisites, conduct the program during story time, math class, gym, parking lot, bus, or during dinner. If modifications need to be made, try starting in the natural setting only for a short time. Find a time when the class is at a special (music, art, etc.) and run the program in the natural location without other students

- If the student is not ready for the target setting, contrive aspects of it as preparation. In a familiar setting where strong responding is already established, simulate instructions, placement of materials, and other aspects of the target environment that will be encountered later. (For an example, see the section "Moving from Discrete Trials to a Group Instruction Setting" in Chapter 8)

- Actively establish pre-requisites by including additional targets and conditions in programs that prepare the student for the target setting. Whenever appropriate and as early as possible, work in a variety of places, include steps to travel from location to location or setting to setting, set up and put away materials, and other incidental tasks that may be important survival skills when the skill is performed in the target setting. For example, while a student may perform well reading from a book, he may have difficulty getting the proper book out and finding a particular page. Include a diversity of program settings and locations in the conditions of instruction

- Identify and program for toleration of sub-optimal instructional conditions for the student. Teach her to tolerate noise and visual distractions. Establish strong attending and performance behavior that survives less frequent opportunities to respond or reinforcement that is less preferred

Managing the Physical Elements of Environments

An area that is efficient and logical in its arrangement of materials and equipment and eliminates unnecessary distractions and competing reinforcers succeeds in enhancing learning. When materials and equipment are arranged in ways that make them easy to use, participants think less about finding and using them and more about the task at hand. In each setting, program writers should take on the mantle of environmental engineer and consider the physical teaching environment:

- How big is the room or teaching space?
- How are desks, tables, and chairs placed?
- How convenient are instructional materials to the teacher who will use them?
- How are materials displayed?
- How will students interact with the instruction? Will they observe, move around, or manipulate materials?
- What comes before and what comes after? Will transitions be smooth?

The Setting of Discrete Trials

When it comes to arranging environments, there are none more exacting than the individualized teaching setting called "discrete trials." Discrete trials are characterized by highly structured, carefully prepared learning opportunities that rely heavily on precise timing and presentation of materials. This highly technical format of instruction has many physical aspects and elements including chairs, desks, tables, easels, boards, and bookcases as well as seating arrangements, placement of tokens, schedules, program books, data sheets, clocks, timers, and other ancillary equipment. The space must be customized to the task but in general, space should:

- Provide enough area so that movement is not awkward or confined and a feeling of claustrophobia is avoided

- Visually screen the student from distracting, irrelevant sights

- Isolate the student from bothersome noise as much as possible

- Afford some degree of privacy

- Provide multiple presentation surfaces (both horizontal and vertical) that are optimal for viewing and manipulation

- Provide enough room to display large arrays and configurations of materials

- Give the implementer easy access to staged materials and other activities on a secondary table to shorten time between trials or activities

- Store unused materials out of the way

- Have enough room to place a program book, timers, counters, data sheets, reinforcers, token boards, communication book, and other paraphernalia conveniently

- Allow the implementer to strategically position materials such as data collection forms and reinforcers to efficiently perform frequent tasks.

- Allow observation by others when necessary and approved

- Allow one other adult or peer to work at the table

Individualized Set-Up

Arrangement of the instructional space allows implementers to start to feel in control over the presentation and flow of events. The consistent positioning of equipment and materials quickly becomes familiar and comfortable with repetition. This is not to say that instructional programs never require alternate configurations to meet the needs of the procedure and student. Just about any aspect of the setting can vary but some aspects are more commonly adjusted.

Seating arrangement frequently varies from program to program, depending on the amount and kind of assistance that the student needs from the implementer, the interaction of the student with materials, and the size of the display area. Several seating configurations are possible that address different instructional needs. Table 1 presents five that are commonly adopted:

Table 1. Seating Configurations for Discrete Trial Instruction

Configuration	
Face-to-Face • Most likely to get attention of student • Easiest to use physical prompts • Requires "mirror" behavior from student • No surface to present materials	
Fully Facing Table • Orients student more to materials • Looks to implementer less probable • Physical prompting a little more difficult	
Angle-to-Table • 45 degree angle of student between implementer and table • Allows easy pivot from implementer to materials • Physical prompting more convenient	
Opposite Table • Maximum exposure to materials and implementer at the same time • Great for visual prompts • Difficult to give physical prompts or ensure in-seat behavior	
Opposite Corner • Good exposure to materials and implementer at the same time • Good for visual prompts • Convenient for physical prompts and to ensure in-seat behavior	

Arrangement of Task Materials

By "task materials" we mean the entire array of stimuli to which the student will respond (in addition to any teacher-based instructions). Depending on the task, the materials may include objects, papers, books, overhead projections, manipulatives, video, or combinations of media. The materials may be arranged in a simple array or a complex, multi-location presentation. The nature of the materials and the intended performance of the student in response to the stimulus presentation will determine the precise configuration for each task. A detailed definition of the target performance or task analysis of each activity is required to adequately plan the design. For example: "When presented with a picture of an airplane, the student will name 3 features." Consult, also, the stimulus conditions relevant to a task which may include the location of the student performance, the location of the task materials, the location of the teacher and student, and other details related to environment:

"When presented with a picture from a set of 10 different airplane pictures *during a whole-class presentation on transportation*, student will raise his hand and volunteer 3 correct features when the teacher asks, "Who can tell me the parts of an airplane?"

Tasks and Fields of Stimuli

Many tasks present samples, choices, or comparisons in an array and require the student to match, identify, or otherwise interact with the display. Samples and arrays can be constructed with various shapes depending on the desired student interaction and the materials involved. Most commonly, simple arrays of objects or pictures are placed in a straight line equidistant from each other but they could just as easily be placed in a semi-circle or in an intentionally haphazard array (called a "messy" array). Large arrays may be placed in rows or spread out in a wider area. Usually, a few common sense rules are generally observed:

- Present arrays of objects in a field that can be visualized all at once by the student without moving their head (unless the student is intentionally being taught to scan a large array)

- Comparison items (sometimes called distracters) within the field should be equidistant from each other and the student

- Present a field of choice objects within reach of the student but not so close that they will casually contact the items

- Present at least three choices to minimize successful guessing whenever possible

Program designers with students who have scanning or other attention issues may elect to present fields on inclined or even vertical surfaces. In severe cases of inattention, fields have been placed in unusual positions like hanging large cards from clothespins on a line strung across the student's field of vision. Sometimes fields are placed so that a student must deliberately lean forward to reach them or even get up and walk a few steps to make a choice.

Computer screens, tablets, and large, touch-sensitive display boards can be very effective ways to present a field of two-dimensional stimuli as long as the implementer is well-versed in manipulating the display and the field is clearly delimited. Obviously, the more complicated the field, the more challenging the display will be for the student. Pages in a book, worksheets, or displays in more than one place can be thought of as complex fields that students may find difficult to navigate. Many times, program designers organize complex fields in ways intended to simplify visual discrimination. Relevant areas or items may be demarcated with borders and backgrounds, or enhanced by making them larger, closer, or otherwise more prominent.[3]

When designing programs that present fields, program writers should ensure that students possess the necessary prerequisite performances. Pointing, picking up an object or card, and placing a card on top of another card are simple enough skills for most students but should not be taken for granted. The same is true for looking where the instructor points and scanning all of the items in a wide array (especially those on the periphery). Occasionally, it is necessary to pause and explicitly teach prerequisites (or improve their fluency) before continuing with the main program. With more complex fields and tasks, more complex prerequisites are necessary. Turning pages, obtaining and managing tools and implements, and organizing one's own workspace are important foundational skills for more advanced programs.

---

[3] Controlling the prominence of relevant stimuli to help students learn is an important area of stimulus control that we will return to in the chapters of Attention and Engagement and Prompts and Prompt Hierarchies.

Section Summary: Writing Programs and Designing Environments, Settings, and Materials

Effective program writers consider the nature and requirements of environments before final specification of target performances and consistently aim to incorporate topographies, conditions, and criteria that are naturally reinforced within the target environment. Programs begin in the least restrictive environment possible and gradually give way in planned stages to the target environment through the application of specific generalization technology. When including information on the design of the general environment, location, and setting for a program, writers choose relevant details from the following:

Target Environment

- What is the name of the target environment for the skill?
- What specific function will the skill play in the target environment?
- What specific topographies, conditions, and criteria must be developed in the new skill for it to function properly in the target environment?
- What is the least restrictive environment in which the program may begin?
- What is the plan for generalizing and incorporating the skill from the starting environment to the target environment?

Starting Environment

- What is the name of the general environment in which the program will start?
- What is the name of the location?
- What is the name of the setting?
- When will the program run?

Setting Details

- Describe the setup of furnishings and equipment
- What will the seating arrangement be for the task?
- Describe the placement of ancillary equipment (data sheet, program book, token boards, timers, visual schedule, etc.)

Task Materials

- What is the general setup of task materials and displays?

- Describe the shape of arrays and number of elements

- Describe any special positions or treatment of comparisons

- Describe the stimulus that will serve as the sample and method of delivery or position of the sample

- Describe necessary pre-requisite performances

Suggested Competencies for Implementers

Program designers ensure that all program implementers are skilled at the set-up and manipulation of setting conditions and instructional materials to properly carry out programs.

Competency: Effectively Design and Manage the Instructional Environment	
Implementer Skill	**Important Qualities of Implementer Performance**
1. Choose and arrange an appropriate setting for the target performance:	• Space allows for easy movement, is not cramped, and provides for convenient and appropriate storage, staging, and task presentation • Minimizes unwanted distractions and promotes engagement • Instructional surfaces, furniture, and equipment adequate to task • Storage and preparatory space convenient and optimized • Instructional materials conveniently located and staged prior to implementation • Data collection, programs, and other informational sources present • Ancillary materials (tokens, PECS materials, visual schedules, etc.) are appropriately located
2. Optimize seating for the task presentation	• Student is accessible for prompts • Student can see and reach materials and all displays. Student can see implementer
Competency: A variety of individualized skill programs are presented that effectively manipulate materials	
3. Present an expressive naming task presenting one object or picture	• Object to be named presented cleanly and easily visible within the student's field of vision

4.	**Present a matching to sample task with a sample and field of choices**	• Appropriate spacing of distracters is exhibited • Distracters are equidistant • Field is within student's field of vision and reach • Sample is presented cleanly and crisply • Position of correct choice is randomized from trial to trial **Positions of incorrect choices are randomized from trial to trial**
5.	**Present a receptive identification task with a field of choices**	• Appropriate spacing of distracters is exhibited • Distracters are equidistant • Field is within student's field of vision and reach • Position of correct choice is randomized from trial to trial **Positions of incorrect choices are randomized from trial to trial**
6.	**Sorting three shapes (e.g., 3 bears, 3 trucks, 3 balls) into three containers with a starting sample of the shape placed in the container. Initiate sort by giving shapes one at a time**	• Student can clearly see sample of shape placed in bin • Bins are arranged equidistant from each other and the student • Shape to be sorted is presented cleanly and crisply within the student's field of vision • Shapes waiting to be sorted are placed out of the way and do not complete for the student's attention
7.	**Present two skill programs consecutively**	• Changeover of materials rapidly and efficiently done without losing the engagement of the student
8.	**Present a fine motor task involving tools or implements** • Cut a paper along a line (any shape) • Color within a shape • Trace letters	• Arrange work surface with adequate space to work and manipulate materials • Position tools so that student can easily find them • Provide place for tools and implements when not in use • Position student so that physical prompts can be delivered as needed

9.	Present a self-help task involving manipulation of clothing	• Choose position for student that is appropriate for task and setting (i.e., standing, seated) • Arrange/Orient starting position of clothing to match learning step • Position student so that physical prompts can be delivered as needed
10.	Present instructional programs in a variety of settings and locations, once initial mastery is obtained in the starting setting	• Within the capabilities of the student, vary set-up, seating arrangement, and presentation of materials to suit the new setting and more closely approximate the target setting

What's Next?
***Put this chapter to work*: MANAGING THE SETTING AND MATERIALS**

- Take a look at recent programs and assess the adequacy of your treatment of information related to the following points discussed in the chapter:
    - General Environment, Location, Setting
    - Setting Details
    - Arrangement of Task Materials

- How does your general environment reflect the priorities and constraints of the culture? How do the priorities and constraints affect your choice of goals and target behaviors? Can you name some specific examples?

- Choose two to three target environments for your students. What are the reinforcers and contingencies present in these natural environments that are accessible to your students? What skills do they need to access these reinforcers?

- What are some ways that you can manage the environment to minimize inconsistencies and variations that exist from environment to environment?

- Add a generalization plan to some of your programs and carry it out. What issues occurred and how difficult would it be to expand the practice?

- What seating plans are used in your program? Why?

- Evaluate the physical environment of your program space using the guidelines in the chapter. How can you improve?

- Evaluate implementers using the suggested competencies. Where should you conduct more training?

Chapter 4

Attention and Engagement

Discussions of instructional methodology within the educational and behavior analytic communities are replete with references to "attending," "attention" and "attention span". It is, perhaps, axiomatic that attention is a pre-requisite for delivering instruction and that a successful learning opportunity depends on it. Yet, many times, specific methods to facilitate the process of "paying attention" within an instructional program may be absent or lack coherence and detail.

This may stem from an insufficient understanding of the nature of attending behavior. The common definition of the verb "attending" includes the following:

Definition: Attending:

1. To pay attention; listen or watch attentively; direct one's thought; pay heed: to attend to a speaker.

2. To be present: She is a member but does not attend regularly.

3. To be present and ready to give service; wait (usually followed by on or upon): to attend upon the Queen.[4]

---

[4]Attending. (n.d.). *Dictionary.com Unabridged*. Retrieved January 25, 2013, from Dictionary.com website: http://dictionary.reference.com/browse/attending

While satisfactory for the purposes of language usage and identifying general behaviors often associated with attending like listening and watching, this definition is inadequate from a technical point of view because it fails to provide information on the topographies, parameters, and functions of attending behavior. In this section, we will discuss the nature of attending behavior from the scientifically-based perspective of behavior analysis and, especially, how attending functions in the acquisition of new skills. With this understanding, we will explore interventions to control the occurrence of attention and engagement and facilitate learning. By turns we will consider several basic questions:

- How is attending adaptive in everyday life and what is its role in learning?
- What is generally meant by "attending" in the language of education and behavior change?
- What are the topographies of attending?
- How is attending behavior established, increased, directed?
- How may this information be integrated into educational applications and program writing?

Attention as a Response to the Environment

At a basic level, attention and engagement involves sensation and perception of environmental stimuli and events. Human capacity to respond to the environment is, perhaps, one of the most fundamental abilities contributing to survival. The ability to adapt – that is, acquire behavior that responds to changing conditions, events, and actions – allows for an almost infinitely flexible process of behavior change that steadily improves the individual's competence in self-preservation tasks, including finding food, shelter, and protection. Survival is no easy task and humans have excelled at it, in part, because our brains are designed to make connections between what we sense (see, hear, feel, taste, smell) and the consequences of what we do.

The Behavioral Timeline

A "Behavioral Timeline" diagrams three critical events that become connected when learning occurs:[5]

$$A \dashrightarrow B \dashrightarrow C$$

The letter A represents *antecedents* – environmental events that are sensed by the individual, B represents a *behavior* that occurs in the presence of those antecedents, and C represents the *consequences* (reinforcement or punishment) that follow the behavior. When we behave in a particular way and receive reinforcement there is a tendency to repeat the behavior in the future. Fortunately for us, our brain is not just paying attention to receiving reinforcement, it is also responding to the conditions under which the behavior was reinforced (the antecedents). For example, randomly looking for berries when we are hungry will be rewarded if and when we find the berries. Tomorrow, if we noticed *where* the berries were located, our task will be easier. Consistently finding berries is facilitated by learning the environmental conditions where berries are found. The association between specific environmental/antecedent conditions and reinforcement is strengthened each time we look for and are reinforced by finding berries.

The world is filled with many sensations, from the sights and sounds of animals to the feel of cold and wet grass. Every waking moment provides a deluge of visual, auditory, tactile, gustatory, and olfactory stimulation. Behavior occurs in the presence of many irrelevant as well as relevant environmental stimuli. Land features, direction of travel, time of day and temperature are stimuli present when berries are found but, so too, are the phase of the moon and the color of our socks. With hundreds of stimuli simultaneously present, it may seem a marvel that only functional stimuli become correlated with successful behavior. Yet, the mechanism is most likely gradual. At first, associations are strengthened between most if not all the stimuli present when reinforcement occurs; for each, the connection is strengthened just a little bit. Therefore, when we find the berries we may tend to over-identify the determining factors for our discovery to include even "superstitious" influences. Over time and many experiences, randomly occurring events do not receive the same number of small increments in their strength of association with reinforcement because they do not occur as often (we still find

---

[5] In behavior analysis, this is called a "three-term contingency."

the berries even when we wear a different color of socks). The environmental stimuli that occur reliably are most strongly associated with desirable or undesirable consequences produced by a particular behavior.

While behavior is centered on obtaining reinforcement, sensation of the environment allows individuals to discriminate the conditions under which behavior is reinforced. What, therefore, does an individual "do" when sensing the environment? Is sensation a behavior? Must a student engage in any special actions of sensation, called "paying attention," prior to behaving in order to facilitate the connection of the environmental event, behavior, or reinforcer: Is the mere occurrence of an event with our field of vision or a sound within our auditory threshold sufficient to qualify as a stimulus that can become associated with reinforcement and occasion the occurrence of behavior? The following discussion will consider these questions.

The Behavior of Attending

Imagine a 4th grade class during a fire drill. The class is seated at their desks when the alarm bell rings. Without being told, they immediately begin to get up, move in an orderly way to the front of the classroom, line up, and exit the building. The teacher accompanies them and supervises their exit, ensuring that all are present and responding correctly, and then closes the door behind them. In the observed chain of events, a bell sound was produced and exit behavior followed. A history of reinforcement for responding to the bell will be assumed to account for this learned behavior. The student's capability to receive auditory sensations is also necessary (i.e. they must be able to hear the bell).

In this case, is hearing the same as attending? Among all of the sounds that were occurring at the time, the students responded to *one* by exiting. Did they engage in "paying attention" to the sound? It hardly seems necessary to insert an additional step in the chain of events. It is most economical to say that there exists a strong relationship between hearing an alarm bell and exiting the classroom because exiting when alarm bells sound has been reinforced in the past. We need not insert the extra step "paying attention" because we note that the characteristics of some stimuli may allow them to be easily distinguished from other stimuli, without additional efforts made by an individual. A bell that is louder than any other sound or a bright flashing light may be sensed regardless of whatever else a student is doing.

Stimulus Saliency

In some cases, the characteristics of stimuli make them relatively indistinguishable from other stimuli. This can be a problem if instruction depends on attention to subtle environmental stimulus attributes. For example, some listeners do not remember the names of characters during multi-page narrations. If the teacher repeats the name several times, emphasizes it in the sentence with a dramatic tone of voice, and points to a picture of the character every time his name is read, individuals may more easily distinguish the occurrence of the name pronounced by the teacher. The enhancement of certain features of a stimulus to make it more distinguishable is called manipulating the "saliency" of a stimulus. There are many techniques for enhancing saliency which vary with the characteristics of the stimulus. For example, to enhance the saliency of spoken words or narration, much has been written about adding visual stimuli, a dramatic tone of voice, or movement.

Consider a situation involving stimuli that vary in saliency. A kindergarten student with autism is directed, with the rest of the class, to move to a group story area. The student in question moves to the story area as directed and seats himself facing towards a shelf of books containing his favorite book. While the students are sitting in a group, the teacher opens a story book and narrates a story while turning pages. During the narration, the target student continues to stare at his favorite book, sometimes makes stereotypic vocalizations, engages in two 15 second episodes of rocking, and looks at his fingers repeatedly. At the end of the story, the teacher asks the class several wh-questions about the story. The student does not volunteer to answer any of these questions. When the teacher asks him a direct question about the story he says, "I don't know."

Some might say that the student did not "listen" to the story. Children who are reported to have "problems paying attention" seem to behave differently from those who are "paying attention." Sometimes it is relatively easy to pick them out in a group. They may not make eye contact or face the speaker; they may not nod their heads or react to a speaker or a notable action. Instead, they may engage in seemingly incompatible behavior—fidgeting, staring off, and/or talking to their neighbors. Similar behavior also occurs in individualized learning formats like discrete trials. Students look down or away from the instructor and materials, they may vocalize repetitively or engage in other stereotypic behavior like rocking or tapping; ultimately, they do not respond when directions are presented or materials are displayed and an observer may comment that the student was not "paying attention."

In this example, there would appear to be some events dominating the classroom environment that are easy to sense, and other events that become available to sense only when the students engage in certain kinds of behavior. First, the teacher delivered a direction to the entire class to assemble in the story area. It would be common for a direction of this sort to be clearly articulated in a relatively loud and authoritative sounding voice. Such a direction stands out from the other sounds of the classroom. In fact, the student in question interrupted his activity and moved to the story area without assistance. Next, the sound of the teacher's voice while narrating the story, the turn of pages, and the visual stimuli of the large pictures shown, are also relatively easy to distinguish, even if the student does not seem to react to them. However, the details of the story, like the names, actions, attributes, sequence of the story (i.e. the "content") are contained within the more subtle aspects of the verbal stimuli produced. A student must discriminate one word from another, particular groups, patterns and sequences of words and sentences, voice inflection, and other complex variations in the vocal stimuli. Even before we ask whether a student "understands" the vocal content, we must ask whether they *attend* to it. If a student, once seated in a group, engages in behavior that interferes with sensing the subtle variations in vocal stimuli produced by the narration, it may well be impossible for him to engage in appropriate target behavior. Therefore, reinforcement from the teacher is unlikely to occur because the student never senses the stimuli that control such behavior.

Directed Sensing Behavior

The term "attending" is common in discussions of instruction and usually used to refer to *specific student actions* that result in sensing environmental stimuli – that is, directed sensation. At a party we may look across the room and see friends engaging in conversation but unless we move closer we do not hear what they are saying. During instruction one must open a book and inspect the pages before interacting with the content. In the process of interacting with the environment we may inspect, regard, stare, strain to hear, "look someone up and down," taste, sniff, palpate, and engage in a variety of other actions that fall into the category of directed sensing or attending. Such behavior brings the individual into contact with stimuli that were not previously sensed. Once stimuli are sensed, the individual may react to them in some way that can be reinforced. As we discussed above, reinforced behavior over time produces a strong association or probability between the occurrence of the stimulus and the occurrence of the behavior.

Summary Points

- **Sensation** of environmental attributes or events is a pre-requisite for learning because only then can such stimuli become associated with behavior and reinforcement and result in behavior change

- **Saliency** refers to the characteristics of stimuli that determine the ability of individuals to sense them. Saliency can be manipulated or enhanced through instructional intervention

- **Salient stimuli** are easily sensed with little effort while stimuli lacking saliency may require additional behavior to permit the individual to sense them

Which Topographies of Behavior?

In many discussions of attending, the topographies referred to implicitly or explicitly often include these well-known and observable topographies:

- Looking at the face of the speaker
- Orienting body towards the speaker
- Looking in response to an instruction like "Look," "Ready," or the person's name
- Looking where the instructor points
- Looking at materials presented

These behaviors are intended to make sensation (e.g. seeing and hearing) of relevant stimuli more probable. Specific topographies of directed sensation are sometimes taught as part of a chain, as in "ready" behavior that is prompted before a learning trial. When a student looks at an instructor with "hands in lap, calm body, and quiet voice," the sensation of relevant instructional stimuli that are about to be presented is more probable.

Sometimes simple "attending" responses like those listed above may not be sufficient for stimuli presented by an instructional task and more specific effort on the part of both student and instructor may be required. For example, concerning the previous example of listening to a story, a rather complex set of presentations and attending interactions may occur. The table below lists some that could occur:

Attending Responses

General Discriminative Stimuli (S^Ds)	Initial Attending Responses	Specific, Related S^Ds	"Engagement" and Responding to content	Reinforcement
Teacher speaking in dramatic tone of voice Book opened to colorful pictures Other students looking at book	Student follows instruction to sit in group Student looks at teacher and book Student listens to story	Name of character spoken when teacher points to picture Teacher names place where character is going Action demonstrated while teacher reads corresponding sentence Consequences of character's actions explained while teacher points to picture	Students repeat name of character while looking at picture. Students answer question, "Who is this?" Students repeat place name, observe picture, Students answer question, "Where is character going?" Students perform action in imitation of teacher. Students answer question, "What is character doing?"	Doing the same thing as others Answering a question correctly and receiving praise Looking at interesting pictures Listening to interesting sentences, actions, events involving interesting characters Avoiding correction for not responding like other students Avoiding boredome Avoiding errors Avoiding doing something different than peers

In the first column, marked "General Discriminative Stimuli" highly salient environmental stimuli are listed that produce responding by the student called "Initial Attending Responses." Attending to the general S^Ds, increases the saliency of more subtle aspects of instruction (in the column marked "Specific, Related S^Ds") such as the sound of the name of the character each time it is spoken. The student may react (as listed in the "Engagement and Responding to Content" column) to the more subtle S^Ds by overt responding (repeating the name, pointing at the character's picture, saying "Look", laughing) or more covertly (shifting eye gaze to features of the character's face, sub-audibly repeating the name that the teacher speaks). As the narration of the story continues and the S^D's evolve, the student continues to shift/direct attention to the unfolding stimuli and respond in overt and covert ways.

The shift of attention and responding to the content of S^Ds during instruction occurs in all teaching formats, not exclusively in groups. While many 1:1 discrete trial programs may be simpler than the task above (especially if we focus only on the single trial), complexity increases exponentially if we consider a series of trials, the inclusion of more complex targets in a session, interspersing mastered trials from different programs, or forming multi-step performance sequences from individual programs. Programs of this type require a strong chain of specific attending behaviors followed by sustained responding to the shifting stimuli of the task or a series of tasks. This has been called "active responding," "responding to content" or "engagement," and may be a more precise specification of what is meant when we advise instructors to "obtain the student's attention" or exhort students to "listen."

More Summary Points

- The "topographies" of the behavior of paying attention can vary widely from passive (just being present in the environment when an event occurs) to highly active

- Simple directed sensing responses like looking, orienting, or assuming a "ready" position may be sufficient to sense simple S^Ds

- More active, complex, sustained, and dynamic directed sensing may be required for complex tasks

Problems in Attention and Engagement

The stimulus-behavior-reinforcement chain can be a rather complex and challenging event to arrange and control. Several potential problems in attention and engagement have been described so far:

1. Failure to sense relevant S^Ds because their characteristics are such that they are indistinguishable from other objects, attributes or events in the environment (saliency)

2. Failure to respond to initial, more salient S^Ds leading to a failure to sense following, more subtle S^Ds.

3. Inability to engage in or avoidance of specific attending topographies for brief or sustained periods

4. (Even if directed sensation results in attention to relevant S^Ds), lack of active responding to relevant S^Ds (content) of instruction that results in an absence of reinforcement, disengagement, and failure to engage in further directed attention

These problems are frequently observed in students that avoid eye contact, engage in high rates of self-stimulatory behavior and other off-task behavior, or have a conditioned aversive reaction to various aspects of the instructional environment and engage in escape behavior. Problems may also manifest themselves when work is too difficult or procedures are instituted in a faulty manner by instructors. In the following section, we will discuss practices for program writers to avoid problems and promote sufficient attention and engagement to facilitate learning.

Increasing Attention and Engagement

This section will focus on three primary strategies for increasing attention and engagement:

1. Increase the discrimination of stimuli

2. Directly shape/reinforce directed sensation behavior

3. Deliver prompts that improve the student's awareness of available reinforcers or improve their momentary effectiveness

1. **Increase the Discrimination of Stimuli**

   Strategies to improve the perception of specific stimuli that are relevant for instructional purposes range from simple to complex and may be classified as socially-based or stimulus-based. Socially-based strategies rely on actions of individuals other than the student which attract attention to the target stimulus:

   Socially-Based Strategies

   - Asking student, "Ready?"
   - Pointing to stimulus
   - Modeling action
   - Giving verbal directions
   - Making an unusual noise or gesture

   Some strategies also involve more specific guidance to interact with the relevant stimuli. These actions by the student are sometimes called "observing responses" and have been a component of many published studies (Shahan & Podlesnik, 2008). Observing responses take several forms including:

   Observing Responses

   - Looking at each item in an array prior to being given an instruction
   - Touching each item in an array prior to being given an instruction
   - Naming each item in an array prior to being given an instruction

   In general, observing responses are most effective when they are closely related to a dimension of the relevant stimulus. For example, touching each item in an array may prompt a student to look generally but not specifically at the items. However, taking each object out of a bag and placing them in a line on the table requires substantially more visual interaction with the stimuli. Nevertheless, observing responses come at a cost. Although they are an effective means of promoting attending to the specific relevant stimuli, observing responses require additional effort that may not be well tolerated in all situations.

Stimulus-Based Strategies

In the larger community as well as in instructional settings, stimulus-based attending strategies focus on targeted aspects of the environment to make them more prominent. We may use all capitals in a text message to help it stand out as more important from normal text, sirens and flashing lights alert us to fast moving emergency vehicles, or a strong odor is added to normally odorless natural gas to warn us of leaks. Manipulation of stimulus prominence is frequently used as part of a prompting procedure to increase attending to particular aspects of instructional stimuli (see Chapter 5: Prompts and Prompt Hierarchies). Stimulus or materials-based practices either act on the stimuli themselves (intra-stimulus) by exaggerating certain aspects, or by adding redundant stimuli (extra-stimulus).

Exaggeration (manipulating specific dimensions of stimuli to increase prominence)

- Larger or smaller size
- Distinctive colors or patterns; bold or underlined text
- Prominent position – in front, on top, set apart from group, higher
- Modify shape to make more distinctive or recognizable (remove background, darken outline, etc.)

Redundancy (adding additional stimuli to increase prominence)

- Arrow points to correct choice
- Circle drawn around stimulus
- Underlined
- Placed in container, on colored square, contrasting background
- Beeping sound as locator
- Distinctive odor
- Flashing light

2. Directly Shape/Reinforce Attending Behavior

While augmenting the prominence of relevant environmental stimuli may reduce the extent to which an individual must engage in directed sensation, it cannot eliminate the need in most settings. Consequently, students must have the various response topographies of attention and engagement in their performance repertoires. If such behavior does not exist, it must be explicitly taught, generalized across people and settings, and maintained through reinforcement. Commonly taught attending topographies include:

Attending (Directed Sensation) Topographies

- Look at a model, speaker, picture, object when directed
- Scan an array
- Listen to a phrase, sentence, story, song
- Touch, hold, manipulate an object
- Shift attention from an object to a person and back
- Imitate a model alone or in a group
- Sustain the behaviors above for varying periods of time when reinforcement and the opportunity to respond is intermittent

Performance of the attending behaviors may occur for some students as a component of other skills. Scanning an array, for example, may occur when a student is asked to match one object with another identical object from a field of three objects. However, in learners when scanning may be severely deficient or non-existent, a more specific and structured programming strategy may be a prerequisite. For example, rather than immediately working on matching, we may start with "finding the x" to establish some instructional control of directed sensing as preparation for matching. Three identical blocks are placed on a table and the student is asked to find the one with an x (or favorite animal figure or sparkly shape, etc.; if necessary, a *preferred* item would be chosen as the object to find).

Other simple attending skills may be shaped similarly. A small, highly preferred toy or edible could be randomly placed inside one of three identical, opaque containers out of view of the student and lined up on the table. An instructor could then teach the student to select and open the container that is tapped or receives a point.

==Strengthening imitation is an excellent means of increasing directed sensation.== Imitation of fun, gross motor actions or actions with objects (often those that make sounds or create obvious consequences) can be gradually extended from single actions to multiple, continuous actions and then, actions in various environments with both adults and peers, eventually graduating to simplified versions of *Follow the Leader* and *Simon Says*.

Shaping Attention to Others

Students who do not look at others fail to "recruit" potentially reinforcing social interactions that are available in an environment containing other individuals. Logically, there could be three basic reasons for this:

1. The student does not find social interactions reinforcing

2. The student does not know that reinforcement is available

3. The student does not know how to recruit reinforcement in this situation

Increasing attention to others ultimately depends on the existence of reinforcing social interactions. Initially, frequent, short, contrived interactions producing reinforcing experiences (based on careful observation of what the student finds pleasurable) are the most beneficial. Programs may involve the instructor exhibiting unusual or amusing behavior to attract the student's attention, covering the eyes of the student and playfully asking, "Where's [student name]?" Highly interactive games such as "Tag" are also attractive to students. Each trial involving these simple games is presented and the student is monitored for eye contact, smiles, approaches, or verbalizations. For example, place a young student in a chair in the center of the room and move to a location 5-10 feet away and, without warning (but with an obvious smile and refraining from doing anything that might frighten the child), rapidly move towards the student and tickle them, dramatically saying, "Here comes the monster." If the student seems to enjoy the experience, the instructor dramatically stalks to a different place in the room and repeats. After several repetitions, the student is often moving his gaze, following the adult around the room carefully, in anticipation. Of course, it is important to stress that activities like this are only useful when one identifies the dividing line between enjoyable and scary activities for a student. While this is true, however, it is also common to observe initial resistance to adult attention that gradually recedes with the right experience, transforming (sometimes rather quickly) into delight.

When walking with a student from one place to another, some tend to lapse into self-stimulatory behavior. With one such student, when he began rotating his head back and forth as we walked down a school hallway, I lightly "bumped" into him, eliciting an interruption in the self-stimulatory behavior and a glance up at me. I smiled and gave the student a high-five. I then switched to his other side as we walked. After a few seconds he began moving his head repetitively again and I bumped into him lightly once more. As he interrupted his self-stimulatory behavior this time, he looked at me with a smile. I smiled back broadly, patted him on the back, and switched sides again as we continued walking. After several repetitions, he began glancing at me every few seconds, smiling in anticipation and did not resume self-stimulatory behavior. To emphasize and encourage continued monitoring, I switched sides a few times at random times as we walked down the hallway. Within two five-minute practice walks the student was exhibiting zero self-stimulatory head movement and was alert to just about every movement that I made. Having shaped strong monitoring behavior, we were then able to improve additional skills like learning the destinations of places within the school, examining displays on hallway bulletin boards together, and greeting familiar people as they passed.

Joint Attention

Simple procedures like those above shape fledgling behavior like eye-contact, listening to others, and even sustained monitoring of a partner. These skills can be built upon in many ways because they establish the partner as a reinforcer and attending as a means of obtaining reinforcement. Such skills form a basis for more sustained and coordinated interactive behavior called "joint attention." Joint attention or shifting attention back and forth between objects and a partner is a cornerstone of interactive play, conversation, and cooperative work in groups. Very young children repeatedly "reference" (that is, look at) their mother or father when venturing out past a certain distance. Other forms of referencing emerge during play and in social situations. Joint attention seems to be at least partially about looking at a partner for a reaction to actions and events. For example, if a pile of blocks falls over, a student may look at a partner and, observing that the partner laughs, begin to laugh herself. During completion of an art project, a boy may repeatedly observe the actions of others, make comments, and show his own work.

Sample Program to Shape Early Joint Attention

Phase 1

Approach the student, maintaining a distance of about three feet, and quietly observe him for 15-30 seconds. If the student tolerates the observation, increase proximity for several 1-2 second intervals by approaching to within one foot of the student, looking closely at whatever he is doing, praising the student, and then moving back to the original observation point. Continue for up to five minutes. Repeat several times.

Phase 2

Approach and engage in highly preferred modes of interaction for brief intervals such as physical play, tickling, enthusiastic praise, silly behavior, high fives; during highly preferred activities, show interest in what the student does and react dramatically to all of his movements, manipulate play materials in amusing ways, etc. Cycle through various actions for 5-15 seconds, and try to attract brief eye contact or head movement away from what the student is looking at. Praise and disengage after a response occurs. Repeat in 15 seconds. Conduct 5-10 trials several sessions per day for 3-4 days. Be persistent in attracting the attention of the student but take care not to annoy him.

Phase 3

Allow the student to choose a preferred activity or, if necessary, direct him. The activity should include enough materials for more than one person to play. Sand or water tables, blocks, train construction sets and other themed play sets, and many other kinds of play materials are suitable. Wait for the student to become highly engaged in the activity, approach and begin to interact independently with the materials in proximity to the student. Slowly begin to initiate simple interactions with the student according to the nature of the activity:

- Hand the student a desired material while saying, "Here" but don't let go of the piece until the student looks at you. Hold the piece up to your eyes if necessary

- Invent fun actions for the student to do: "Fill up my bucket." If the student is not inclined to comply right away, fill up the bucket yourself and act like you're having a great time. Keep cycling through novel actions that entice the student to join. Be alert for attracting the gaze of the student to your actions, materials, or facial expression and reinforce all approximations

- If other peers are in the same location, play with them as well, clearly having fun by smiling and laughing, to attract the attention of the target student

Section Summary

From the perspective of attention and engagement, we have discussed pre-requisites to a correct performance:

- The student *must be* able to sense the relevant S^Ds (instructions, materials, etc.)

- The student must engage in directed sensation and engagement behavior with relevant SDs wherever they are not sufficiently prominent

- Shaping the various topographies of attending behavior to both instructional materials and other individuals may require separate and explicit programming prior to its incorporation as a component of a more complex performance

3. Attention and Engagement Prompts

Even when programs address the steps above, teachers and behavior analysts have seen how the actual attending performances of students can vary considerably from learning opportunity to learning opportunity and session to session. Attention and engagement *prompts* are antecedent procedures designed to manipulate/accentuate the discriminability of the available reinforcer and the conditions under which it will be delivered to facilitate the occurrence of a target behavior. During instruction, attention and engagement prompts connect the student with the reinforcer *before* a direction is given, in an attempt to initiate approach behavior to the reinforcing stimulus. When initial engagement with the reinforcer is obtained, the normal S^Ds (direction, presentation of work materials, etc.) is then interposed while there is a momentary spike in the student's motivation to obtain the reinforcer. Described in this way, attention and engagement prompts act in a manner equivalent to *motivating operations* (Cooper, Heron, & Heward, 2007). Some attention and engagement prompts are similar to reminders:

- Display/manipulate reinforcer
- Offer small sample of reinforcer
- Describe/remind of contingencies of reinforcement
- Give sample of reinforcement

Performing one of the steps above brings the individual into contact with the reinforcer briefly before the stimulus is removed. This potentially increases the student's motivation to work to get it back. Even powerful reinforcers may, at times, require manipulation in this way, especially if long periods of work are required between reinforcer deliveries.

Other types of prompts may facilitate attention and engagement by introducing a series of highly preferred response opportunities that transform into the target response opportunity. For example, an instructor may present an easy mastered task to a student that has been associated with strong reinforcement. The student may readily engage with a few repetitions of the task, attending strongly, before the instructor switches to presentation of the first trial of the actual task. This presentation scheme has been described as a "high-probability request series" (Hock & Mace, 1986) and will have a prominent place in future discussions (e.g. Chapter 8). Several attention and engagement prompts are based on high-probability request series principles:

- Compliment/Praise Student
- Instruction to Perform Incidental Task
- Incidental Comment or Question to Student
- Instructor Engages in Task

Summary of Strategies

A consolidated list of 19 simple prompts for promoting attention and engagement is summarized below, based on the previous discussion. All prompts are delivered as antecedents to instruction and behavior. The strategies generate attention and engagement through:

Type	Strategy Description
1	Prompting directed sensation to relevant instructional stimuli
2	Attracting the student's attention through delivery of exaggerated or redundant stimuli
3	Directing the student's attention to potential reinforcers
4	Manipulating reinforcers to increase their effectiveness

Individual strategies may be combined into a hierarchy or multi-step procedure where progression through the steps of the procedure depends on how easily attention and engagement occurs. For example, the teacher may begin by waiting for ready behavior, progress to physically establishing it (if ready behavior is not exhibited in two seconds), then attract eye contact by manipulating the task material in front of the student. Some combinations may be natural for certain students such as those who love (and require) dramatic, fast-paced interaction. Some instructors may start out with a simple strategy but include additional prompts as the circumstances warrant. Regardless, proficiency with all prompts is important for teachers who work with a variety of students with attention and engagement difficulties.

Summary Table of Attention and Engagement Strategies

Strategy	Type	Description
Wait	NA	When an established history of scheduled reinforcement is strong, pausing at the right moment (i.e. interrupting the schedule) may result in attending to the instructor or task materials, or exhibiting "ready" behavior
Give Instruction for Eye Contact	1	A direct verbal or gestural prompt given by instructor to look at instructor or task materials
Instruction to Attend to Materials	1	A verbal statement or gesture directing student's attention to a task-related stimulus array
Prompt Student Point to Stimulus Array or Sample	2	**An observing response** in which student is verbally or physically prompted to point to predetermined parts of the task's stimulus array such as each member of a choice set or a sample
Prompt Student Touch to Stimulus Array or Sample	2	**An observing response.** Same as above except that the student touches the materials
Have Student Manipulate Sample	2	**An observing response.** Student is prompted verbally or physically to pick up and explore (visually and tactilely) members or parts of the task materials
Prompt "Ready" Behavior	2	An instructor prompt for student to assume a pre-taught attentive position, usually including placing hands on table or knees, head and eyes oriented towards instructor, and remaining quiet and motionless
Give Physical Touch/ Positioning Assistance	2	Any physical touch designed to elicit attentive behavior from the student. May depend on previously established routines such as when instructor has physically assisted student to assume a "ready" position and has gradually faded the guidance to a more abbreviated touch

Strategy	Type	Description
Unusual Noise or Event	3	A stimulus whose qualities and onset is engineered to attract the attention of the student—e.g., tapping the table. May capitalize on the student's curiosity or a previous experience with such noises. May include rapid onset at an intensity that varies markedly from the general noise level to facilitate discrimination and increase effectiveness
Display/Manipulate Reinforcer	4	The instructor holds actual reinforcer object or picture of reinforcing event so that the student observes it. Instructor may manipulate the object so that it makes noise or lights up. (This procedure is sometimes followed by reminding the student of the reinforcement contingencies)
Offer Reinforcer	4	The instructor holds out to student reinforcing object or picture representing the reinforcing event and asks if the student desires the stimulus with words like, "Do you want this?" Actions are tailored to produce some sort of affirmative response like saying "Yes," nodding head, or reaching for stimulus. Instructor then directs student to finish work task while repositioning stimulus in its normal space (or possibly, in a more prominent location)
Describe/Remind of Contingencies of Reinforcement	4	The instructor states contingencies of reinforcement for present task: "Remember, if you do five more steps you get to play with the puzzle!" May be used with the visually-oriented procedure Offer Reinforcer.
Give Sample of Reinforcement	4/5	The instructor gives sample of reinforcing stimulus non-contingently to student, usually followed by a statement like, "Let's work for more now." When sample of non-edible is given, procedure requires withdrawal of stimulus, which can provoke undesirable behavior. Also requires that instructor avoid giving sample following inattentive behavior. Typical occasion and function for delivering reinforcer sample is when attentive behavior has already been established and a more extensive level of engagement is desired

Strategy	Type	Description
Compliment/Praise Student	4/5	Before giving instruction, instructor praises student, using general language or language specific to the task, such as "You're so smart!" or "You're working so fast!" As in giving a sample of reinforcement, requires that instructor avoid giving compliment or praise following inattentive behavior and that an initial level of attention to instruction is established that will be accelerated by the procedure
Instruction to Perform Incidental Task	5	The instructor directs student to perform action unrelated to primary task. Incidental action is usually short, already in the repertoire of the student. May be useful to maintain attention to teacher during pauses in instruction (such as when new materials are being set up) or to achieve behavioral momentum which makes following task-related behavior more likely
Incidental Comment or Question to Student	5	Similar to *Instruction to Perform Incidental Task*. Designed to elicit a response that may facilitate continued responding on the target task. Comment or question must provoke responses more readily than the regular task instruction in order to be worthwhile. Example: [Instructor points to task materials] "Do you see this?!! Wow, what's this?" [Student looks at materials and reaches for them—instructor helps student into a ready position and then gives instruction]
Instructor Engages in Task	4/5	The instructor completes a portion of the task in a manner that facilitates subsequent engagement by the student. May function by initiating an established chain whose partial completion then enlists the student's participation. Also, by decreasing initial performance requirement for reinforcement, may temporarily lower the "threshold" for performance initiation
Engage in Task in Novel/Interesting Manner	4/5	Identical to *Instructor Engages in Task* except that instructor performs steps of task in manner that attracts attention of student such as by exaggerating or emphasizing certain actions, making dramatic comments ("Here I go...!"), or reinforcing herself on completion of a step

Some Final Advice on Maintaining Attention and Engagement

Most instruction is still presented socially. In order to capitalize on the intrinsic social opportunities within every instructional experience, implementers need to establish that interactions are expected and fun:

- **Begin by establishing a social "connection" and sustain it for the *entire* teaching session.** It is common for me to recommend that instructors begin a session by playing with the student or engaging in some other brief, but fun, socially engaging activity. Tickles, high fives, holding hands and jumping together, spinning, and other gross motor activities are good at immediately gaining the attention of some students. Surprise, silliness, gentle teasing, and other exaggerated interactions can provoke smiles and giggles, as well as sustained eye contact. Other, quieter activities may be more appropriate for some students like talking about favorite activities or complimenting them. Social engagement is an important start when preparing to give instructions and it shapes the child into monitoring the teacher frequently throughout the session for fun interactions.

- **Help the child to be an active responder.** This is accomplished by asking the child to respond frequently in a variety of ways to verbal and nonverbal interactions initiated by the teacher. Each time the child listens and responds to the teacher and is reinforced, overall social engagement is strengthened. Prepared learning trials are, of course, one source of opportunities to respond but not the only source. Incidental opportunities to respond can be added after a correct response to the main program, which prolong engagement without adding much to the difficulty of the experience. Interspersed trials of mastered programs that require language and social engagement can be rather seamlessly integrated into a session. For example, after correctly answering a question involving a flash card, the teacher might also request that the child give him a high five, pick something up, or put something on a shelf. Sometimes a teacher may pick up a new item and dramatically say, "Look at this!" A number of simple behaviors that are easily elicited can be improvised by the teacher and are especially handy in maintaining social engagement before and after a trial, when engagement tends to be more difficult. This does not mean that the teacher engages in so many off-task activities that the student is confused or cannot concentrate on their work. It also does not mean that incidental interactions become contingent on inattention or inappropriate behavior—quite the reverse. It does mean that the teacher engages the student socially and maintains engagement for as long as possible. Adding incidental tasks or instructions should facilitate completion of work if it increases the likelihood that students remain engaged with the teacher since errors due to inattention would be expected to decrease

Case Study

A short case study may serve to illustrate the benefits of integrating learning trials and incidental opportunities to respond. Chuck is a three year-old student with autism. He has already learned to sit for up to five minutes in a discrete trial session and has "mastered" a few basic drills. He imitates five gross motor actions with objects, imitates seven gross motor actions, matches many different identical objects, and is doing pretty well on matching identical pictures. Chuck can also build a tower, scribble with a marker, and follow three instructions to perform gross motor actions. Finally, Chuck can identify two objects from a field of three when the teacher says, "Show me the ___."

During observation of Chuck in several short discrete trial sessions, he appears somewhat resistant to instruction, whining when trials are presented and sometimes trying to leave the table. Instructors report that, on several of his programs, he rapidly learned three or four of the individual targets but now is making many mistakes. Indeed, on observation, Chuck is not regarding the stimuli often and sometimes makes selections randomly. Even when Chuck is working for his strongest reinforcer—watching short clips of his favorite video—he protests and seems distracted during the trials.

Remaking Chuck's Session

Given the previous discussion, let us modify the discrete trial session and describe how we might integrate some of the concepts in this chapter to improve Chuck's performance. When it is time to start trials, Chuck is usually playing with a favorite toy 2-5 feet from the work area. The teacher might sit down next to Chuck and engage in play with him briefly. Several techniques to get his attention are possible but no instructions should be given until he begins spontaneously monitoring the teacher during their play. After a few moments of fun interaction, the teacher can give the instruction to move to the work area. The teacher should continue the fun interaction as Chuck moves to his chair. This is important because Chuck is leaving a preferred activity; why would he want to begin a non-preferred activity (work) unless we remind him that other reinforcement, exemplified by our play, is available? Of course, the teacher may need to give physical prompts for Chuck to begin to move but these should be done quickly and can be disguised to improve tolerance. For example, we might gently assist Chuck to his feet, hold his hands, and jump together in place for three seconds, before continuing to hop to the chair. One way or another, it is important to get Chuck moving and away from his toy playing without incident.

With Chuck seated in his chair, we have only a few seconds before we will begin to lose his attention, so we must wisely prepare all of our next moves in advance. First, we spend a few seconds continuing to play with Chuck. We will do this until we are sure that he is strongly monitoring us. Then, we will begin one of a number of possible actions depending on the session. The most common next step in our present scenario would be to show Chuck the stimuli for the first trial of our first task. We show him the stimuli because we are maintaining a social connection with him. Sometimes, just taking the time to place three cards on the table is enough to lose a student's monitoring of the teacher. Therefore, we seek a way to place those stimuli before our student in a way that maintains the student's attention to the teacher and extends that attention to the teaching materials. In addition, we are also signaling that the previous enjoyable and motivating social interaction is continuing. Various techniques may accomplish these dual purposes with Chuck—we might playfully put the cards on the table. We could dramatically thump each card down, sing out "One, two, three!" rhythmically, or we could simply place the cards on the table while exchanging glances with the student and smiling. Whatever is done, we must expect that Chuck will respond and, at least, continue to monitor us while noticing the stimuli. He might also repeat what we say, point to the card, laugh, etc. If he does not continue to monitor, it is up to us to proceed with efforts to regain his attention because we cannot go on to our planned activity (the probable next step would be to give Chuck an instruction) unless we have the prerequisite attentive behavior from the student. Doing so simply leads to errors.

Given that Chuck continues to regard his teacher and the stimulus materials, the next minute or so will be occupied with a series of learning trials that are presented as rapidly as optimal. If Chuck is attending and the task is not too hard, he will respond correctly on several consecutive trials. This will often build an excitement and tendency to continue. After each trial the teacher will try to maintain engagement and attention to the task with social and, possibly, extrinsic reinforcement like edibles, time with a favorite toy, or tokens. Smooth and rapid presentation technique facilitates this engagement. However, the longer the series of trials, the more there is a tendency on the part of the student to disengage or make an off-task response. It is, therefore, important for us to accurately estimate how long Chuck is likely to continue without disengaging and to anticipate his disengagement by ending or changing the task. In this way we can terminate the first series of trials without errors, a highly desirable goal.

Perhaps, however, we would like to extend Chuck's session in order to give him additional necessary practice on a set of learning targets. We could certainly deliver his reinforcer, give him a short break, and start another series of trials. However, a break may be costly in terms of momentum. We would usually expect that the transition from break back to work would require another warm-up before achieving the level of attention and effort necessary to really be "on." Therefore, instead of a full-fledged break, we might add a short social task at the end of successful trials that allows Chuck to "rest" but maintains his social engagement with the teacher:

- After the last correct trial, ask for a high five, and play a short game with Chuck for about 30 seconds, looking at an interesting toy together

- Ask Chuck to put away the cards we just used

- Ask Chuck to help set up for the next task

Any short action will suffice as long as it involves reciprocal interactions—looks, handing things back and forth, joint attention to a material, etc. It should also be fun and easy for Chuck to readily accomplish. When our short interlude is finished Chuck will be directed back to the educational materials to begin additional trials.

Training Competencies for Attention and Engagement

Competencies for implementers in this area include: (a) maintaining attention and engagement during longer or more complex task performance conditions such as across multiple trials or tasks, (b) facilitating coordination of student attention and engagement during a task that requires both manipulation of materials and observation of the teacher (joint attention).

General Target Performance: The competent implementer will attract the attention of the student and maintain social engagement

Implementer Behavior	Important Qualities	Designed to Elicit
• Use engagement strategy from 19 core techniques to attract attention of student to implementer • Direct attention of student to specific area or material including prompting observing responses • Using toys or games, establish joint attention with student for 30 seconds	• Presentation is fast-paced • Presentation is enthusiastic • Implementer movements are coordinated with student's response • Engagement with student is maintained between presentations of trials, data collection, manipulation of materials, or other extraneous activities	• Eye-contact • Head turns to instructor • Monitoring instructor movements • Smiles • Approach, reach to instructor • Follow instructor's point or other prompt to focus attention on specific area or material

Instructional Format and Procedure:

Lesson 1: 60 minutes.

1. Trainee will receive written list and descriptions of 19 strategies to obtain the attention of students with autism. Trainee will observe competent model performing six of the strategies and ask questions about the strategies. Trainee will practice appropriate strategies with a student to complete the specifications above under the supervision of the competent model. Model will give corrective feedback and suggestions to trainee until mastery is achieved

Lesson 2: 30 minutes.

Same as above with next six strategies

Lesson 3: 30 minutes.

Same as above with final six strategies

Lesson 4: 30 minutes.

(A) Same as above practicing the direction of attention of student to various media

(B) Trainee will discuss and practice strategies involving observing responses

(C) Trainee maintains attention and engagement of student for a series of 5 trials.

Lesson 5: 30 minutes.

Same as above practicing establishment and maintenance of joint attention with student for 30 seconds or more.

What's Next?
Put this chapter to work: **ATTENTION AND ENGAGEMENT**

- Analyze the presentation of directions and materials in your programs. Where do you need to improve the prominence of stimuli?

- What are ways that you address "paying attention" in your programs? Discuss integrating the attention and engagement prompts into your programs. Use the *Training Competencies* as a general training program

- Observe a student who has demonstrated problems in attention and engagement and suggest remedial procedures

- Observe and analyze a student in a group instructional setting and create a table that documents the following:
    - General S^Ds
    - Initial Attending Responses
    - Specific, Related S^Ds
    - Engagement and Responding to Content
    - Reinforcement

- Observe implementers and/or videotape a teaching session. Evaluate whether a social connection between the student and teacher is established and maintained for the entire teaching session

Chapter 5

Prompts and Prompt Hierarchies

Prompts are an integral part of teaching students with intensive needs, used in one form or another in just about every teaching program. It is vital that instructional programs contain clear and effective prompting procedures and that implementers become proficient in the use of the various forms of prompting as well as the protocols governing their use in a typical intensive program. This section will present information and examples on how to design and implement prompting procedures, including stimulus and response prompts, prompt hierarchies and task analyses, within an overall errorless teaching paradigm.

This chapter is divided into seven sub-sections:

1. **Errors Beget Errors!** Errorless teaching and avoiding errors

2. **A Little Help Please?** Types of instructor-based and environmentally-based prompts

3. **Less is More:** Prompt hierarchies, fading prompts and following prompting criteria:

    a. Least-to-most

    b. Most-to-least

    c. Time delay

d. Graduated guidance

e. Prompt criteria

4. **Trial by Trial:** Documenting prompts with discrete trial instruction

5. **By the Numbers:** Task analyzing a performance into steps:

    a. Differences between Discrete Trial Instruction and Task Analysis

    b. Backward chaining

    c. Forward chaining

    d. Total task chaining

6. **Error Correction:** Responding when the performance is inaccurate

7. **Conclusion**

Errors Beget Errors!
Errorless Teaching and Avoiding Errors

When first approaching instructional design, program authors must carefully answer a fundamental question: "Is making a mistake a bad thing in the process of learning to do something?" Consider a student learning to play the piano. The student practices a musical passage all week only to find at his lesson that he has been practicing it the wrong way. Of course, once corrected, he sets out to practice the passage in question in the correct manner but soon finds that his errors come back to haunt him. Each time he approaches the target musical passage he hears the correct way to play it and intends to play it the correct way but, somehow, his fingers just don't cooperate. Only with great effort and painstaking repetition does he pull himself out of a vicious cycle of errors. And no wonder he has studiously practiced the wrong performance each day for a week before beginning to practice the right one. Consider a four-year-old learning to ride a two-wheel bike. Would a parent be expected to allow the child to fall until he gets it right? "Errors beget errors," as the behavior analyst Lawrence Stoddard frequently advised. Errors practice an incorrect performance and make it stronger.

Herbert Terrace described a type of instruction called "errorless teaching" that has been used with fledgling learners of all types (Terrace, 1963a; Terrace, 1963b; Moore & Goldiamond, 1964; Skinner, 1968; Sidman and Stoddard, 1967; Holland, Solomon, Doran and Frezza, 1976). The methodology breaks a skill into easy to perform component parts and gradually assembles the component parts into the final target performance as the student shows mastery of the individual components. While the new performance is fragile, assistance is given to ensure a stable performance free of errors.

The term "errorless teaching" is somewhat of a misnomer—more of an intention and objective on the part of the program writer than an expected outcome. While educators and behavior analysts use precise methodology to avoid errors as much as possible, there is no way to guarantee that the student will always receive instruction that perfectly predicts his or her needs at every moment; nor is this absolutely necessary to achieve positive teaching results. Nevertheless, in errorless teaching every effort is made to avoid the disruptive effect of practicing the wrong performance.

A Little Help, Please?
Types of Instructor-Based and Environmentally-Based Prompts

"Prompts" can be anything that helps a person to perform a response correctly. Examples include giving verbal directions on where to find something, physically assisting a young child to ride a two-wheel bike, demonstrating how to use a tool, traffic signs, clocks, underlined text, sirens, and announcements. Prompts can be instructor-based or environmentally-based. Instructor-based prompts are sometimes called *response prompts* (Cooper, Heron, and Heward, 2007) because they occur slightly before or while the response occurs to ensure that it happens correctly. Response prompts involve actions directly performed by the instructor including verbal prompts, gestures, modeling, or physical guidance.

Environmentally-based prompts, sometimes called "stimulus prompts," are any type of stimulus – event, object, material, noise, etc. that helps the student perform a target response correctly. These stimuli are arranged to be present in the student's environment prior to the target response so that they affect performance. Many types of environmentally-based prompts can be arranged; this type of prompting is very powerful. In general, instruction that uses stimulus prompts usually makes some modification to the presentation or materials to make the correct answer obvious, such as underlining, bolding, pointing to the answer with an arrow, making the correct answer larger than other choices, or making it closer. (We'll have more to discuss on this subject later.)

Less is More

Prompt Hierarchies, Fading Prompts and Following Prompting Criteria

The word *hierarchy* simply refers to a list that is ordered in a particular way. A prompt hierarchy is a list of prompts arranged in the order in which they are applied. Protocols or procedures are developed that control the application and fading of prompts in the prompt hierarchy. Refer to Table 1 below, entitled "Response Prompt Hierarchy" for an example. Notice that there is a list of prompt names and a description of how to implement the prompt. Also note that the prompts are arranged in a particular order. This particular group of prompts is sometimes called a "physical prompt hierarchy" because it starts with physically-based prompts like hand-over-hand guidance. This is a rather streamlined set of prompts but many variations of instructor–based prompts could be added. For example, a physical prompt that is given only once, called "initial touch," might be inserted above "Touch Prompt" or we could separate point prompts from model prompts and make them two distinct prompt levels.

Table 1. Response Prompt Hierarchy

+ F or – F	Full Physical Prompt	Continuous contact of instructor's hand which grasps wrist or other body part of student and guides correct response
+ P or – P	Partial Physical Prompt	Continuous contact of instructor's hand to wrist or body part of student as above but open-handed pressure
+ T or – T	Touch Prompt	Intermittent brief touches any place along the hand, wrist, arm, back, etc. No limit but touches must be no more than 1-2 seconds.
+ G or – G	Gestural Prompt	Points, taps on the materials, or model of behavior to initiate or continue the completion of the target step
+ or –	Independent - No Prompt Given	Completes target step without any prompts defined above - may receive verbal praise during completion.

Another useful response prompt hierarchy could be created with just verbal prompts. Refer to Table 2 below entitled "Verbal Prompt Hierarchy – Most to Least." Here the program writer listed a prompting strategy that might be useful for teaching students certain kinds of expressive labeling tasks like answering wh-questions (e.g., "What is 2 + 2?"). The highest level of prompting starts with modeling the whole answer in response to the instruction. Then the prompt is faded away in successive steps, first supplying only the first syllable of the answer and then only the first sound.

Table 2. Verbal Prompt Hierarchy – Most to Least

+ FV or – FV	Full Verbal	Implementer provides complete verbal model of answer
+ S1 or – S1	First Syllable	Implementer provides first syllable of answer
+ L1 or – L1	First Letter	Implementer provides first letter sound of answer
+ or –	Independent	Implementer provides instruction only

The term "prompt hierarchy" in ABA has been generally applied only to instructor – based (response) prompts although there is no reason why it would be improper to think about environmentally-based (stimulus) prompts in a similar hierarchical fashion. Look at the tables below entitled "Stimulus Prompt Hierarchy" for examples of hierarchies of environmentally-based prompts. Three different methodologies are illustrated that manipulate materials to prompt the student to perform correctly. For the hierarchy using a "Position Cue," the prompts are embedded in the array of materials by putting the correct choice further forward than the incorrect choices. In subsequent prompting steps, the correct choice is placed increasingly closer to even alignment with the incorrect choices.

Table 3. Stimulus Prompt Hierarchy – Position Cue

+ 6 or – 6	Six Inches Forward	Place three choice items in a row equidistant from the student and equally spaced apart. Randomize the position of the correct choice among the three available positions (left, right, center). Move the correct choice six inches towards the student
+ 4 or – 4	Four Inches Forward	Same as above but four inches forward
+ 2 or – 2	Two Inches Forward	Same as above but two inches forward
+ 1 or – 1	One Inch Forward	Same as above but one inch forward
+ or –	In Line	In line with other choices

Many kinds of stimulus prompts may be arranged into hierarchies. A "Size Redundancy Cue" (Table 4) increases the size of the correct answer and gradually decreases the size back to normal as the student correctly responds.

Table 4. Stimulus Prompt Hierarchy – Size Redundancy Cue

+ T or – T	Triple Size	Place three choice items in a row equidistant from the student and equally spaced apart. Randomize the position of the correct choice among the three available positions (left, right, center). Display the correct choice twice as large as the other choices
+ D or – D	Double Size	Same as above but double size forward
+ H or – H	1.5 Times Normal	Same as above but one and one-half size
+ Q or - Q	1.25 Times Normal	Same as above but one and one-quarter size
+ or –	Same Size	Same size as other choices

The "Arrow Cue" hierarchy (Table 5) draws an arrow pointing to the correct answer and gradually fades it out:

Table 5. Stimulus Prompt Hierarchy – Arrow Cue

+ F or - F	Arrow Full	Place three choice items in a row equidistant from the student and equally spaced apart. Randomize the position of the correct choice among the three available positions (left, right, center). Display a black arrow pointing to the correct choice
+ 50 or – 50	Arrow Fade 50%	Same as above but arrow is 50% grey
+ 75 or – 75	Arrow Fade 75%	Same as above but arrow is 25% grey
+ 90 or - 90	Arrow Fade 90%	Same as above but arrow is 10% grey
+ or –	No Arrow	Same as above but no arrow

Prompt Fading

To optimize errorless teaching, the steps of both response prompt hierarchies and stimulus prompt hierarchies are arranged in a particular order that start with the most extensive or obvious use of prompts and step down gradually to less prompting and, finally, no prompting at all. A prompt hierarchy always reflects a particular directional strategy for applying and fading prompts. Two strategies are:

- **Least-to-Most**: prompts are applied starting with the *least* amount of prompting and adjust to higher levels of prompting

- **Most-to-Least**: prompts are applied starting with the *most* amount of prompting and adjust gradually to the *least* amount of prompting

Least-to-Most Prompts

Least-to-most prompts are typically used when the student already has a certain level of proficiency in performing the target skill. With least-to-most prompts, students are allowed to initiate the target performance and, if it does not occur, prompts are given starting with the lowest level of prompting on the hierarchy. If the target performance does not occur, the next highest level of prompting is initiated, and so on, until the correct performance is obtained. For example, a least-to-most prompting hierarchy might be implemented in a program concerned with answering wh-questions about state capitals (See Table 6, "Verbal Prompt Hierarchy – Least-to-Most"). If the student has previously studied and memorized the answers to the question, "What is the capital of..." we could ask a question and begin the prompt hierarchy by waiting for the correct answer. If the student pauses, the first level of prompting might be supplied, such as pronouncing the first letter of the answer. If the correct answer is still not forthcoming, the next level of prompting might involve pronouncing the first syllable of the answer. At that point, if the correct answer is not given, the instructor might supply the answer.

Table 6. Verbal Prompt Hierarchy – Least-to-Most

+ or –	Independent	Implementer provides instruction only
+ L1 or – L1	First Letter Sound	Implementer provides first letter sound of answer
+ S1 or – S1	First Syllable	Implementer provides first syllable of answer
+ FV or – FV	Full Verbal	Implementer provides complete verbal model of answer

Most-to-Least Prompts

A most-to-least prompting direction is most commonly associated with errorless teaching. For example, if we would like to use response (instructor-based) prompts to teach a student to color in a shape, we could start with our hand completely enveloping the student's hand holding a crayon and making a back-and-forth motion until the student begins to move cooperatively. In succeeding coloring trials, as the student gradually becomes more independent, we would slowly withdraw support and guidance. In the prompt hierarchy illustrated in Table 1, prompts began with "full physical" prompts and moved to "partial physical," "touch," "gestural," and, finally, to no prompting at all.

Remember, there are many variations in the strategy of fading prompts. For example, with response prompts, instead of gradually decreasing the extent of the grasp of the instructor around the student's hand, program writers may prefer to change the location of the prompts. One method to accomplish this would be to define prompts that begin by holding a person around the hand (as above) and fade by moving the location of the prompt to the wrist and then the forearm and, finally, the elbow before removing the prompt altogether.

Fading Using a Stimulus Prompt Hierarchy

As we saw in the stimulus prompt hierarchies illustrated above, most-to-least prompting is applied to stimulus prompts in the same ways as it is applied to response prompting – only the nature of the prompts is different. In the position cue hierarchy, the distance that the correct choice is put forward gradually decreases and, therefore, the prompt becomes less obvious. When the size of the correct choice is increased as a prompt, successive prompting steps decrease the size slowly back to normal. When an arrow is added as a prompt, it is faded away until it disappears.

Fading Using a Time Delay

Another common method of fading prompts uses a time delay (Touchette, 1971). To prepare a time delay prompt hierarchy, a prompt is first chosen that will reliably prompt correct performance. This prompt can be anything including a response prompt (e.g., point, verbal prompt, touch, etc.) or a stimulus prompt (e.g., showing a card with the printed answer to a question) but, whatever prompt is given, it must be sufficient to enable the student to respond correctly. Initially, the chosen prompt is immediately delivered after the instruction is given. Then a short time delay (e.g., 1 second) is introduced between the instruction and the prompt. During the "pause," the instructor looks to see if the student will anticipate the prompt and perform the target step independently. If not, the prompt is delivered and the correct performance is reinforced. Trials continue and if the student does not anticipate after a given period of time, the delay is increased. Seconds continue to be added as required until the student successfully anticipates. Table 7 presents an example of a prompt hierarchy using a time delay and a point prompt:

Table 7. Time Delay Prompt Hierarchy

Designated prompt: Point to correct choice after delay

+ D0 or – D0	0 sec. Prompt Delay
+ D1 or – D1	1 sec. Prompt Delay
+ D2 or – D2	2 sec. Prompt Delay
(Steps continue…)	
+ D9 or – D9	9 sec. Prompt Delay
+ or –	No Prompt

Applying and Fading Prompts Using Graduated Guidance

Graduated guidance (Azrin & Foxx, 1974) is yet another strategy for applying and fading prompts. When using graduated guidance, prompts are applied at the level necessary to achieve a correct performance at that moment and then modified from moment to moment depending on the performance of the student. Graduated guidance generally uses a version of the least-to-most prompting strategy. So, for example, if a set of response prompts similar to those in the physical prompt hierarchy (Table 1) is used with graduated guidance, an instructor would give an instruction and wait to see if the student responded. If not, the instructor immediately applies the first level of prompting. If the student does not respond, the next level of prompting would be applied and the process continues in this way until the student correctly performs the target behavior. In contrast to strict least-to-most prompting protocols where a certain number of trials are administered at a given level of prompting before fading, graduated guidance modifies the amount of prompting momentarily. If the student shows some degree of independence when performing a target behavior, the instructor adjusts the level of prompting to suit the performance. In practice, the movement from one prompt to another, both forward and backwards, may be very rapid, in order to adequately assist the student and avoid incorrect performances or gaps in performance.

Criteria for Fading Prompts

In summary, a set of prompts may be defined and arranged into hierarchies for a particular teaching task, specifying a direction of prompt movement – that is, how prompts change and become less or more intrusive according to the student's response. In addition to the prompt name and definition, prompt hierarchies also include *criteria* for fading or reinstating each prompt level and *data codes* for documenting the student's performance on a data sheet. Each of the prompt tables presented included data codes in the leftmost column. Let's take a look at criteria for fading and reinstatement.

In many protocols[1], criteria set the number of accurate[2] trials to be achieved at a certain prompt level before fading. For example, the criteria might state that the instructor should obtain five consecutive accurate performances at a given prompt level before moving to the next prompting step. This is called the "fading criterion." The procedure could also state that if the student performs a target step inaccurately two times in a row, the previous (more extensive) prompting step will be reinstated. This is called the "reinstatement criterion." If the reinstatement criterion is triggered, the student will not only receive more extensive prompts, he will need to meet the fading criterion *again* before prompts are returned to the previous level. Common criteria for fading and reinstatement vary. The specific number of accurate trials chosen has to do with finding a level of performance in which we have confidence that the student is ready to advance. On the other hand, the criterion number should not require the student to repeat a learned

---

[1] The term "protocol" refers to a standardized procedure devised by a program author that specifies how implementers perform common tasks. Protocols are generic processes that ensure consistency, simplify complex workflow, and reduce training costs and are extremely useful in ABA programs. Many sample protocols are provided throughout this manual. For additional discussion of the use of protocols see Chapter 10 on ABA Project Management.

[2] The term "accurate" signifies that the student performed the target behavior correctly (as defined in the objective or task analysis) *with* a prompt. If the student performs the target behavior correctly *without* a prompt, the performance would be called "independent."

performance to the point of boredom.

Trial by Trial
Documenting Prompts with Discrete Trial Instruction

When implementers follow fading and reinstatement criteria to use prompts in a systematic way, program supervisors can evaluate the use of prompts as an indicator of the performance of the student. Even though the use of prompts is what the instructor does (called an *independent variable*), taking data on the delivered prompt may give a reasonable picture of the student's performance if:

- The use of prompts follows a strict set of rules

- The use of prompts is ultimately connected with the student's behavior

This "set of rules" corresponds to the prompt hierarchy, including the criteria for fading and reinstatement as well as the precise definitions of the prompts that appear on the hierarchy. A sample protocol may help the reader to understand the means by which prompt use is controlled and quantified through prompt definitions, hierarchies, fading and reinstatement criteria, and data codes. Refer to the following page illustration entitled "PC3 Data Sheet: Recording Prompt Data."[3] At the top of the page, part of a data sheet is shown with the name of the program, goal performance, and instructions on how to present the program. Using the data codes from the prompt hierarchy, the implementer writes in the prompt used on each trial, following the procedure and criteria written below:

Prompting Procedure

1. Give instruction to the student to complete the target step

2. Apply the beginning prompt from the hierarchy immediately. Start with the highest level of prompting (Full Physical) unless another prompt level is specified in the program procedure

3. Fade to the next lower prompt level when student accurately completes the target step with the instructor's prompt, **five consecutive times**

---

[3]Some sample protocols use materials from the ABA Program Companion 3.0 software, an online ABA program creation and implementation environment available for purchasers of this manual.

4. If student makes an error (performs any part of the target step inaccurately), repeat the trial with a full physical prompt

5. If student incorrectly completes target step two times in a row, reinstate the previous prompt level and again require 5 consecutive correct trials at that level of prompting

At the bottom of the illustration, data has been entered for five trials with full physical prompts, five with partial physical, and four trials with touch prompts. The instructor has written his initials and the date of the session above the data grid. According to the *Response Prompt-Physical Prompt Hierarchy* data code column, mistakes or inaccurate performances are designated by a minus sign followed by the code for the prompt level – in the case of full physical prompts, the inaccurate performance code would be – F.

According to the procedure, when inaccurate performances occur, it is up to the instructor to repeat the trial and ensure that the repeat performance is accurate using a full physical prompt. After two inaccurate performances, according to the prompt protocol, the reinstatement criterion is invoked and the fading criterion is reset. Therefore, the previous, more extensive level of prompting is given on the next trial and five more accurate performances at that prompt level will be necessary before fading is resumed. For example, if a student is receiving partial physical prompts but performs the steps inaccurately on two consecutive trials, he would be returned to full physical prompts and the criterion for fading would be restarted.

Issues with Prompting Protocols

Overall, data collection using prompting codes is a rather simple process since the criteria determine in advance what prompt will be supplied and the implementer must determine only whether the target step was performed correctly or not. Yet, implementers may find it difficult at first to recall definitions and codes. Program writers should place prompt definitions, fading and reinstatement criteria, and data codes prominently within written program materials so that implementers may quickly refer to them when necessary. Prompt hierarchy information may also be placed on a separate sheet that is conspicuously posted.

ABA-PC3 Data Sheet: Recording Prompt Data

Sample Data Sheet with Data Grid

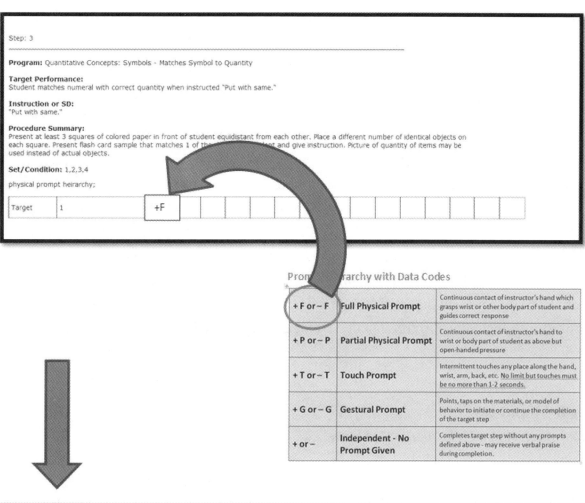

Program writers should also keep in mind that prompts like those on the physical prompt hierarchy are often difficult to implement reliably. The exact topography and timing of actions involved in complex movements like response prompts is often hard to precisely specify and repeat consistently from session to session or instructor to instructor. Therefore, training including modeling, observation, and feedback should be a regular part of every implementation including formal procedural reliability assessment.

Another possible issue concerns prompt fading criteria. While the criteria for prompt fading and reinstatement provide simple guidelines controlling implementer behavior towards students, such guidelines may not provide the means for satisfactory decision-making. For example, a single, standard number of trials to be performed accurately may not succeed as a criterion for some prompt fading circumstances; likewise, standardized rules to return to previous prompt levels after errors may not be sufficient to re-establish correct performance. Thankfully, protocols are not intended as replacements for data-based decision making. Data revealing errors or sustained lack of progress provides important information that should be used by decision-makers to revise implementation procedures, including the creation of custom criteria for fading and reinstatement of prompts.

By the Numbers
Task Analyzing a Performance into Steps

So far, the discussion of prompts has been confined to their use with single-step target performances. For example, a student may be required to match a yellow card to another yellow card in a field of several colored cards. Other instructional programs are concerned with performances of multiple steps, such as the twelve steps to wash one's hands shown below. Many programs taught to students including academic tasks and self-help skills involve multi-step processes. Target performances that are composed of more than one step are analyzed and placed in a list of component performances called a "task analysis." Table 10 presents an example of the handwashing task analysis:

Table 10. Handwashing Task Analysis

1. Walk to sink
2. Turn on water
3. Get hands wet

4. Pump soap into hands
5. Rub hands together
6. Rub tops of hands
7. Rinse soap
8. Turn off water
9. Get paper towel
10. Dry palms of hands
11. Dry tops of hands
12. Throw paper towel away

The number of steps of a task analyzed performance varies and is determined in part by the person writing the task analysis. Usually, a task is broken down into individual steps that are easily remembered and practiced. If a student has trouble with a step, it can be further broken down into several smaller steps. Several practical considerations accompany the creation of task analyses:

- What are the optimal task steps for the target students?
- Are steps clearly and objectively defined?
- Is the order of steps appropriate? Are there points where the order may vary?
- Does the task analysis apply to all current settings? Are some steps different in different settings?

A task analysis should be thought of as a "chain" of performance steps leading to a target outcome. During acquisition of the chain, the task of the instructor is to help the student (a) perform the individual steps and (b) perform them in the correct order to accomplish the target function. There are three common programming methods to build chains: *forward chaining, backward chaining, and total task chaining.*

Forward Chaining

A sample protocol from the ABA-PC3 system is provided below, illustrating the process of forward chaining. The task analysis for handwashing is shown on a data sheet. Below the identifying information of the program, each step of the task analysis is

Teaching Using a Task Analysis - Forward Chaining

Type	Item
(TA-Target)	A. Walk to sink.
TA	B. Turn on water
TA	C. Get hands wet
TA	D. Pump soap into hands.
TA	E. Rub hands together
TA	F. Rub top of hands
TA	G. Rinse soap
TA	H. Turn off water
TA	I. Get paper towel
TA	J. Dry palm of hands
TA	K. Dry top of hands
TA	L. Throw paper towel away

Chaining Step 2

Type	Item
TA-Maintain	A. Walk to sink.
(TA-Target)	B. Turn on water
TA	C. Get hands wet
TA	D. Pump soap into hands.
TA	E. Rub hands together
TA	F. Rub top of hands
TA	G. Rinse soap
TA	H. Turn off water
TA	I. Get paper towel
TA	J. Dry palm of hands
TA	K. Dry top of hands
TA	L. Throw paper towel away

Chaining Step 3

Type	Item
TA-Maintain	A. Walk to sink.
TA-Maintain	B. Turn on water
(TA-Target)	C. Get hands wet
TA	D. Pump soap into hands.
TA	E. Rub hands together
TA	F. Rub top of hands
TA	G. Rinse soap
TA	H. Turn off water
TA	I. Get paper towel
TA	J. Dry palm of hands
TA	K. Dry top of hands
TA	L. Throw paper towel away

Chaining Step 9

Type	Item
TA-Maintain	A. Walk to sink.
TA-Maintain	B. Turn on water
TA-Maintain	C. Get hands wet
TA-Maintain	D. Pump soap into hands.
TA-Maintain	E. Rub hands together
TA-Maintain	F. Rub top of hands
TA-Maintain	G. Rinse soap
TA-Maintain	H. Turn off water
(TA-Target)	I. Get paper towel
TA	J. Dry palm of hands
TA	K. Dry top of hands
TA	L. Throw paper towel away

placed in the data grid. Next to each step is a designation called the "type" which contains information about the step related to acquisition. Prior to starting the program, all steps are designated "TA" for "task analysis." When teaching begins in forward chaining, just the first step of the chain is taught while the student receives full physical prompts by the instructor to perform all of the subsequent steps of the task. In the illustration, notice that the type of the first step is "TA-Target," or "Task Analysis – Target" which means that teaching has actively begun on the first step. The other steps still have "TA" as a type, meaning that they are NOT presently taught and that the instructor should fully help the student to perform the step. Teaching (prompt fading) on only the first step continues until the student is independent in carrying out the first step. Once the first step is mastered, the student is allowed to perform the first step independently while the second step is taught. As before, the instructor helps the student on all of the following steps and does not fade prompts to those steps. In this way, the second step is added to the first and the chain of steps moves forward. On the data sheet marked "Chaining Step 2," the first (mastered) step is now marked with "TA-Maintain" and the second step now has "TA-Target" for a type. When the first and second steps are independent, the third step is added as a target (see the box, marked "Chaining Step 3"), then the fourth, etc. until all of the steps are performed to criterion in the proper sequence. The third box, marked "Chaining Step 9," shows the chaining process near its completion.

Backwards Chaining

The process of backwards chaining is identical to forward chaining except that the order of acquisition of steps is reversed. That is, the process begins with teaching the LAST step and adds steps one at a time in a backwards fashion.

Table 11. Backwards Chaining

Chaining Step 2	Chaining Step 3	Chaining Step 9
Type / Item: TA — A. Walk to sink. TA — B. Turn on water TA — C. Get hands wet TA — D. Pump soap into hands. TA — E. Rub hands together TA — F. Rub top of hands TA — G. Rinse soap TA — H. Turn off water TA — I. Get paper towel TA — J. Dry palm of hands TA-Target — K. Dry top of hands TA-Maintain — L. Throw paper towel away	Type / Item: TA — A. Walk to sink. TA — B. Turn on water TA — C. Get hands wet TA — D. Pump soap into hands. TA — E. Rub hands together TA — F. Rub top of hands TA — G. Rinse soap TA — H. Turn off water TA — I. Get paper towel TA-Target — J. Dry palm of hands TA-Maintain — K. Dry top of hands TA-Maintain — L. Throw paper towel away	Type / Item: TA — A. Walk to sink. TA — B. Turn on water TA — C. Get hands wet TA-Target — D. Pump soap into hands. TA-Maintain — E. Rub hands together TA-Maintain — F. Rub top of hands TA-Maintain — G. Rinse soap TA-Maintain — H. Turn off water TA-Maintain — I. Get paper towel TA-Maintain — J. Dry palm of hands TA-Maintain — K. Dry top of hands TA-Maintain — L. Throw paper towel away

Backwards chaining has some advantages over forward chaining for some students because the completion of the task (and reinforcement) is closer in sequence to the student's independent performance. For example, with the handwashing steps, the first teaching step in a backwards chaining procedure would be *throwing away the paper towel*. A teaching session is conducted by assisting the student to complete the first 11 steps of the task and then fading assistance on the last step. Any effort towards independence made by the student on the last step is immediately reinforced by completion of the task as well as the delivery of whatever extrinsic reinforcement is scheduled. In contrast, with forward chaining, independent efforts on the first step are followed by eleven prompted steps before completion of the task and reinforcement.

Total Task Chaining

In total task chaining, all steps in the chain are targets at the same time and the instructor actively teaches them using and fading prompts that are individualized for each step. Table 12 shows the handwashing task analysis with several steps already mastered (TA-Maintain) and several receiving active instruction (TA-Target).

Table 12. Total Task Chaining

Type	Item
TA-Target	A. Walk to sink.
TA-Target	B. Turn on water
TA-Maintain	C. Get hands wet
TA-Target	D. Pump soap into hands.
TA-Maintain	E. Rub hands together
TA-Target	F. Rub top of hands
TA-Maintain	G. Rinse soap
TA-Target	H. Turn off water
TA-Target	I. Get paper towel
TA-Maintain	J. Dry palm of hands
TA-Maintain	K. Dry top of hands
TA-Maintain	L. Throw paper towel away

Total task chaining is advocated by some as more efficient in that all steps are taught at the same time and, therefore, the student may be expected to learn the task faster. Little in the way of established evidence exists for this assertion. Since fading occurs simultaneously on all steps, use of this strategy is more complex than the other chaining methods. Sometimes total task chaining is used in conjunction with graduated guidance, a practice that multiplies the number of momentary judgments and adjustments made by implementers from step to step and which makes reliability and procedural integrity a distinct issue.

Error Correction

While error correction is not a prompting strategy, it is a natural part of a prompting procedure. As we have seen, inaccurate performances may occur even when prompts are offered. Eventually, when prompts are eliminated, the student is "allowed" to freely respond to a direction, like "Touch your nose" or expected to independently turn on the water after approaching the sink. If these target performances have been well practiced, there is reasonable probability that the correct response will occur. Nevertheless, probability is not certainty. Errors may occur at any time due to a variety of factors including inattention, changes in the environment, or previous errors. Since, over the course of instruction at least some errors can be expected, even after mastery, program writers should plan for their occurrence. In the protocols displayed so far, specific correction procedures have been included for errors that occur with or without prompts. According to the sample procedure, after an error, the student is asked to repeat the target performance with full prompting to ensure a correct response:

When an Error Occurs:

A. Interrupt the performance if possible. Return the student and materials to the ready position

B. Repeat the same trial with a prompt to ensure a correct performance (the prompt should be chosen to guarantee as much as possible that further errors do not occur)

C. Repeat the trial without a prompt

If the student performs correctly on Step C, instruction resumes as before. If another error is made, the error correction procedure is repeated. However, according to this protocol, it is not applied more than twice. If the student makes two errors in a row, instruction is resumed and the instructor makes a notation to discuss the session with program supervisors later.[4]

Conclusion

In this chapter, we have explored one of the most important aspects of highly structured teaching – errorless instruction. While we know now that "errorless" doesn't always mean total elimination of errors, it does mean using instructional methodologies that minimize them. We have reviewed the nature and types of prompts including those based on instructor actions (response prompts) as well as those based on manipulation of environmental events and instructional materials like size or position (stimulus prompts) and how such prompts may be organized into hierarchies and implementation protocols. Task analysis or breaking skills into smaller, component parts to simplify acquisition, comprises another part of a detailed protocol, in concert with implementation criteria, error correction procedures, and performance evaluation strategies.

Delving into the complexities of prompting requires a step into the technology of teaching. This may be somewhat intimidating for some implementers – interacting with students and following the rules of protocols at the same time can be difficult and even a bit messy. Nevertheless, as educators we should remember that with practice the proper instructional behavior becomes second nature and the benefits of a powerful technology far outweigh any temporary discomfort.

---

[4] The concepts, supporting scientific literature and strategies of error correction will be discussed in Chapter 7.

Training Competencies for Prompts and Prompt Hierarchies

General Target Performance: The competent implementer will consistently use and fade prompts according to specified protocols

Verbal Skills

- Define the term "prompt" and provide examples of instructor-based (response) and environmentally-based (stimulus) prompts

- Discuss why errors interfere with skill acquisition and how "errorless" procedures are structured to prevent errors

- Based on a sample hierarchy provided, list prompts in order of intrusiveness

- Describe how the steps of a time-delay prompt hierarchy are implemented and faded

- Define the term "task analysis" and give an example

- Describe how steps of a task analysis are chained together using forward chaining and backward chaining

- Locate the prompt hierarchy and data codes on a data sheet

- Given a stimulus prompt hierarchy, set up and demonstrate presentation of trials for each step

- Given a printed prompt hierarchy and data sheet with prompt descriptions, fading criteria, and data codes, describe and demonstrate the steps in taking data for programs involving:

    o A task analysis using backward chaining

    o A discrimination task taught with discrete trial instruction

Performance Skills

Implementer Behavior	Important Qualities	Designed to Elicit
Demonstrate the use of each prompt in a **physical** prompt hierarchy	Prompt execution consistent with definition and procedure	Accurate response without error
Demonstrate the use of each prompt in a **verbal** prompt hierarchy	Prompt execution consistent with definition and procedure	Accurate response without error

Demonstrate the use of each prompt in a **time-delay** prompt hierarchy	Prompt execution consistent with definition and procedure	Accurate response without error
Carry out a discrete trial sessions with a student using prompts according to a prompt hierarchy	• Use correct prompt according to information supplied on data sheet and prompt hierarchy • Follow protocol criteria and fade and/or reinstate prompt when appropriate • Document prompt and student performance using code from protocol	Accurate response without error
Present sessions of a program using **stimulus prompts** according to the hierarchy	• Set up and present materials according to the protocol • Follow protocol criteria and fade and/or reinstate prompt when appropriate • Document prompt and student performance using code from protocol	Accurate response without error

What's Next?
Put this chapter to work: **PROMPTS AND PROMPT HIERARCHIES**

- List the prompts and prompt hierarchies used in your program

- Analyze your students' current success in their programs and determine if further prompt hierarchies would be helpful

- Analyze the frequency of errors during prompt use. Are prompts used effectively?

- Are stimulus prompts used in favor of response prompts wherever possible to maximize consistency?

- What additional stimulus prompts could be used in your program?

- How are you currently fading the use of prompts? Analyze your programs and try one of the following:
    - Position cues
    - Time delay

- Do you have a criterion in place that determines when fading and/or reinstatement is necessary?
    - Does the criterion require the student to unnecessarily repeat a learned performance?
    - Is the criterion easily measured and directly connected to student behavior?

- Do written prompt protocols exist including prompt definitions, fading and reinstatement criteria, and data codes prominently displayed either on the data sheet or on an attached sheet?

- If not, develop prompt protocols similar to the samples in the chapter for your most common prompt hierarchies and train all implementers

- Implement a fixed schedule of procedural integrity observations for all prompting procedures. Calculate and share results

- Assess existing task analyses for current target performances:

- Is the task broken down into individual steps that are easily remembered and practiced?

- What programming method is most useful to your student: forward chaining, backwards chaining or total task chaining? Why?

• How is student performance with prompts documented? Compare your methods to the methods in the chapter and consider how you might improve them.

Chapter 6

Developing a Solid Reinforcement Strategy
What's in it for ME?

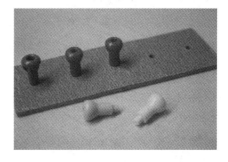

*Much of the foregoing discussion has been devoted to issues of stimulus control – arranging the **antecedent** conditions of instructional performance via attention and engagement strategies, materials, and prompts. We now turn to the **consequences** side of the behavioral timeline. Learning is dependent on the delivery of a reinforcing stimulus immediately after the target behavior. However, a given stimulus, regardless of its intrinsic characteristics, may or may not act as a reinforcer. The term "reinforcer" is reserved for stimuli that increase the probability of occurrence of a behavior, when delivered contingently and immediately after the behavior occurs. There is no guarantee that candy, praise, money, or free time will act as reinforcers for a behavior. The occurrence of reinforcement depends on dynamic conditions in the student's environment. Whatever reinforcement value exists depends on a complex interaction of several variables including:*

- The student's "history of reinforcement"

- The characteristics of the stimuli delivered as reinforcers including quality and quantity of reinforcement

- The student's state of satiation and deprivation with regard to potentially reinforcing stimuli

- The characteristics and potential reinforcement value of other stimuli available

- The contingencies in effect in the instructional environment governing the behavior necessary to obtain a given stimulus/reinforcer

In this chapter we will discuss each of these variables, how they influence the behavior of the student, and how instructional programs may be designed to maximize the effectiveness of reinforcers.

The Past as Present: Effects of a "History" of Reinforcement

Just as, biochemically, "you are what you eat," behaviorally, you are *what you do* and *what you have done.* That is to say, our present behavior does not just depend on our present environment. It is also affected by past experiences and associations – a "history of reinforcement." Biology (sensations, emotions, and other neurological responses) allows each organism to experience the world in a way that changes the organism's future behavior. This chronology of biological interactions with the environment partly determines the student's general tendencies to "like" certain foods, toys, people, and events. For example, while we may tend to like all sweet foods, history will play a role in which box of breakfast cereal we prefer (the one with the Captain on it!). Sometimes history determines *if* a stimulus will act as a reinforcer: if small round coins have been strongly associated with purchasing highly preferred activities, awarding the coins will probably act as reinforcement for many behaviors. If a small child encountered a group of aggressively trumpeting ducks and was frightened when she was young, pictures of pretty birds may not act as reinforcers. Sometimes history determines *when* a stimulus may act as a reinforcer: while praise may be very effective in reinforcing social interactions when the student is participating in a group of friends, it could be quite ineffective when reinforcing completion of homework problems. Over time, the interaction of our sensory organs with the environment builds up a multitude of interconnected experiences that affect how each stimulus functions for an individual.

Characteristics of Stimuli that Act as Reinforcers

Stimuli that can act as reinforcers take many forms beyond the often used praise and candy. The particular quality or reinforcing dimension of a stimulus can appeal to any sense as seen in the following table:

Reinforcing Dimension of Stimulus	Examples
Social	Being with a person, eye-contact, smiles, interactive games, talking to a person, parties, winning
Gustatory	Pizza, Burger King, candy, soda, salty, swallowing, chewing
Auditory	Music, singing, novel sounds, ocean sounds, bird sounds
Visual	Colors, bright lights, motion pictures, art, attractive people
Tactile	Hugs, roughhousing, tickling, massage, cool breeze on a hot day, vibration, warm blanket
Proprioceptive	Exercising, throwing a ball, stretching, bowling
Olfactory	Perfume, flowers, food aromas
Vestibular	Rocking, amusement park rides, swings, rides in vehicles, bicycle riding, running, trampolines

Each stimulus varies in *quality,* that is, the character and configuration of aspects of the stimulus that affect its potential reinforcing properties. A smell might be subtle or strong (intensity), floral or citrus (character). The colored lights of a toy might be white or multi-colored (character), bright or dark (intensity), and positioned on the toy's extremities or interspersed throughout (configuration). Students show great variation in preferences for stimuli based on even small differences in qualities such as intensity, configuration, and character.

Reinforcement value may also vary based on the quantity or frequency of delivery of the stimulus. Delivery of three minutes of a preferred activity may have a different reinforcing value than delivery of one minute; receiving two crackers may be more motivating than receiving one cracker. The effectiveness of reinforcement is also affected by the *schedule* of delivery of a stimulus. For example, reinforcers may be delivered after one correct response (continuous reinforcement) or several responses (intermittent reinforcement). Schedules can be based on the ratio of responses required (reinforcement occurs after 2, 3, 5, 10, or 100 responses) or the time that elapses between responses (5 seconds, 20 seconds 45 seconds, 2 minutes, etc.).

Other Stimulus Characteristics that Enhance Reinforcement Value

Apart from physical characteristics, quantity, and schedule of delivery, other attributes of stimuli may affect their capacity to act as reinforcers. Sometimes *novel* stimuli may reinforce behavior simply because they are novel. For example, changing the location of a task, the color of a worksheet, or the method of delivery of the directions may augment intrinsic reinforcement of engaging in the task. *New* toys, games, people, flavors, smells, dances, or songs may be preferred for a while, regardless of their design or specific character.

Sometimes, the reinforcement value of a stimulus depends on its characteristics *relative to other stimuli in the environment.* Premack (1959) described behavior in terms of its probability of occurrence in a given setting. When individuals are allowed to respond freely, the frequency of each exhibited behavior can be identified and ranked in probability of occurrence from the highest (most probable) to lowest (least probable). Highly probable behavior tends to act as a reinforcer when it follows lower probability behavior. For example, Jane may spend more time reading her favorite books than doing homework. If the opportunity to read a favorite book is only presented upon completion of homework, she may be more likely to complete her homework because reading is a higher probability behavior than completing homework.

High probability behavior tends to be more independent and error-free than lower probability behavior, probably in large measure because reinforcement is under greater control of the individual. Errors and a need for assistance disrupt or delay reinforcement. In fact, there may be some additional reinforcing qualities about independent, competent behavior that add to its probability of occurrence. For example, children as young as two-years-old may insist, "Me do!" when offered help to perform a task or students may call attention to themselves when completing a project, "Look what I did!" Adults report satisfaction with competence and independence at tasks that are not even likely to be preferred like being on time to work appointments or completing their responsibilities. Conversely, requiring help to complete a task is sometimes seen as a loss of status. Undoubtedly, a history of associations between independent, competent behavior and social or other forms of reinforcement must be included in any explanation of reinforcement value. In any case, the opportunity to engage in behavior that is independent and competent may be a noteworthy source of reinforcement.[1]

Satiation, Deprivation, and Programming for Variety

We have discussed that the reinforcing value of a given stimulus varies with its individual characteristics, novelty, and history of reinforcement. Yet the sum of those factors, if it could be calculated, would not provide a definitive determination of reinforcement value because the value *varies from moment to moment*. A student's state of *deprivation* and *satiation* with a particular stimulus has much to do with its ability to act as a reinforcer. Saying that a student that has had "too much of a good thing" suggests that an item is less desirable at the moment due to excessive contact. This is called satiation. With a long enough period of absence (deprivation), the value of a stimulus as a reinforcer rebounds. Stimuli vary in their resistance to satiation. Computers, favorite videos, and other items may act as potent reinforcers for days or months. Eventually, however, the reinforcing effects of all stimuli are degraded by overuse. This may manifest by sluggish drill performance, inattention, protest, increased errors, or other behaviors.

Using a variety of reinforcers provides one needed countermeasure to satiation. Though programming with a variety of reinforcers may not always use the strongest reinforcer available in a given trial or session, more benefit is gained in the long run by preventing a weakening of the reinforcing effect that may eventually necessitate total exclusion of a once powerful stimulus. While individuals may sometimes reject offered alternatives or their responding may suffer when their favorite reinforcers are not constantly used, the danger of satiation is real and variety in reinforcement must be considered crucial as a long-term strategy to effectively motivate students every day, week, and month.

The most crucial step in explicitly incorporating variety into schedules of reinforcement and avoiding overreliance on tried and true stimuli is to establish protocols for regularly testing and ranking stimuli as potential reinforcers. Some procedures are

---

[1] In the area of instruction, independent, mastered tasks, as high-probability behaviors, may be programmed to reinforce behavior in acquisition. A student is asked to perform one or more trials of a task in acquisition and successful performance is followed by presentation of one or more trials of the mastered task. Such "task interspersal" arranges the mastered task as a potential reinforcer for the task in acquisition. For some students, interspersed programs can be extremely effective as well as efficient because they allow maintenance of mastered programs, reinforcement of acquisition programs, and the establishment of more complex heterogeneous performance chains. We will return to this concept in detail in Chapter 8.

more informal than others but each should be firmly built into the daily workflow of the program. On an ongoing basis:

1. Ask the student what (s)he likes

2. Train implementers to observe, recognize and document student expressions of preferences including choices and other behavior around items, events and people throughout the day

3. Create a running list of potential reinforcers and review it with implementers. Encourage all implementers to add to the list

4. Interview other knowledgeable sources (parents, inclusion teachers, etc.) to discover preferred items in other settings

5. Formally test preferences

Preference Assessment

There is no alternative to conducting data-based preference assessments; they are essential to providing effective services because the crucial information they provide is not available through any other means. Contrary to the occasional assertions of some implementers, data-based preference assessments do not merely confirm what we already know. More often than not, the conventional wisdom about how and whether a stimulus functions as a reinforcer is at least incomplete. Devoting the time to explicitly consider and provide empirical support for using stimuli as reinforcers appropriately reflects the prominence and priority status of reinforcement within a three-term contingency.[2] Such effort pays dividends in the discovery, conservation, and effective employment of reinforcing stimuli. In addition, regular assessment helps ensure that decisions are based on current information within a decidedly dynamic system.

Two basic questions are answered by an explicit inquiry into preferences:

1. What stimuli are preferred?

---

[2] A "three-term contingency" refers to the arrangement: discriminative stimulus→behavior→reinforcement, in effect, the behavior timeline. The word "contingency" implies that the last term (reinforcement) is contingent on the occurrence of the first two terms. Reinforcement is the event most responsible for the occurrence of the first two events.

2. What is the degree of preference of each stimulus compared to others?

Typically, as discussed above, Question 1 is approached through observations and brainstorming with those who are familiar with the student (Steps 1-4). The evaluator assembles a list of potentially reinforcing stimuli, each noted as preferred, from as many sources as possible. Considering that individuals will require reinforcement for sustained efforts over the entire school year, there can never be too many candidates.

Once potential reinforcers are identified, the next phase of a preference assessment protocol provides data about a student's interaction with listed stimuli in a particular setting. Commonly, there are four methods of arranging such interactions presented either in trials or more extended observations:

1. **Single Stimulus Presentation**: trial-based presentation of each reinforcer candidate in isolation from other stimuli and noting a student's interactions and engagement. The stimulus is placed in proximity to the individual and the individual is allowed to freely interact with it. The evaluator notes (a) whether the item was touched and (b) how long the interaction with the item lasts. This method can be adapted to any stimulus that can be discretely delivered to the individual including edibles, toys, or some activities that involve materials (e.g., bowling). When used with a series of reinforcer candidates, the individual assessed may become satiated as the process continues, thus impacting the validity of interaction data with later stimuli. In addition, since no choice is involved, preference between stimuli is not easily ranked

2. **Paired Stimulus Presentation**: a trial-by-trial procedure where stimuli are paired and presented in all possible combinations. The student is asked to choose one stimulus for each presentation. Choice is recorded and the individual is allowed to engage with the stimulus briefly before another pair is presented. The number of times each stimulus was chosen is used to calculate the percentage of trials and the stimulus is ranked against all other stimuli presented. Paired stimulus presentations allow individuals to directly express preference; over repeated measurements, a relatively stable ranking tends to emerge as long as the order of presentation of trials is as random as possible. Paired stimulus presentation can require a lengthy process of trials when many stimuli are assessed. Some students object to

disengaging with highly preferred items when instructed

3. **Multiple Stimulus Presentation:** a trial-by-trial procedure where an entire set of stimuli are presented and the student is encouraged to choose one. Some methods of multiple stimulus presentations ("multiple stimulus *with* replacement" or MSW) interfere with relative ranking of stimuli contained within the set because individuals tend to persistently choose the most highly preferred items and not choose less preferred items. Therefore, in contrast to paired stimulus assessment, some stimulus combinations are never evaluated. This may result in the domination of the most highly preferred stimuli and the underestimation of the value of less preferred stimuli as reinforcers. A version of the multiple stimulus presentation assessment called "Multiple Stimulus Without Replacement" (MSWO) presents a set of stimuli at the same time but eliminates a stimulus after it is chosen, thus forcing the individual to choose from the remaining set items. MSWO assessment methods are briefer and tend to be as accurate as paired stimulus assessment. They allow more accurate ranking of set items than MSW assessments

4. **Free-Operant Presentation:** in a contrived or natural setting, sets of potential reinforcers are displayed and individuals are allowed to freely select and interact with them in any way they would like. Selection and duration of engagement with stimuli are recorded. This method can be brief and accurate and, compared to paired stimulus preference assessments may elicit fewer problem behaviors because stimuli are not withdrawn. It is also useful when students have difficulty making meaningful choices and tend to select items based on position or order of presentation. As with MSW-type presentations, the free-operant method tends to accurately identify the most preferred items most accurately if it is always available. Therefore, different sets of items must be created to rank less preferred items. Data collection can be more complicated in a free-operant presentation. Since multiple stimuli can be engaged simultaneously, some data collection systems use partial interval recording with

short (~10 seconds) intervals. For example, a data sheet spanning five minutes in total containing 30, ten-second intervals requires implementers to place a check in all boxes of stimuli that were engaged by the student during the interval. Less exacting data collection methods may simply record the duration of the student's interaction with each stimulus

Preference Assessment Protocols

Generally, assessment protocols ensure that the student has had a sample of all the items prior to making a choice in the assessment. Protocols may specify additional details depending on the abilities and needs of the individual assessed and conditions of assessment. For example, some preference procedures may present choices between pictures of potential reinforcers, speeding up the process and allowing a greater range of stimuli to be conveniently presented.

Implementers have been easily trained to perform preference assessments (Lavie and Sturmey, 2002) using written preference assessment protocols as the focus of training, such as the sample provided below:

Sample Protocol

Multiple Stimuli without Replacement (MSWO) Preference Assessment[3]

1. Allow the student to sample each item prior to initiating the assessment

2. Assemble items to be assessed and record them on the data sheet

3. Seat the person to be assessed in a chair positioned in front of a table

4. Present items on the table in a straight line equidistant from the student and each other. Make sure all items fit on the table without overcrowding with space between each

5. Instruct the student to "pick one"

6. Place a check in the row of the selected item on the data sheet

7. Remove the item that is selected and present the remaining items. If the selected item was a consumable like food, do not replenish it

8. Randomly rotate the remaining items. Continue to ensure that they are equally spaced and equidistant from the student

9. Repeat Steps 5-8 until all of the items are selected or until the student does not make a selection within 30 seconds of the instruction. If a student makes no selection, mark all remaining items as "Not Selected" and terminate the assessment

10. Calculate the percent of trials where each stimulus was chosen when available. The first item chosen was available for 1 trial before it was removed. The second item chosen was available for 2 trials, the third item chosen was available for 3 trials, etc. Use the following table to choose a value for each stimulus tested:

Item Chosen on Trial:	Value:
1	1/1 or 100%
2	1/2 or 50%
3	1/3 or 33%
4	1/4 or 25%
5	1/5 or 20%
6	1/6 or 17%
7	1/7 or 14%
8	1/8 or 13%
Item not chosen	0/total trials or 0%
(Continue up to the number of items presented)	

11. Combine the values if multiple sessions are completed by adding the numerators and denominators of all values. For example, if an item was tested on 2 occasions and received 1/1,

---

[3] See the data sheet supplied for an MSWO preference assessment included in the Appendix.

1/3, and 1/4, add the numerators (1 + 1 + 1 = 3) and denominators (1 + 3 + 4 = 8 to get the value (3/8). Divide and multiply the result by 100 to calculate the percentage (38%)

12. Use the percentage score calculated for each item to rank the items from most preferred to least preferred

Is a Preferred Stimulus Also a Reinforcing Stimulus?

By definition, stimuli are only called reinforcers if the probability of occurrence of a particular behavior increases after the stimulus is contingently delivered. When freely available, students may express a strong tendency to choose a particular item but this does not necessarily mean that the item will motivate any behavior beyond reaching. For example, even if playing with the computer is the most highly ranked preference in a list of stimuli, there is no guarantee that access to the computer would successfully reinforce writing an entire paragraph of several sentences. Highly preferred stimuli exist as potential reinforcers whose effectiveness depends, at least in part, on the nature of the behavior that precedes it. Therefore, preference assessment is a provisional process that should be followed by reinforcer effectiveness evaluation. This naturally occurs when we use preferred stimuli in an actual teaching situation. However, program designers should not wait for wholesale errors and prolonged lack of progress as a means of discovering ineffective reinforcement. Rather, constant, careful review of response rates, latency, and other student interactions with the potential reinforcers should occur as soon as they are incorporated to ensure that possible deficiencies are identified.

In addition to the level of preference for a stimulus, four limiting factors or parameters related to the nature of the target response can be identified which impact whether the response will be reinforced by a given stimulus. Evaluating these possible factors may help to inform program authors of needed adjustments to reinforcement or the targets themselves:

Determining if Reinforcement will Occur: Limiting Factors

Factor 1: The Difficulty Required in Performing the Target Response may be High

- Actions may be complex, require sustained attention, or frequently lead to errors, restarts, and imperfect results

- Responses may be required to occur rapidly, for long durations, with high magnitude or short latency

Factor 2: Engaging in the Target Behavior may be Aversive

- Performing actions may be uncomfortable or painful

- Conditions under which the behavior is performed may be extreme, unsafe, unsanitary, fearful, or repetitive

Factor 3: Frequency or Quantity of Reinforcement may be Low

- The schedule of reinforcement may require long intervals or a high frequency of responses before reinforcement is delivered

- The amount, intensity, or duration of the reinforcing stimulus may be low

Factor 4: Concurrently Available Contingencies of Reinforcement may Exist and Compete for the Responding of the Individual

Factors 1 and 2 increase the response *effort* and tend to require upward adjustments in reinforcement quantity, quality and/or frequency. For example, prolonged writing is often cited as non-preferred for some students because they must expend sustained effort to laboriously form all the letters that form the words and sentences. When reinforcement is inadequate, instructors may observe starts and stops, complaints, frequent mistakes, erasures, or a degradation in letter formation as time goes on. Difficulties may be ameliorated if the instructor increases the type, amount, quality, and/or schedule of reinforcement. For example:

- Change the stimulus used as a reinforcer to one that is more highly preferred (type)

- Increase the reinforcement given from one minute to three minutes (quantity)

- Add a highly preferred person as partner during play period (quality)

- Add a system of checks and praise for each word written (schedule)

Changing the nature of the required behavior and adding prompts may also reduce response effort and, therefore, affect the potency of potentially reinforcing stimuli:

- Break target responses up into easier, component behavior until the behavior occurs easily with available reinforcers

- Use prompts to eliminate errors and inaccurate performances and speed correct behavior

- Shorten practice sessions

By reducing errors, aversive aspects of the teaching situation may be reduced. In some cases, program designers may also opt to discard or change procedures:

- Eliminate aversive consequences such as repeated error correction, response cost, or penalties for non-responsiveness or errors

An Expectancy of Reinforcement – Establishing Effective Contingencies

In summary, effective instructional procedures contain effective reinforcers which are identified through formal and informal assessment processes. The identification of strongly preferred stimuli and the careful choice of a suitable amount of response effort optimizes the probability that reinforcement will occur when target behavior and instructional stimuli are arranged in a contingency. However, success only occurs when the arrangement and execution of a "contingent relationship" between the target behavior and the reinforcer is structured effectively. Difficulties can also arise in the schedule of delivery of reinforcers which can impair the formation of a solid contingency. Examples include:

- Reinforcement delivered non-contingently (not immediately, inconsistently)

- Undefined or vaguely defined targets for reinforcement

- Unpredictable amounts of work required for reinforcement

- Long gaps in opportunities to respond for reinforcement

- Tokens or other secondary reinforcement that is weakly connected with primary reinforcement

It is distressing and, perhaps, surprising, how often contingencies collapse in instructional situations. Procedural integrity issues such as those listed above are far too commonplace and have a corrosive effect on the power of any instructional contingency to succeed.

Implementation problems frequently relate to the immediacy of delivery or the conditions under which reinforcement is delivered. For learning to occur, a connection between completion of target behaviors and delivery of preferred items must be firmly established. This connection occurs relatively easily when reinforcing stimuli are immediately available *only* for performance of the specified target behaviors. Optimally, reinforcement should be delivered within one second of the occurrence of the behavior to properly ensure that reinforcement is associated with behavior. Often, at the start of programs, a behavior requirement will be simple and brief—one repetition of one action (e.g., one trial of matching a yellow card with another yellow card) followed by immediate reinforcement. This constitutes the basic building block that, with repetition, strengthens the student's tendency to independently repeat the behavior. Continuous reinforcement (reinforcing after every correct response) facilitates the development of consistent student performance as long as the reinforcing stimulus is potent, the response requirement is clearly defined, and the level of effort is realistic, especially when the contingency is new. Reinforcer delivery confirms that the response was correct as well as motivates the student to continue to respond in the future.

Implementer training to achieve competent delivery of reinforcement initially focuses on the definition of the target behavior and the mechanics of timely delivery of the reinforcing consequences. The formulation of precise and practical definitions of the response may require some ingenuity when responses do not have easily recognized beginnings and endings. For example, defining a "correct" response when matching a card to another card in an array of three cards may seem relatively simple at first glance – the student must simply place the sample card on the corresponding card in the array. However, some students may place the sample card in front of the corresponding card rather than on top of the card or place the card so that it lies between or touching two of the array cards at the same time. Alternatively, the student may place the card on one card and then move it to another card. Conventions governing the treatment of each of these ambiguous responses are required to ensure consistency in implementation such as:

- A response is defined as occurring after the student releases the sample card. If the student does not release the card and moves it (even several times), no "response" has occurred until the card is completely released

- Cards in a choice array are separately placed in individual plastic trays with shallow sides. Sample cards that will be matched to a choice are required to be placed completely inside one of the choice trays

Delivery of the reinforcer may also pose certain logistical challenges to an implementer depending on the size, shape, or other characteristics of the reinforcing stimulus as well as the characteristics of the instructional space. This can be daunting if instruction involves manipulation of other materials closely in time to delivery of reinforcement. Program writers and implementers, therefore, may often find themselves collaborating in the choreography of movements during a trial to ensure that everything happens efficiently and effectively. Certain practices can help:

- Keep items to be delivered conveniently positioned

- Use immediate praise to bridge the gap between a correct response and delivery of an item, edible, or event. Other stimuli that may effectively serve as "gap fillers" include ringing a bell, checking a box, or delivery of pictures of items and events. Note, however, that such stimuli are usually conditioned reinforcers and, therefore, must acquire reinforcing value by being systematically paired with backup reinforcers. This process will be discussed below in more detail

- Practice all procedures until they are smooth and become second nature. Give and receive feedback from others to improve consistency

Intermittent Reinforcement

While continuous reinforcement can be necessary and effective, program writers may adjust the schedule of reinforcement for target responses during the course of instruction for a variety of reasons. As we discussed in the last section, immediate delivery of reinforcement is sometimes logistically difficult. In addition, mastered tasks usually require less effort than tasks in acquisition and, therefore, lowering the amount of reinforcement maintains a consistent balance between effort and amount of reinforcement. As the task becomes easier, it is likely that the student performs it more quickly and receives more reinforcement and, potentially, a student may become more quickly satiated if adjustment does not occur. In some cases, adjustments in the rate of reinforcement can result in stronger behavior than if reinforcement is delivered continuously. For example, if a student is given a deck of cards to sort and reinforced with a small edible after each correct card is placed in the correct sorting pile, there is a noticeable inter-trial interval where the student receives the edible, consumes it, and makes a transition back to work. However, if the student is reinforced after 5, 10, or 20 cards are sorted (assuming that he can wait for reinforcement), the sorting process will occur more rapidly because there is less interruption.

Non-continuous reinforcement (or *intermittent reinforcement*) has been extensively studied by the science of behavior analysis for its effects on the behavior of organisms (Ferster and Skinner, 1957). It may be classified into two major types: intermittent schedules that vary in the *ratio* of responses required for reinforcement and intermittent schedules that vary in the amount of time that must elapse (the "*interval*") before reinforcement becomes available. For example, ratio schedules may require 3, 5, 10, 20, or 100 individual responses before reinforcement is delivered (compared to continuous reinforcement that requires only a single response). In an instructional situation, a student on a ratio schedule may have to complete three problems before receiving one sticker. In contrast, interval schedules require a certain period of time to expire before reinforcing the first target response that occurs. During a class presentation, a teacher may pause and ask questions every three minutes. Students who raise their hand and answer correctly are praised.

In the examples above, procedures presented an opportunity for reinforcement based on a *fixed* number of responses performed by the individual or after the completion of a *fixed* time interval. Researchers have also studied the effects of *varying* the ratio or interval rather than keeping it consistent. For example, on one trial the student may be required to complete three problems but on the next trial he may have to complete two or four. Variable schedules require specifying the *range* of value used to deliver reinforcement. For example, a variable ratio schedule needs to specify the range of responses required for reinforcement, such as 4-7 or 3-5.

Four basic variations of intermittent schedules of reinforcement are created by combining ratio and interval schedules with the attributes "fixed" or "variable":

- **Fixed Ratio**: reinforcement is delivered after a consistent number of target responses

- **Variable Ratio**: reinforcement is delivered after a variable number of target responses

- **Fixed Interval**: reinforcement is delivered for a target response that occurs after a consistent interval has elapsed

- **Variable Interval**: reinforcement is delivered for a target response that occurs after a variable interval has elapsed

Benefits of Intermittent Schedules

The various intermittent reinforcement arrangements are common to settings like schools, home, work, and the community and building them into instructional procedures is frequently desirable. Each has unique effects on responding and may have a place in the acquisition or maintenance of target behavior. For example:

- Gradually increasing the ratio of required responses in a sorting task from continuous reinforcement to two responses then three, four, and five responses may result in more rapid and even more accurate completion of the task

- Withholding reinforcement during the completion of the various steps of a chain of behavior (e.g. handwashing, participation in a basketball game, singing a song) may reduce or eliminate disruptions

- Interval schedules may increase monitoring and sustained attention as students learn to pace their performance and attentively wait for reinforcement opportunities

- Variable schedules may help students break out of an abnormally strict expectancy of reinforcement that results in protest or disruption when even small discrepancies in delivery occur

- Intermittent reinforcement arrangements approximate those in the natural environment and their intentional incorporation within instructional programs enhances generalization and survival of emerging skills

Nevertheless, intermittent reinforcement presents its own set of implementation issues that require consideration. Chief among them are the limits of a given reinforcer to effectively strengthen behavior. We have already discussed how the amount of effort required by a behavior interacts with the strength of the reinforcing stimulus at a given moment. With continuous reinforcement the amount of effort expended by the student for a single trial is the total amount of effort reinforced. However, with intermittent reinforcement, required behavior spans multiple trials or repetitions of the behavior with longer intervals between reinforcement. When the amount of work required for reinforcement is stretched beyond the toleration of the student or becomes too unpredictable, extinction effects[4] may result in undesirable behavior and the impact to an instructional program may be disruptive. This phenomenon is sometimes called "ratio strain" (Reynolds, 1975). In addition, by failing to provide a reinforcer after every correct response, intermittent schedules give less feedback to the individual that correct behavior has occurred and that reinforcement will eventually be delivered.

Token Reinforcement

Token reinforcement systems are commonly used procedures used to facilitate effective intermittent reinforcement schedules within a variety of programming situations. "Tokens" such as poker chips, pennies, stickers, checks, tickets, stars, or the like may be awarded as convenient stand-ins or replacements for continuous reinforcement which help bridge a delay between a target response and the actual delivery of reinforcement. For example, when three responses are required for reinforcement, a token is delivered immediately after each response and the actual reinforcer is delivered after the third token is earned. Using tokens provides an immediate confirmation that a correct response has occurred and, if done correctly, facilitates continued responding up to the actual point of

---

[4] "Extinction effects" refers to the appearance of strong, disruptive or agitated behavior that occurs when reinforcement is discontinued. In the situation discussed above, changing reinforcement schedules radically may be tantamount to discontinuing reinforcement from the perspective of the student.

reinforcer delivery on an intermittent schedule. Tokens are constructed from any relatively portable, self-contained stimulus that is easily delivered to the student. Tokens are generally chosen to be:

- Highly visually discriminable. For some students bold colors and simplified drawings are preferable to photographs with complicated backgrounds[5]
- Durable, inexpensive, and easy-to-clean
- Sized so that multiple tokens can be conveniently manipulated, delivered and displayed, (enough to span the required reinforcement period)
- Attractive or interesting to the individual receiving reinforcement
- Easy-to-reproduce

The identity and physical characteristics of tokens are mainly a practical concern for program designers because tokens are not required to possess any initial value as reinforcers[6], often starting out as neutral stimuli. Token training procedures pair the initially neutral token and "backup" reinforcers. Backup reinforcers are highly preferred stimuli that are already established as reinforcers due to intrinsic characteristics or a history of reinforcement. They can include any reinforcing stimulus such as food, drinks, tactile stimulation, games, social stimuli, toys, etc. By repeatedly pairing tokens and backup reinforcers, tokens acquire the ability to reinforce behavior as well, earning the designation "conditioned reinforcer." The strength of the association and, therefore, the strength of the conditioned reinforcer (token), depends on the quality and number of pairings of the two. Breakdowns in the effectiveness of tokens can be an inevitable occurrence in clinical practice if common problems are not successfully addressed:

1. Failure of the system to frequently and consistently pair the token with the backup reinforcer during initial introduction of the token

2. Failure to take enough care while increasing the interval or ratio of responses required and "leaning out" reinforcement

---

[5] In order to empirically test the student's ability to discriminate the token from other things, have her match it to another identical token in a field of objects or pictures.

[6] It may be important for program designers to choose tokens that do not possess a history of reinforcement to avoid possible undesirable associations with past programming efforts.

3. Failure to maintain a consistent relationship between tokens and strong backup reinforcers over the life of the contingency

4. Failure of the backup reinforcer when backup reinforcers are not potent enough relative to the required target behavior or if they become satiated

Above all, backup reinforcers must support strong response rates of the target behavior for the duration of the instructional period, even when they are delivered on intermittent schedules matching the requirements of the contingency at hand. Often, identification of a *variety* of the most highly preferred stimuli and providing the student with a choice of backup reinforcers is necessary to strengthen the contingency and compensate, to some extent, for the day-to-day fluctuations in preference and reinforcer strength.

Token Training Procedures

After selecting a backup reinforcer (or array of choices), training is initiated to integrate tokens into a contingency. There are many variants of token training, depending on the type of tokens used, the way in which tokens are accumulated, and the method of trading in tokens for backup reinforcers. However, all methods usually begin by teaching individuals to exchange tokens for backup reinforcers. For example consider the following sample procedure:

Training Step 1

1. Instructor presents a plastic container with a slot cut into the top

2. Instructor presents the student with a token and points to the slot

3. Student inserts the token into the slot

4. Instructor immediately presents praise and small backup reinforcer

5. After reinforcement is complete, the instructor repeats Steps 2-4, ten additional times[7]

---

[7] Ten trials are provided as a sample only. The actual number of trials should be dependent on how long the student will eagerly participate. End a session *before* the student becomes tired or bored. With some students the author has dismissed the student to a 30-second "break" after just a single trial and then repeated the cycle.

While some minimal prompts may be necessary at first to communicate the requirement for inserting the token into the slot, the student is soon likely to eagerly anticipate the delivery of tokens and independently perform the insertion, depending, of course, on the desirability of the reinforcing stimulus. The minimal behavioral requirement ensures a strong response and, therefore, optimal pairing between token "redemption" (insertion) and reinforcement with the backup reinforcer. Over the course of several sessions, a sufficient number of trials should be conducted to ensure that totally independent behavior occurs consistently with the shortest possible latency. The second step of token training then begins by adding a small response requirement prior to delivery of the token:

Training Step 2

1. Instructor gives student instruction to perform a simple single-step mastered task ("clap", "do this", "give me block")

2. Instructor presents the student with a token

3. Instructor calls out, "You finished!" and presents plastic container with slot cut into the top

4. Student inserts the token into the slot

5. Instructor immediately presents praise and small backup reinforcer

6. After reinforcement is complete, the instructor repeats steps 2-5, ten additional times

The specific additional response requirement is selected because it is highly likely to occure when the student is instructed to perfrom it. In a way, the contingency is slightly elaborated without endangering the pairing that occurs between performance of the small chain of behaviors (following a one-step instruction, putting the token into the slot) and backup reinforcement. Again, a sufficient number of trials are conducted to ensure consistent, totally independent and short latency behavior over a reasonable number of trials. The third step of token training introduces a means of saving tokens when more than one response is required before token redemption.

Training Step 3

1. Instructor places token "jig" on desk, consisting of a strip of cardboard with two round Velcro dots placed in a line, one inch apart

2. Instructor gives student instruction to perform simple mastered task ("clap", "do this", "give me block")

Three designs of token jigs

3. Instructor immediately presents the student with enthusiastic praise and a token

4. Instructor points to Velcro dot and guides student to place token on dot (token has a matching Velcro dot that sticks to the dot on the cardboard strip

5. Instructor gives student instruction to perform another simple mastered task ("clap", "do this", "give me block")

6. Instructor immediately presents the student with enthusiastic praise and a token

7. Instructor points to Velcro dot and guides student to place token on dot

8. Instructor calls out, "You finished!" and presents plastic container with slot cut into the top

9. Student inserts both tokens into slot (instructor provides assistance as necessary)

10. Instructor immediately presents praise and small backup reinforcer

11. After reinforcement is complete, instructor repeats steps above, up to 10 times

Step 3 of token training permits the program designer to increase the number of responses required for backup reinforcement by gradually incrementing the number of Velcro dots placed on the cardboard strip until the desired number is reached. However, in the early stages of Step 3, the instructor should be careful to give (and gradually fade) assistance so that the student learns to place the tokens in the jig and trade them in when the token receptacle (slotted plastic container) is presented. It is crucial to delay moving on until the student is considered to be fluent in the mechanics of manipulating the tokens – usually indicated by independence in performance of each step without hesitation (short latency). Additional signs of effectiveness include anticipation of placement of the plastic container as soon as the jig is filled or immediately showing "ready" behavior after the first response (anticipating the next instruction).

It may take some time for students to do well with schedules of reinforcement that require a high number of responses or long intervals before backup reinforcement is delivered. In this case, the integrity of the token performance is paramount. Only a slow and gradual progression of increases in the response requirement, an extremely consistent token delivery procedure, and constant attention to the potency of the backup reinforcer will produce acceptable outcomes. This is good advice to follow after the desired ratio or interval schedule is reached as well. Token programs, like all reinforcer systems, rely on a balance between the amount of effort required and the amount of reinforcement delivered. As a student makes progress and contingencies are added or modified, the balance can easily become unstable. The value of a single token, for example, may decrease as more responses are required for backup reinforcement, eventually diminishing to a level that does not support continued responding. New performances may be more difficult or require more effort, and the student may be entitled to expect a little "renegotiation" in the number of tokens required for trade-in.

Competition of Concurrent Schedules and the Matching Law

Reinforcement contingencies presented by instructional programs are not the only contingencies in existence at a given moment in the student's day. Whether a student sits at a desk in a classroom, a table in a restaurant, or in a sandbox on the playground, there are multiple contingencies competing for his behavior. Such contingencies may or may not be mutually exclusive – that is, the student may be able to do several at the same time or may be required to distribute his behavior between available contingencies, one at a time. Regardless, the individual has a range of choices. For example, when seated in a professional sports arena, a spectator's senses are assaulted by multiple stimuli – the action on the field, the hawking of vendors, the public address announcements, the scoreboard, the crowd, and the discussion of companions, to mention a few. Each stimulus is available simultaneously and represents a potential reinforcer whose delivery depends on a choice of behavior. Spectators may speak with friends, scan the scoreboard, buy a hot dog, cheer with the crowd, or watch the players, depending on the strength of each potentially reinforcing stimulus. Most likely, they will engage with *all* appealing stimuli, some simultaneously and some sequentially, in an elaborate series of selections intended to create the maximum enjoyable experience. *The Matching Law* (Herrnstein, 1961) states that students generally choose to behave in a manner that maximizes their reinforcement based on what is available in a given environment (Cuvo, 1998). Concurrent schedules of reinforcement (contingencies that are in force at the same time) are a natural part of every environment.

Each setting presents a different range of reinforcers and set of expectations for the behavior required to obtain them. Indeed, the behavioral requirements or constraints of the contingencies that govern the availability of stimuli are as important as the presence of the stimuli themselves. At the sports arena, hotdogs are not freely available but must be purchased. In a classroom, each reinforcement opportunity (some created by instructional personnel, others not) rests within a contingency (if you want that, you must do this) that competes successfully or unsuccessfully to engage the student's behavior.

In the following section, we will employ The Matching Law to analyze and quantify how reinforcers compete for student behavior. Imagine a student responding in a classroom during a free choice time. In this setting, like many others, different behaviors tend to receive differing levels of reinforcement. In order to simplify things, let's say that all responses are equally preferred and that the only reinforcement available is the receipt of a cookie. After a period of data collection, some statistics have been calculated on the delivery of reinforcement to the student during the free choice time. Five different behaviors occurred over a period of days that were reinforced at different rates:[8]

1. Complaints –> Reinforced **4** times

2. Reading task –> Reinforced **9** times

3. Screams –> Reinforced **3** times

4. Draws a picture –> Reinforced **2** times

---

[8] Note that a combination of appropriate and inappropriate behaviors is listed, just like a real environment where (unfortunately) inappropriate behavior is sometimes reinforced.

5. Asks for cookie –> Reinforced **6** times

A behavior analyst would like to understand how the contingencies that are in effect in the environment are likely to affect a student's future behavior. Her first step would be to calculate the total reinforcement available.[9] This may be accomplished by adding the individual rates of reinforcement delivered for *all* behavior. Therefore:

Total reinforcement: 4 + 9 + 3 + 2 + 6 = 24

Next, the relative reinforcement percentage for each behavior is calculated by dividing the individual reinforcement rate by the total rate and multiplying by 100:

1. Complaints: 4 out of 24 = 4/24 *100 = 17%

2. Reading task: 9 out of 24 = 4/24 *100 = 37%

3. Screams: 3 out of 24 = 3/24 *100 = 13%

4. Draws a picture: 2 out of 24 = 2/24 * 100 = 18%

5. Asks for cookie: 6 out of 24 = 6/24 * 100 = 25%

While some mathematics has been necessary to get to this point, we now possess information that may be useful both in understanding the present situation and deciding how to intervene. First, we now plainly see the range of reinforcement for the various behaviors. Reading was reinforced most frequently followed by requesting a cookie, complaints, screaming, and drawing a picture. In the future, we would expect that the relative rate of reinforcement available will be generally matched by the individual's rate of behavior. In other words, the frequency distribution of complaints, reading, screaming, etc. is likely to correspond to their individual percentages of relative reinforcement (17% of responses will be complaints, 37% of responses will be reading, 13% of responses will be screams, etc.).

Changing the contingencies by changing the relative rate of reinforcement is likely to change the relative rate of responding for any of the listed behaviors. For example, training

---

[9]Herrnstein's original (1961) method of calculation will be used for the sake of simplicity in this example.

implementers to redirect or ignore complaints and screams may, by itself, *increase the time spent drawing or any of the other behaviors on the list* as the individual shifts responding to maintain maximum reinforcement. Increasing the delivery of reinforcement for drawing decreases relative reinforcement for inappropriate behavior in favor of drawing and will likely result in a corresponding increase in drawing relative to other behavior. If the relative rate of reinforcement for other behavior is lower, their rate of occurrence may decrease. One of the most important lessons of The Matching Law is to make every effort to try and understand that the range of reinforcers available in a given environment is an interconnected system that includes many concurrent contingencies. Changing one contingency usually impacts others; focusing on one contingency in isolation and ignoring others may produce unexpected results.

The Role of Discriminative Stimuli in Successful Contingencies

Effective instructional contingencies that successfully compete with off-task contingencies available in the environment depend on *discriminative* as much as reinforcing stimuli. A strong discriminative stimulus (S^D) clearly sets the occasion for behavior that will be reinforced. These antecedent events are said to "elicit" behavior, an ability that comes about through a history of pairing with reinforcers. In other words, stimuli that have been present when behavior is reinforced eventually tend to increase the probability that a behavior will occur whenever they appear. The stimuli are not reinforcers themselves but they become associated with reinforcement. For example, if dark clouds are frequently present when it rains, and taking an umbrella prevents us from becoming wet, we might take an umbrella when dark clouds appear in the sky. The appearance of dark clouds has become a discriminative stimulus that elicits the behavior of taking an umbrella which is (negatively) reinforced by avoiding becoming wet. While the greatest factor in determining whether a behavior will occur is the relative potency and magnitude of reinforcement that follows, factors related to discriminative stimuli are also crucial:[10]

- Discriminability of the stimulus signaling the availability of reinforcement

- Strength and consistency of association between the antecedent stimulus (S^D) and reinforcement

---

[10]These factors are similar to those discussed in the creation of tokens and any process involving pairing/associating one event with another.

Problems with these factors may result in weak discriminative stimuli that act inconsistently or stimuli that completely fail to elicit the target behavior. The discriminative stimuli of task presentation should be associated with the opportunity to obtain relatively strong reinforcement but may fail if:

- Reinforcement is seldom offered, inconsistent, or delivered long after completion of the task

- It is unclear from the antecedents what behavior is required, how much work needs to be done, what reinforcement will be delivered, etc.

In some cases, problems like those above create discriminative stimuli that come to signify an *absence* of reinforcement, effectively transforming the settings, materials, and implementers of instructional programs into conditioned aversive stimuli, resulting in protests and other escape-related behavior when they are presented (Carbone, 2009). Therefore, when establishing contingencies, discriminative stimuli should be carefully structured and established. For most instructional purposes, stimuli should be easy to discriminate, consistently present, and associated with potent reinforcement schedules. Such procedures establish discriminative stimuli that communicate:

- What behavior(s) will be reinforced, where, with whom, etc.

- How much work is expected for reinforcement and the quality of work expected

- What materials should be used and where to get them

- How much work remains prior to reinforcement at any given time during the activity

- What reinforcer(s) will be available

- Where, when, and how to obtain reinforcement

- What choices and options within the activity are allowed

- What ancillary behaviors (concurrent contingencies) are permitted and which will be discouraged

- The appropriate way to interrupt or stop the activity, refuse, protest, and solve problems

- What's coming next

Arranging Discriminative Stimuli to Facilitate Strong Instructional Contingencies

The list above may seem like a lot to ask of discriminative stimuli but each item directly affects the ability of the contingency to deliver reinforcement for the target behavior. Each aspect of the task-related environment should facilitate task completion by directing the student towards reinforcement and removing problems, questions, or frustrations that may interfere with reinforcement as well as removing unnecessary dependencies on others that may result in waiting, pacing problems, or other sorts of breaks in the continuity of task completion:

- **Establish Effective Discriminative Stimuli Related to Reinforcement**
    - Augment task to enhance progression of task and discrimination of reinforcement arrival:
        - Tokens fill up a defined number of spaces
        - Pegs fill up all available holes
        - Puzzle pieces fit together to complete a picture
        - Counter counts down to zero
        - Counter counts up to target number
        - Verbal alert: "Five more to go"
        - All materials or components of task to be completed displayed:
            - Mixed bin of materials to be sorted until empty
            - Pile of flash cards to be matched until gone
            - Pile of cards to be named and placed all at once on table
            - Problems to be completed checked off on worksheet
    - Enhance task materials to improve discrimination of reinforcement interval:

- Countdown timer shows time remaining in work interval
- Clock displays end time of teaching session
- Verbal alert: "Two more minutes"

o Enhance discrimination of identity of reinforcer:
- Item displayed
- Icon/picture of reinforcer displayed
- Printed word of reinforcer displayed
- Place reinforcer on pedestal, in clear box, close to student

- **Establish Effective Discriminative Stimuli Related to Performance of Target Behavior(s)**

    o Use stimulus prompts to achieve errorless performance during acquisition (see Chapter 5 – Prompts and Prompt Hierarchies)

    o Construction and layout of task materials:
    - Optimal size
    - Placed in proximity to student and related materials
    - Visually prominent and clearly defined, separated
    - Arrays configured to facilitate visual inspection
    - Orientation of manipulatives emphasizes ease of movement

- **Establish and Incorporate Discriminative Stimuli to Guide Auxiliary Performances**

    o Use a visual list of ingredients or parts to be assembled

    o Place materials in standard locations and teach their locations

    o Label locations and materials

    o Provide a "completed" folder or table

- **Exploit Social Interactions Inherent in Instructor – Student Relationship to Strengthen Instructional Contingency**

- Prior to presentation of program, establish the instructor as a strong social reinforcer by frequently pairing instructor with preferred stimuli in non-demand settings

- Prior to presentation of program, establish history of instructional control with preferred, low effort activities

- Establish accepted and effective means of communication of distress or protest and permissible conditions of escape

- Employ preferred interaction styles:
    - Tone of voice
    - Eye contact
    - Facial expressions
    - Means of delivering praise and encouragement (high-fives, pats on back)
    - Novelty
    - Playfulness
    - Quiet vs. dramatic, active vs. sedate, rapid vs. slow presentation style
    - Employ competition when appropriate ("Bet you can't do it faster than me...oh, you beat me!")
    - Employ choice when appropriate:
        - Choice of reinforcer ("What do you want to work for?")
        - Choice of order of work tasks ("Which one do you want to do first?")
        - Allow temporary rejection of non-preferred task ("I don't want to do that now, please")

- **Employ Motivating Operations**
    - Control availability of preferred stimuli

- Give opportunities to engage in common off-task behavior in non-work settings
- Reduce coerciveness of procedures
- Disguise limits when necessary

Towards a Long-Term Reinforcement Strategy

With 360 minutes in a six hour school day, 1800 minutes in a week, and 9000 minutes in an average month, writing skill programs for student instruction must take a long-term view of behavior change and maintenance. Program presentation is a long chain of related events that starts one morning and continues into the future beyond the limits of the cubby, classroom, program, schedule, school day, and even school year. As such, effective education is continuous and cumulative and should be concerned with a long-term reinforcement strategy. Larger time spans require us to be mindful of arranging our methodology to keep the student going.

A day of educational programs is a real-life example of a *chain* of schedules of reinforcement (Reynolds, 1975). Each component is accompanied by a discriminative stimulus that is associated with an independent schedule of reinforcement. In a chained schedule, completion of one component becomes an S^D signaling the start of the next component. Student performances continue to interact as the hour, day, and week progresses. The nature of such interactions between programs in a sequence is something that is of concern to program writers and may be controlled to some extent by manipulating characteristics of individual sequence elements (programs). For example, program characteristics may vary along several dimensions:

- Task difficulty
- Task duration
- Task preference
- Task reinforcement

In addition, characteristics of sequence components may also vary *relative to other sequence components*:

- Position of tasks within a sequence of tasks

- Relative preference of task compared to preceding or following tasks

Chapter 8 will provide an in-depth discussion of issues related to sequencing tasks which will not be duplicated here. However, with regard to the issue of reinforcement and chains of programs, it may be appropriate to make at least some suggestions for approaching the structure of long-term reinforcement. Therefore, when planning for a student's ongoing participation, it is suggested that educators routinely identify five time frames within a student's overall learning experience[11] as potential targets of reinforcement:

Suggested Time-Frames for Reinforcement

- ***Response Level:*** The relationship of a single target response to a reinforcer. Considerations at this level are concerned with how to assist the student in discriminating whether his behavior was correct or not

- ***Series Level:*** The relationship of one response to another within a group of responses. A series is a string of responses from one program or several programs that are reinforced together. At this level, program authors consider how many responses will be required for intermittent reinforcement. Depending on the student and complexity of the programs, the series may last at least several minutes

- ***Segment Level:*** The relationship of one series to another within a group of series. Program authors consider what programs will be placed before and after a given program as well as how many programs will be required before a break or change of location. Segments typically last 20-60 minutes

- ***Schedule Level:*** The relationship of one segment to another within a group of segments. How will segments be dispersed in time throughout the day? How will

---

[11] The terms used in this list are descriptive and do not refer to any inherent organization other than a simple breakdown and categorization of convenient time frames relevant to reinforcement. A greater or fewer number of levels could be defined, depending on program circumstances.

events like lunch, recess, therapies, or inclusion times be integrated to maximize performance? Schedules may last two to three hours or more – up to the entire school day

- ***Phase Level:*** The relationship of one schedule to another within a group of schedules. What changes occur from day to day? How will daily progress in programs change the difficulty and need for reinforcement? How will satiation affect the student's progress over the course of the week and month? Phases last several days to several weeks

In this kind of comprehensive reinforcement planning, each phase is part of an overall reinforcement strategy that aims to motivate behavior within *all phases*. This requires explicit planning to avoid satiation, build momentum from one part of the schedule to the next, avoid "trouble spots" in the day (e.g. non-compliant periods after lunch), and encourage the student to persist all the way through complex learning tasks.

Complex Visual Systems of Motivation

One approach to long-term management of reinforcement is to adopt a token system that includes several layers of reinforcement contingencies and uses a consistently themed, highly visual set of program materials. While some students work well with simple schedules like stickers, charts, penny tokens, and the like, other students tend to become unmotivated with simple exchanges after the novelty has worn off and extra layers of reinforcer exchange may be necessary. For example, if a student exchanges ten work icons for a reinforcer during a morning, she may also get a star for completing all of the morning work. While continuing to exchange the work icons she may eventually be given a "special" reinforcer after accumulating five stars. This second layer of reinforcement, while slightly more complex, adds variety and interest to a simple system and, as discussed above, additional levels of reinforcement may be helpful to sustain student responding. Another challenge for motivation systems presents itself when a variety of behaviors are targeted for change but are unrelated to each other in either the nature of the behavior or the location/time of its occurrence. This requires a motivation system that is implemented in multiple locations and under different circumstances.

Effective token systems may be designed that address these and other motivational challenges (Kazdin, 1982). For example, using an amalgam of strategies including elements of social stories (Grey, 2000) and *Power Cards* (Gagnon, 2001) in conjunction with behavior analytic principles, the author created a multi-layered motivational system called "Super Hero Cards."

Super Hero Cards Motivation System

The design of *Super Hero Cards* incorporates several important features of a practical motivation system:

- **Portability**—able to be implemented across a variety of settings

- **Flexibility**—easy to use with any number of target behaviors regardless of the nature of the behavior

- **Suitability**—especially relevant for classroom settings and classroom related behaviors

- **Durability**—system is sufficiently complex to maintain student interest and motivation

- **Customizable**—allows for individual preference and reinforcer variety

Phase 1: Establishing Contingencies of Reinforcement

The first part of the program involves organizing and explaining the contingencies of reinforcement to the student. A visual schedule is constructed with each scheduled event for the day clearly depicted. The teacher displays the schedule and describes each item in a positive way. The criterion for success and the independence level expected of each item also needs to be clearly described. The criteria will be one of two types: (1) completion of a schedule item alone or (2) completion of a schedule item *plus* absence of a problem target behavior. *Each* successfully completed schedule item should be followed by reinforcement on whatever schedule is necessary to establish and maintain good behavior. For example, young students may require reinforcement after each event while older students may earn stickers that accumulate for the morning and then are cashed in. Some students may start with immediate reinforcement and gradually progress to reinforcement that is more delayed. Even if students receive immediate reinforcement they should also receive a check, sticker, or some other token on their schedule that accumulates until it is time to cash them in for a backup reinforcer. Backup reinforcers are more desirable stimuli that are available for more effort and after a longer period of good behavior. Sometimes even higher level reinforcers are included like those awarded for an entire week of successful behavior. Consider the previous discussion on reinforcement time-frames when establishing levels of reinforcement for the student.

For example, imagine an eight-year-old student named Tom, who is working on a number of things. In addition to generally requiring extrinsic reinforcement for completing all items on his daily schedule, Tom is specifically working on participating more often in circle group, completing work sheets independently, moving from activity to activity without reminders, and raising his hand rather than calling out in class. Tom loves the stars and planets and knows the names of many of them. He loves pictures and books involving planets and space. His teachers have chosen stars, planets, and space as Tom's theme for the motivation system. For the first phase of his token program, Tom's teachers have discussed the target behaviors and settled on the following contingencies:

- When Tom completes an activity on the schedule, he gets a blue star

- Each time Tom raises his hand three times in circle, he gets a blue star (named Polaris)

- Each time Tom does not call out during the entire circle activity, he gets a blue star

- Each time Tom completes three assigned worksheets, he gets a blue star

- Each time Tom moves from activity to activity with the class, without a reminder from his aide, he gets a blue star

- To begin with, stars will be traded in for backup reinforcers every 60 minutes. A classroom aide and Tom will go to the resource room for 15 minutes and Tom will get to trade his stars for his favorite activities. Some activities cost more than others. At the end of 15 minutes Tom and the aide will return to the classroom. If successful, the trade-in interval will be gradually lengthened to 90 minutes

- For every 10 stars, Tom earns he gets a Big Red Star (named Cassiopeia).

At the end of the day, he collects his Big Red Stars and brings them to the bulletin board where he keeps track of his progress towards the BIG BLAST-OFF REWARD at the end of the week (see below). He needs 5 Big Red Stars to earn the BIG BLAST-OFF REWARD

Phase 2: Integration of the Contingencies with Super Hero Cards

Many students have favorite story characters from books, TV, or videos, or have strong special interests like cars or dinosaurs. These interests can form the basis for a motivation system if students will work for access to fun activities involving these characters or interests. In addition, special interest in characters or topics can be used to increase student attention to rules and reminders. In Phase 2, the student is asked to listen to a story about an imaginary character that is related to his interest area. Each target behavior is paired with one imaginary character. An adult makes up (and writes down) a problem-oriented short story about the character related to the target behavior. The story should be interactive and dramatically told. The adult asks the student questions like, "What's going to happen?" and "What should he do instead?" and incorporates the student's answers into the story, as appropriate. After the story, the student draws two pictures of the character. Once picture shows the character smiling and is labeled with the character's name and the desirable behavior. The other picture depicts the character frowning and is labeled with the character's name and the problem behavior. Place both pictures back to back and laminate them. (Alternately, baseball card protectors are very sturdy and convenient and will accommodate a 3 in. by 4 in. drawing.)

Tom's teachers are beginning Phase 2 of his token program. They have written several stories, each involving space characters and a particular target behavior. One is illustrated below:

"Captain Armand Lap is traveling in a spaceship from Earth beyond the Galaxy. He is going in the fastest space ship ever made and visits unknown planets and meets all sorts of alien creatures. But every time he meets a creature he talks and talks and talks and doesn't let anyone else talk. Sometimes he interrupts the aliens and yells out what he wants to say. The poor alien creatures don't get to talk at all and they just blast off in their space ships because they are sooo sad and kind of frustrated that they couldn't get their turn to talk."

Teacher: "What should the captain do?"

Tom: "I don't know."

Teacher: "Well, in our group what do we ask the students to do so they all don't talk at once and everybody has a turn?" (Teacher raises her hand.)

Tom: "Raise your hand?"

Teacher: "Right! That's exactly right! I wonder if Captain Armand could do that. Do you think he could?"

Tom: (Smiles) "I think that the aliens would like it if the Captain let them talk and they would be friends and they would blast off together and be happy."

Teacher: "O.K. Let's make a picture of Captain Armand showing how he never raises his hand and lets anyone talk."

[Teacher coaches student to draw picture of any size and stresses the character *not* raising hand and the sad aliens. The character should be obviously sad with a down turned mouth, sad expression.]

Teacher: "Great. Now let's draw the captain after he starts raising his hand."

[Teacher coaches student to draw a picture of any size with hand raised. Draw *happy* aliens and a happy expression on the character's face.]

The teacher may use a color copier or computer scanner to reduce the drawings to a size that can be conveniently carried around. They should be laminated back to back or placed back to back in a single clear card holder. The original story and drawings should be placed together in a thin three ring binder for future reference.

The *Super Hero Cards* are integrated with the contingencies through the stories. The target behaviors (e.g., not calling out, completing three worksheets, independently moving from activity to activity) are identified and described through the story-generating process and a character representing the target behavior is made. Participation by the student may enhance recall and understanding. The interest theme from the stories can be used to construct the tokens and visual schedule. Thus, stickers could be spaceships and the visual schedule could include a track winding through the galaxy. The cards and stories should be reviewed each day along with reminding the student of the contingencies. During activities, the card face with the smiling character can be "flashed" to silently reinforce the student for engaging in a desirable target behavior. Conversely, the frowning face side of the card can be flashed as a warning or reminder if the student is beginning to engage in problem behavior. (Remember to warn as early as possible, before the problem behavior gets started.)

Progress Display Board

A colorful display should be posted on a bulletin board representing the student's progress towards a larger, more desirable activity or item. The display is visited regularly but not too frequently by the student (usually once or twice daily) to update their progress. Tom's team implemented this aspect at the start of the program. Tom's teacher and Tom made an outer-space bulletin board with stars, planets, and rocket ships on it. Tom wanted to name some of the stars and planets with their proper names, so some time was spent researching the names. Tom's teacher told him that they would make only *part* of the universe now and that, if Tom did well on his program, he could come back and make more parts. The teacher was careful to help Tom enjoy the process of making his bulletin board "world" and responded to Tom's comments and interests as often as possible. Three separate 20 minute sessions were conducted over two days to make this part of the bulletin board. During the construction process the teacher had Tom make and decorate several spaceships and suggested that the spaceships could travel to parts of the universe that Tom wanted to go. At the end of the third session, three large, decorated planets including the Earth (at the starting point), five named stars, 10-15 dots representing unnamed stars, and one spaceship were arrayed on a black background that measured two feet high by four feet wide. Cotton balls representing space gas were glued here and there and a title "The Universe" was placed above the artwork decorated with markers and glitter. The teacher was careful to leave about six more feet of unused space to the right and about two feet of unused space underneath. Because of the teacher's enthusiasm and Tom's natural interest, Tom asked several times to go back to his "space board" during the process of creating it.

At the end of the last space board creation session, the teacher showed Tom the characters that he had had previously created (his "card men") and told Tom that his characters were on a space voyage from Earth to somewhere in the universe. Tom was asked, "Where are they going?" and he chose the planet Mars as the destination. The teacher then removed the planet Mars from the board and placed it about one foot from Earth. A path (similar to that found on a board game) with 10 large spaces was placed between Earth and Mars and Tom was told that his "men" would all travel together in one of the spaceships to Mars. When they arrived they (and Tom) would get a big prize and Tom would get to choose the prize. The teacher asked Tom, "What do you think the prize should be?" and Tom immediately said, "A trip to McDonald's." Since this reinforcer was one of the things that Tom often talked about, his teacher had discussed including this activity on the list of larger reinforcers with Tom's parents. Therefore, she could immediately say to Tom, "Great, when you all get to Mars you can go to McDonald's. Now *how* are you all going to get to Mars? You know what?—every time you get a BIG RED STAR you can come here and move your spaceship one space. And when you get to Mars you'll all go to McDonald's."

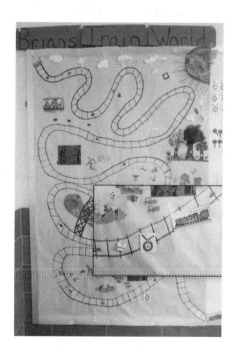

The bulletin board evolves as the student progresses, so some additional space for expansion is necessary. In Tom's case, the teacher dedicated a fair amount of room but smaller spaces can also be used if necessary. Classroom space can be used but it is preferable that a location outside the classroom be chosen so that visiting the board is viewed as "special" by the student. Once the first destination is achieved by the student another location is chosen and an additional path is placed on the board to the new location with an appropriate number of spaces. The number of spaces may increase if desirable. When the allotted space for the bulletin board is filled, previous paths should be removed and replaced with new paths. If the student has some free time or if an extra reinforcing activity is desired, time spent decorating the board with new items (scenery, characters, etc.) may be scheduled. Access to the board should be highly controlled, however, and the frequency should be limited so that satiation does not occur.

Starting the Program

So far, the first three major steps of implementing the motivation system have been accomplished:

1. Discussing the system with all implementers, including parents, and making decisions regarding the interest theme, the location of the bulletin board, the target behaviors, the short-term reinforcers and reinforcement schedule, and the longer-term reinforcers and reinforcement schedule

2. Obtaining materials for the project, writing the stories attached to each target behavior, going over the stories with the student, illustrating the stories by making the character cards, and explaining the short-term contingencies to the student

3. Designing and constructing the theme-related bulletin board *with the help of the student*, and explaining the longer-term contingencies to the student

The program can now start at any time. It is wise to choose a time near the beginning of the week so that the student has time to complete the requirements for both short- and longer-term reinforcement at least once. Go over the stories, the meaning of each card, and the contingencies with the student at the start of each day. Start with no more than one to three cards (target behaviors) and add to them only when the student is positively responding to all the previous cards. In the author's experience about eight to nine cards are the maximum number of target behaviors that can be conveniently used concurrently. After a period of suppression of the problem behavior and mastery of the new alternative behavior, characters can be retired and replaced with others.

Checklist for Implementation of the Super Hero Cards System

1. Choose a special interest of the student that will form a theme for the motivation system.

2. Make a list of the target behaviors for modification and prioritize them.

3. Make a list of 10 strong reinforcing activities, items, or edibles that can be quickly delivered within the context of the student's educational setting. Procure these items.

4. Make a list of 5-10 special activities, items, or events that will comprise the longer-term reinforcers. Procure these items or make arrangements with those who will deliver them (e.g., parents, special friends or teacher, etc.).

5. Write a story for each target behavior and choose a name for the "Super Hero."

6. Gather materials for drawing, decorating, and protecting the super hero cards.

7. Gather materials to construct and decorate a theme-related bulletin board that measures progress of the student in the program. Choose a dedicated location for the bulletin board that will be accessible to the student when needed. Make sure the board has enough room for expansion.

8. Choose a target date for implementation and make sure all personnel interacting with the student are aware of the program procedures. Choose one person who will be mainly responsible for maintaining the system. Schedule several meeting times during the first two weeks to review and revise the procedures.

9. Make the special interest bulletin board over several sessions.

10. Go over the stories with the student and make the super hero cards. Put the stories and drawings in a binder.

11. Explain the short-term contingencies to the student.

12. Explain the longer-term contingencies to the student.

13. Start the program with 1-3 target behaviors.

14. Meet with program decision makers after the first day and other times as necessary to make revisions to contingencies or program materials.

What's Next?
***Put this chapter to work*: DEVELOPING A SOLID REINFORCEMENT STRATEGY**

- Improve student response to reinforcement
    - Optimize quality, quantity and schedule of delivery
    - Adjust difficulty of required behavior
- Increase the novelty and variety of reinforcers in your program
    - Offer a choice of reinforcers
    - Identify 10 new reinforcers
    - Establish a budget and regular shopping time for new reinforcers
- Implement an explicit strategy that rotates reinforcers to avoid satiation. On an ongoing basis:
    - Ask the student what (s)he likes
    - Train implementers to recognize student expressions of preferences throughout the day
    - Create a running list of potential reinforcers and review it with implementers. Encourage all implementers to add to the list
    - Interview other knowledgeable sources (parents, inclusion teachers, etc.) to discover preferred items in other settings
    - Throughout the day, observe and record the student's choices and other behavior around items, events, and people
    - Formally test preferences
- Institute regular data-based preference assessments
    - Single stimulus presentation
    - Paired stimulus presentation
    - Multiple stimulus presentation

- Free-operant presentation
- Create a protocol to integrate the results of preference assessments into instruction
- Improve implementers ability to competently deliver reinforcement
    - Ensure that the choreography of movements during the trial happens efficiently and effectively so that reinforcement is optimal
- Conduct a reinforcer effectiveness evaluation
    - Do any adjustments to reinforcement or the targets themselves need to be made? Consider the following factors:
        - The difficulty required in performing the target response may be high
        - Engaging in the target behavior may be aversive
        - Frequency or quantity of reinforcement may be low
        - Concurrently available contingencies of reinforcement may exist and compete for the responding of the individual
- Use The Matching Law to quantitatively analyze the reinforcement environment of your setting
    - List as many instructional and non-instructional contingencies available to students as possible
    - Measure the frequency of student responding on each contingency for a defined period of time
    - Use the method outlined in the chapter to compare the relative frequency of reinforcement of each contingency
- Develop a long-term reinforcement strategy
    - Establish multi-level contingencies of reinforcement
    - Use complex visual systems of motivation

Chapter 7

Errors and Error Correction

Regardless of the strength of the reinforcer, simplicity of the task, or prior achievement of mastery criteria, from time to time, errors may occur. At their most basic level "errors" refer to performances that do not satisfy the conditions for reinforcement that are in effect. For example, when a student sits at a desk in school during reading or math, she is likely to act in some specific way to obtain reinforcement. She may read a passage, answer a question about the story, or attempt to solve a math problem. In these cases, we could identify behavior that would receive reinforcement as well as behavior that would not. From our perspective, volunteering the wrong answer to a math problem or retelling a story out of order may be called "errors" in the sense that reinforcement, as we define it, would not be delivered.

Errors and Contingencies

An instructional contingency for students on a playground during a soccer game might specify the antecedents (playground, soccer game, approaching the goal with the ball), the behavior (kicking the ball into the soccer goal) and, finally, the reinforcer (roar of the crowd, praise from teammates and coach). Such a contingency could motivate a student to run fast, avoid the defenders, and kick the ball into the goal. However, if the student runs and kicks the ball but it does not go into the net, reinforcers besides those specified in the contingency could be operating. The student might want to:

- Make a joke
- Help friends on the other team win
- Avoid hurting the feelings of the other team's goalie
- Avoid attracting unwanted attention

From the point of view of a student strongly motivated to avoid unwanted attention, no error is made by kicking the ball away from the goal. However, a performance desirable to the team did not occur and the coach might certainly identify the student's performance as deficient. From an instructional perspective, the definition of an error is determined by the program writer who specifies target performances and the conditions under which they should occur. Programs arbitrarily define behavior as "correct" just as they refer to behavior that does not conform to the stated contingencies as "errors."

What to Do About Errors? Contingencies Applied to Errors

Errors, as defined above, occur because one or more parts of a specified contingency do not occur properly:

- The student is unable to perform the behavior
- The student is unable to discriminate the conditions under which behavior would be reinforced
- The stimulus contingent on behavior is ineffective as a reinforcer

In the previous chapters, "Attention and Engagement" and "Using Prompts and Prompt Hierarchies," we discussed methods of assisting the student to achieve an adequate performance of the behavior under the proper instructional conditions. In the present chapter, we will discuss procedures that are designed to decrease the future probability of errors. When such procedures occur as consequences to errors they are known as "error correction." We will also continue our discussion of the design of "errorless" teaching methodology and how it may contribute to error-free performance.

Error Correction Studies

A variety of procedures to reduce errors ranging in complexity from minimal to elaborate has been described in the ABA literature (Rodgers and Iwata, 1991) as well as those procedures that have been handed down from clinical practice. The most minimal procedure possible, of course, is no error correction. Reinforcement-only procedures provide reinforcement for correct responses and withhold it for errors, referred to as "differential reinforcement" (Cooper, Heron, & Heward, 2007). This procedure, common in early laboratory studies to develop simple performances (Skinner, 1938, Ferster & Skinner, 1957) has also been reported as effective in studies of instructional procedures (Lazar, Davis-Lang & Sanchez, 1984, Bennett, 1974, Gatch & Osborn, 1978). In these studies, reinforcement was delivered for a specified response and not delivered if any other response occurred. For instance, in an instructional setting with students, three cards with shapes are presented to the student and an instruction given to touch one of the shapes. If the student touches the correct shape, reinforcement is delivered. If an incorrect shape is touched or no response is made, the cards are silently withdrawn and another trial is presented. Some studies found that overall effectiveness of the instruction improved if a delay (~10 seconds) was introduced after incorrect responses and before the start of the next trial to accentuate the difference between reinforcement and non-reinforcement (Touchette & Howard, 1984, Barton, 1970, and McReynolds, 1969).

Stoddard and Sidman (1967) built in automatic adjustments of the difficulty of trials following both correct and incorrect trials. Trials following an error were made slightly easier while trials following success became progressively harder. They found that subjects' errors backed them up in the program to a point where responding was easy enough to re-establish correct responding and, then, successful performance continued even past former error points. An adjusting contingency of this type was found by Altman, Hobbs, Roberts, & Haavik (1980) to be least associated with disruptive behavior.

Possibly the most traditionally accepted benefit of error correction is its presumed remedial nature (Axelrod, Dramer, Appleton, Rockett, and Hamlet, 1984; Rodgers and Iwata, 1991; Cuvo, Ashley, Marso, Zhang, and Fry, 1995). The term "remedial" can be applied to error correction when procedures include practicing a corrected version of a performance after an error. Karsten & Carr (2009) provided "hand-over-hand or full verbal response prompts" contingent upon errors to help the student practice the correct performance. When students made errors in the process of learning conditional discriminations, Murphy et al. (2005) "gently took the child's hand and guided it physically to the [correct] stimulus," saying, "This is the one you should point to" (p. 450). Other remedial corrective actions have included exposure to a correct video model after an error (Goodson, Sigafoos, O'Reilly, Cannella, & Lancioni, 2007). Worsdell et al. (2005) studied the nature of the remedial error correction procedure by comparing "relevant" practice vs. "irrelevant" practice as a consequence for errors. Relevant practice consisted of prompting the student to repeat the correct performance – pronouncing a sight word correctly – after making an error on reading it. Irrelevant practice consisted of prompting the student to say a *different* word after making an error. Paradoxically, all subjects improved with both relevant and irrelevant error correction, although some subjects made better gains with relevant practice. Like Worsdell et al. (2005), Fabrizio and Pahl (2007) found that relevant and irrelevant practice conditions were both effective in decreasing reading errors but also concluded that the simpler relevant correction procedure was more efficient than the multi-step irrelevant practice procedure. In the discrimination practice condition, if the subject read a word incorrectly, both the incorrect and correct responses were written on a piece of paper and the subject was prompted to read the correct and incorrect words sequentially. In the contrasting condition, after a reading error, the subject was simply prompted to read the word correctly.

Worsdell et al. (2005) and others (Ollendick, Matson, Esveldt-Dawson & Shapiro (1980); Schumaker & Sherman (1970) have also looked at the number of repetitions of the error correction as an independent variable, comparing no error correction with single repetition vs. prompting repetition up to five times. All three studies reported data suggesting that the repeated error correction procedures were more effective than non-repeated procedures.

Clinical Practice

ABA manuals on the creation of instruction have recommended composite error correction procedures that incorporate various parts of the data-based literature. A much-discussed procedure described by Leaf and McEachin (1999) is sometimes called the "No-No- Prompt." Contingent on an error, the student is told "No" (or an equivalent word is used) and prompted to repeat the trial. If another error occurs, the student is again told "No." At that point the trial is re-presented and a prompt is given to help the student perform the response correctly. According to the authors:

"The first incorrect response allows the student to learn from the feedback. Therefore, the second trial would provide the student an opportunity to make the correct response. More than two incorrect responses indicates that the student is not learning from negative feedback. It may also exceed the student's tolerance for failure and the lack of reinforcement may lead to an escalation of negative behaviors."

Empirical studies reporting effective use of the No-No-Prompt method have been conducted with students learning to label facial expressions (Leaf, Oppenheim-Leaf, Dotson, Johnson, Courtemanche, Sheldon and Sherman, 2011) and other receptive language tasks (Leaf, Sheldon, and Sherman, 2010).

Fovel (2002) recommended an error correction procedure for discrete-trial teaching containing six basic steps:

1. Interrupt the incorrect action (if possible)

2. Withdraw materials if relevant

3. Return student to "ready" position

4. Re-present the trial with a prompt to ensure a correct response. In matching-to-sample tasks, the configuration of the choice array is maintained as in the previous trial and only limited, verbal praise is given for a correct response

5. Re-present the trial without a prompt. In matching-to-sample tasks, a new, randomized position of the choice array is presented. Correct performance is reinforced with full reinforcement

6. If a second error is made when the trial is re-presented without a prompt (Step 5) the procedure is repeated but if a third error is made, further error correction is eliminated for the trial and training moves on to the next training stimulus

The inclusion of a second presentation of the trial without a prompt in Step 5 has been the subject of some discussion. Carbone (2005) describes this as a "transfer trial" and proponents have suggested that it may serve to reinforce the connection between the target discriminative stimulus and the target response. In other words, simple correction with a prompt (Step 4) reinforces the performance of the target behavior under stimulus conditions that *include the prompt*. This is mitigated by a further presentation of the task so that the student may respond under unprompted conditions and be reinforced for independent behavior. In theory, this avoids increasing prompt dependency and enhances the transfer of control of a correct response from the prompts to the proper discriminative stimuli (e.g. directions, materials, etc.).

Turin, Croteau, and Moroz (2010) compared a "delay" error correction procedure with an "independent probe" procedure. Following an error, the delay procedure consisted of:

1. No feedback and a five second delay

2. Presentation of the instruction again with a prompt to ensure success. Successful performance by the student was not reinforced

3. Presentation of the next training stimulus trial

The independent probe condition consisted of:

1. No feedback and a three second delay

2. Presentation of the instruction again with a prompt to ensure success. Verbal praise for correct performance

3. Presentation of a "distractor" trial. Distractor trials were instructions to perform mastered behaviors similar to (but not part of) the present learning set. For example, if the program involved receptive identification of animals ("Touch cat", "Touch dog", etc.) a distractor trial might be "Touch nose"

4. Presentation of the original trial again (as in Step 2) without assistance and with a new, random presentation of the training array with reinforcement for a correct response

While both methods were reported as successful, the "distractor" trial of the independent probe condition was a unique aspect of the error correction procedure. While the procedure in Fovel (2002) moved directly from a prompted error correction trial to an unprompted error correction trial for the same target performance, Turin et al. hypothesized that, for some students, there may be an advantage to eliciting an *intervening* correct independent response between a prompted correction trial and an unprompted correction trial.

Table of Error Correction Steps

For comparison purposes, the table below presents a compilation of individual error correction components implemented in the published sources cited. Procedures cited were built from one or more steps:

Table 1. Procedures Implemented Contingent on the Occurrence of an Error

Step	Description
No error correction	Instructor does not respond after error except to move to the next trial. No reinforcement is delivered
"Informational No" or No equivalents	After error, instructor says, "No" or "Not that one" and moves to the next trial without reinforcing student
"Try Again" (Similar to re-presenting trial)	Student is encouraged to continue to respond until a correct response occurs using statements like "Try again"
Delay	An inter-trial interval of several seconds (3-10 seconds) is observed before the next trial is presented
Return to easier step	Following an error (or error criterion), the student returns to the next easiest step in the following trial
Interrupt Incorrect Action (if possible	Physical prompt is delivered to interrupt the student from completing the incorrect behavior
Return to "Ready" Position	Instruction or prompt is given to place hands in lap and look at the instructor or materials in anticipation of the next trial
Withdraw Materials	As soon as error is committed, task materials (all or some) are quickly removed
Repeat Trial	Trial where error was committed is re-presented

Repeat Trial with Prompt	Trial where error was committed is re-presented with a prompt that ensures a correct response
Repeat Trial without Prompt and New Stimulus Arrangement ("transfer trial")	Trial where error was committed is re-presented without a response prompt. If task is a matching-to-sample task, the array of choices is randomly shuffled
Distractor Trial	Trial of a mastered performance not associated with error is presented
Repeat EC Procedure	Contingent on an error, the error correction procedure is repeated a specified number of times
Response Cost	Contingent on an error, student loses all or part of a given reinforcer. Alternatively, student may lose tokens or points counting towards reinforcement

Discussion of Contingent Error Correction Procedures

Various procedures have been employed as error correction ranging from minimalist differential reinforcement-only approaches to multi-step corrected practice procedures. Empirical studies focused on several parameters and provoke a thoughtful consideration of how errors are approached in instructional programs. Several points are supported:

1. Differential reinforcement alone (that is, no additional programmed consequence other than withholding reinforcement after an incorrect performance) proved effective in some studies

2. Contingently-delivered procedures (procedures implemented after an error) were also shown to be effective and, indeed, some studies found that contingent error correction procedures were more efficient and effective in producing skill acquisition when compared to differential reinforcement alone. Consequently, many researchers and clinicians continue to recommend correction consequences for errors including:

    - *Immediate correction* contingent on errors
    - Corrected practice of the *relevant* behavior
    - *Repeated* practice

3. The possibility was raised that effective error correction functions because it is aversive:

- Delays of up to ten seconds were programmed in several studies similar to time-out for the student

- Error correction procedures were repeated. Three studies found that up to five repetitions were more effective than a single repetition although one study (Cuvo et al.) found that five repetitions of error correction were just as effective as 10 or 15 repetitions. In the studies that compared the result of "relevant" practice with "irrelevant" practice, *both* types of practice resulted in improved performance

Students varied in response to different error correction procedures and, ultimately, program authors decide which procedures are appropriate based on the needs of the student and the nature of the instruction. Turan, Corteau, and Moroz (2010), mindful of the differences between students, their reinforcement history, and the possible effects of various error correction contingencies, recommended conducting an "error correction functional analysis" by comparing potential error correction procedures via an alternating treatments design.

The use of a potentially aversive error correction procedure should be evaluated against the potential benefits. While even simple differential reinforcement and shaping contains an extinction component (withholding reinforcement for incorrect responses) that may be frustrating for subjects, establishing an error correction procedure that contains a marked delay or practice component (relevant or irrelevant) may be similar to adding response cost or overcorrection for some students. Program writers should be especially sensitive to embedding aversive procedures in programs unless absolutely necessary, at the risk of provoking avoidance behavior on the part of students.

It is not always easy to recognize potentially aversive contingencies when in the midst of busily writing programs for challenging students. Recently, when considering the design of a teaching session for a student with severe task avoidance behavior, the author and an experienced ABA teacher discussed how many trials should be run. We especially wanted to motivate the student to maintain attention to the task without having to interrupt him with corrective practice (which usually occasioned screams). One idea was to simply ignore errors and continue the session until the student performed correctly on the step five consecutive times. We discussed various ways of visually communicating the criterion to the student who had limited language, so we imagined drawing a grid with five squares on a piece of paper and having the student award himself a penny for each correct response, putting each penny inside one of the squares. When the squares were full the student would be done.

However, we realized, when he makes an error, he would have to start over, which meant that the pennies would have to be taken off the grid. As we further considered the procedure we decided that sweeping the pennies away would constitute a form of response cost[1] for errors. Since errors were already the occasion of problem behavior we concluded that the student would not react well to the potential procedure. Instead, we decided to specify a fixed number of trials per session, ignore errors, and trust that the cumulative effect of differential reinforcement would suffice (it did).

Errorless Design Principles - Revisited

In actual practice, it is often difficult to exclude the possibility that *any* procedure contingent on errors involving delays or practice is, at least, somewhat aversive. Before programming any error correction contingencies, it is wise to make every effort to adopt an instructional design that results in a performance that is as error-free as possible. We have already discussed errorless teaching methods and using prompts in prompt hierarchies in Chapter 5. We also talked about breaking the task into smaller, component parts that are easier to perform. However, there is much more that can be said on the subject. Sometimes described as "programmed learning" or "stimulus control" (Skinner, 1968; Keller, 1968; Holland et al. 1976), so-called "errorless," antecedent-focused procedures represent a mature and robust technology. The process of program creation based on stimulus control techniques is, essentially, a shaping process and, therefore, rests on careful design of:

---

[1] Response cost is a Type 2 punishment, such as losing a privilege or other reinforcer that has been delivered but not yet consumed (Cooper, Heron, & Heward, 2007).

- The initial response requirement

- The target (terminal) response requirement

- The series of intermediate responses that will gradually transform from the initial response to the terminal response through a carefully controlled *shift of stimulus control* from one intermediate response to the next

The Initial Response Requirement

One of the most important design aspects of successfully minimizing errors is to begin with an initial performance that is *already* in the repertoire of the student. In other words:

1. The topography, frequency, duration, latency, and magnitude of the required initial response as well as the conditions of its occurrence must be within the established capabilities of the student

2. The schedule of reinforcement must be adequate to guarantee that the initial response will be strongly emitted under instructional control

Starting with independent performances allows procedures that are free of extensive error correction or intrusive instructor-based prompts and eliminates much of the risk that instructor behavior or the instructional setting will function as a negative reinforcer. Moreover, as discussed in the previous chapter, independent behavior may be an intrinsic or conditioned reinforcer. Initial behaviors should be high-probability, strong, persistent actions that occur even under unfavorable conditions. Such behavior is best suited for shaping and stretching into new, more elaborate responses. Contingencies controlling high-probability behavior compete more effectively with off-task behavior and task-related attention and engagement is high. With high-probability behavior, even when errors and delays in reinforcement occur, students quickly rebound and re-engage in attempts to produce correct behavior rather than emotional behavior.

Watching a student explore an iPad or similar device provides an interesting example of how simple high-probability behavior under highly reinforcing contingencies can produce elaborate and even sophisticated discrimination behavior with minimal intervention. With pressure-sensitive screens and bright, colorful graphics, simple finger touches and movements can produce a stunning array of visual effects. Sometimes, simply through trial and error, the child discovers how to independently perform amazing feats of navigation through layers of nested menus to start and operate their favorite programs. With additional practice, new responses and discriminations follow and, eventually, without a single formal lesson, the child operates the device like a sophisticated user. The contingencies producing this behavior are, conceptually, among the simplest. Start with a powerful reinforcer (visual display) and make it contingent on high-probability behaviors already in the repertoire of the individual (touching and pressing). Then, create simple conditions under which the behavior must occur (sounds and sights occur only for certain sequences of presses) and sit back and watch the student try to discover them. If the reinforcer is powerful, the required behavior highly-probable, and the conditions under which the behavior is reinforced simple, correct behavior will emerge, strengthen, and gradually transform into whatever routines are built into the system. Other than differential reinforcement, the learning system places few or no contingencies on errors or off-task behavior. If correct responses emerge, the system (instructional program) is ultimately validated. If they do not, the system (contingencies) must be redesigned to function more successfully.

While errors may not receive direct consequences, they do provide a convenient means of analyzing the student's performance with respect to the contingencies. The existence of errors marks areas of potential inefficiency and inconsistency in the program and the instructional design process should place a premium on optimizing procedures by eliminating flaws that produce errors.

Intermediate Responses and Transfer of Stimulus Control

Once a strong initial response under instructional control is established, the response characteristics and/or response conditions are gradually shaped into the terminal response over a series of steps. The changes involved in each new intermediate response and the stimulus conditions under which it occurs must be carefully designed – changes should be small and the new response likely to occur without much external intervention. Effectively, the new response requirement is "communicated" to the student by delivering a modified set of stimuli and withholding reinforcement for the initial response. The modified stimuli retain enough similarity to the old set to maintain the student's responding even under new stimulus conditions. For example, a student was refusing to complete educational tasks at his work area and only wanted to play on the computer, which was located on a table 15 feet away. A program to gradually shape increased work time was designed using stimulus control principles:

Work Completion Program, Phase 1:

Initial Response and Conditions	Given one peg, puts peg in a peg board held out by the behavior analyst
Intermediate Response 1	Given one peg, puts peg in a peg board **placed on chair next to student**
Intermediate Response 2	Given one peg, puts peg in a peg board placed on chair **two feet from student**
Intermediate Response 3	Given one peg, puts peg in a peg board placed on chair **five feet from student**
Intermediate Response 4	Given one peg, puts peg in a peg board placed on chair **ten feet from student**
Intermediate Response 5	Given one peg, puts peg in a peg board placed on chair **13 feet from student**
Intermediate Response 6	Given one peg, puts peg in a peg board **placed on desk in work area**

The initial response was chosen based on the behavior analyst's familiarity with the student's repertoire and motivation. At the beginning of the session, the student was allowed to seat himself in front of the computer for three minutes. At the end of the interval, the behavior analyst handed a peg to the student and held out the peg board, slightly blocking the computer screen. While a bit reluctant, the student took the peg and immediately placed it in the pegboard. The pegboard was quickly withdrawn and the student was allowed to return to the computer for another two minutes. Thereafter, Intermediate Responses 1-6 were successively presented to the student every two minutes. While the behavior analyst was ready to present a given intermediate response step more than once, the changes in stimulus conditions (moving the pegboard to a new location) were tolerated by the student errorlessly. After approximately 15 minutes the session was ended. Later in the day, a second session was conducted starting with the final intermediate step. After successful completion of the step, the second phase of the program was presented:

Work Completion Program, Phase 2:

Intermediate Response 6	Given one peg, puts peg in a peg board **placed on desk in work area**
Intermediate Response 7	**Peg board held out of view by behavior analyst in work area. Mastered matching task set up on desk with 1 picture to be matched**
Intermediate Response 8	Peg board held out of view by behavior analyst in work area. Mastered matching task set up on desk with **2 pictures to be matched**
Intermediate Response 9	Peg board held out of view by behavior analyst in work area. Mastered matching task set up on desk with **3 pictures to be matched**
Intermediate Response 10	Peg board held out of view by behavior analyst in work area. Mastered matching task set up on desk with **4 pictures to be matched**
Intermediate Response 11	Peg board held out of view by behavior analyst in work area. Mastered matching task set up on desk with **8 picture to be matched**
Intermediate Response 12	Peg board held out of view by behavior analyst in work area. Mastered matching task set up on desk with **15 pictures to be matched**

In Phase 2 the behavior analyst held the peg board out of view in the student's work area until the student completed the work on the desk. On the first trial of the phase, the behavior analyst pointed to the matching task. Since matching was familiar to the student, he completed the task quickly and the behavior analyst presented the pegboard, allowing the student to insert the peg and return to the computer. Phase 2 was completed in 20 minutes. Sessions were errorlessly repeated over the following three days. Even at this early point, the student's performance represented significant progress since previously, *any* attempt to instruct the student away from the computer resulted in crying and even aggressive behavior. At the end of Phase 2 (total program time: 35 minutes during one day), when given a peg, the student interrupted his time at the computer, moved to his desk, and spent about two minutes independently completing a matching task. Further phases were presented over the following month, successfully extending the student's work time and the variety of tasks presented without provoking extended protests.

The success of the program is based on the incorporation of the program design principles previously discussed. An initial response requirement was chosen that was well within the student's capabilities and conditions for the response were arranged that fell under the instructional control of the behavior analyst. A strong reinforcer was contingent on completion of the response. Transformation of the initial conditions and response through the intermediate steps was gradual, required minimal prompts, and no error correction.

Avoiding Coercive Prompts

Using stimulus-based techniques to gradually and errorlessly transfer control of responding from one step to another is preferable to using response prompts under some circumstances. For example, a response prompt like partial physical guidance might be employed to assist a student to perform a task and obtain a designated reinforcer. Suppose, however, that the student is more interested in playing with the computer than engaging in the task at hand and resists a bit. Adapting to the student's resistance, the instructor momentarily increases the amount of physical pressure delivered to "help" the student complete the action. As the session continues, if student resistance is consistently followed by an increase in physical guidance by the instructor, the student eventually gets the message that performing less independently will result in more prompting. If the student finds physical force aversive, a secondary source of (negative) reinforcement is present. The student now works to avoid prompting as well as obtain the nominal reinforcement. Prompting scenarios such as these illustrate how instruction can subtly but quickly slip into a coercive methodology. Alone or combined with aversive error correction, such prompting runs the risk that the student will engage in task avoidance. While both response prompts and stimulus prompts help students engage in target behavior to obtain reinforcement, stimulus prompts such as those presented above or those discussed in the previous chapter (position, size redundancy, arrow cues) are easier to consistently present and fade and are minimally intrusive. Nevertheless, response prompts such as pointing, modeling, verbal prompts, and well-defined physical guidance is indispensible and efficient when used in the proper context. Program developers using potentially intrusive prompts, therefore, should develop protocols that sensitize implementers to issues of coercion and avoidance.

Section Summary

The best errorless procedures capture strong, independent responding from the very beginning of sessions. This requires starting with high-probability behavior that is shifted and shaped by the gradual modification of stimulus characteristics of the task materials and criteria for reinforcement. Inevitably, errors will appear, but an emphasis on rapid program redesign and adjustment helps to eliminate them; as a result, the need for coercive consequences to errors is minimized.

Issues with Antecedent-Focused Procedures

As strong as stimulus control technology may be, there are disadvantages in employing it:

- **The design/redesign process is time consuming.** Changes to materials to avoid errors may require reconstruction of existing materials. For example, stimulus prompt strategies such as underlining the correct choice could be adopted in a program to teach a discrimination. After the student correctly chooses the card with a line that is 100% black for a certain number of trials, the program fades the line to 80% black for the second phase. If the student starts making errors, the program author could decide that the line was faded too quickly and needs to be 90% black, requiring a modified set of materials. While the line prompt is implemented far more consistently than response prompts and the degree of control over fading much more precise, more effort is required than simply adopting a bit more physical prompting or pointing after a shorter delay

- **The fading process is time consuming**. In order for an antecedent-based program to avoid errors and start with solid control of a response, a very simple initial target must be chosen. This requires many small fading steps and, potentially a prolonged fading process. On the other hand, starting at an early point creates a very strong history of reinforcement from which to proceed and contributes to the future absence of errors. Programs need to start with performances that can be easily established and then shaped into more elaborate performances. Of course, the starting point should be as close to the final target performance as possible but it is better to start too early and risk boring the student than starting too late and forcing errors

- **There is no way to guarantee that responses occur, especially when the student's emerging behavior is weak.** Programs using physical response prompts are better able to ensure that responses occur, albeit at the risk of being coercive. Antecedent-based procedures rely on strong control of prerequisite behavior and reinforcers, which carries far less risk of coercion. Sometimes stimulus control programs employ minimal physical and response prompts (modeling, gestures, verbal prompts) to bring the student into initial contact with the reinforcer

- **If there are few high-probability behaviors in the repertoire of the individual related to initial target responses, control over an independent performance is difficult to establish**. The student is required to have some pre-requisites in their repertoire on which a program is based. Tasks such as putting on a pullover shirt need to start with at least some fine motor ability to grasp, raise arms, and pull down. If movements such as these are difficult or inconsistent, the student can benefit from a combination of strategies including some antecedent design of the materials as well as physical response prompts. For example, pulling a shirt over one's head is made far easier if the shirt is slightly oversize (antecedent strategy), oriented with the tag on top (antecedent strategy), and if the back, bottom edge of the shirt is pulled up slightly so the student can easily see where to grasp it (antecedent strategy). In addition, the student may benefit from a back-chaining strategy where the shirt is initially placed over the student's head by the instructor and the student has only to pull the shirt down with some physical guidance (response prompt strategy)

Using Error Correction

When a program author designs an instructional contingency with specific consequences for the commission of errors, the structure of the contingency must be carefully operationalized. First, the behavioral definition of correct and incorrect responses should be carefully described including the response topography for correct and incorrect behavior. There are a surprising number of nuances to getting it right and avoiding confusion and lack of procedural integrity on the part of implementers. The program author should take the chance to consider the range of response topographies that could be encountered during the conditions of instruction, such as those that follow. Consider the answers to the following questions:

- What is the definition of "correct" and "incorrect" behavior in observable and measureable terms?

- What is the definition of "no response?"

- When has a "choice" been made? What should happen if the individual hovers over one choice without touching it?

- What should happen if the student is asked to touch a choice but gives it to the instructor instead – is the response correct or incorrect?

- What happens if the student touches the space near a choice but not the choice itself, places a card so that it overlaps both possible matching choices, or puts the card in front of the choice rather than on top of the choice?

- What happens if the student makes a correct response and immediately does something inappropriate before reinforcement is delivered?

- What happens if the student makes a correct response and immediately makes an incorrect choice or "scrolls" through all the options?

- What happens when the student's verbal answer contains more information than asked for?

- What happens if the student answers incorrectly but then answers correctly?

Creating written procedures in advance will help prepare implementers to confidently address variations in a student's response in a consistent manner. Explicit definition of all parts of the instructional package also assists when evaluating the success or failure of the methodology. When choosing the actual error correction procedure, keep in mind the following options:

- Will a delay be imposed between the error and the presentation of the error correction or the next trial?

- Will the procedure re-present the same trial or a different trial?

- How many times will a re-presented trial be repeated?

- Will the procedure contain relevant or irrelevant practice?

- What will be done with materials after an error?

- Will the re-presented trial be reinforced or not?

- Will corrected trials be reinforced?

- What will occur on repeated errors?

- Will prompts be used during error correction to ensure a correct performance?

- Will response cost or other punishment procedures be needed?

- How will disruptive reactions to the EC procedure (side effects of potentially aversive procedures) be reported and evaluated?

What's Next?
Put this chapter to work: **ERRORS AND ERROR CORRECTION**

- Survey how you currently use contingent error correction in your programs. Try to observe implementers carrying out the procedures. Analyze how current error correction procedures *actually* function (as opposed to how they are *intended* to function)

- Meet with team members to discuss errors and decide which contingent error correction procedures are appropriate based on the needs of the student and the nature of the instruction:
    - Establish a "default" error correction protocol and train all implementers
    - Take care with remedial repetition of trials to avoid undesirable side effects of coercion

- Investigate where coercive practices may be creeping into your programs. Look closely at the use of physical prompts, error correction implementation, and any practice that results in avoidance behavior on the part of the student

- Assess the overall frequency of student errors. Use stimulus control techniques to revise instructional designs to result in performances with fewer errors:
    - Choose an initial response requirement under strong instructional control
    - Identify a series of intermediate responses that will gradually transform from the initial response to the terminal response through a carefully controlled shift of stimulus control
    - Experiment with exaggeration and stimulus redundancy to facilitate transfer of stimulus control
    - Try to build in a "backup" contingency that makes the task a little easier after an error

Chapter 8

Generalization and Incorporation –

Establishing Functional Competencies in Natural Settings

Designing programs to teach a single, isolated skill is the initial step on a path which, ultimately, must lead to functional behavior. Pivotal education promotes generalization and incorporation of individual skills into more complex competencies capable of succeeding under conditions found in real-world settings and positively impacting a person's quality of life. To achieve this impact, the program designer uses behavior analytic principles to analyze natural settings and create an explicit plan that systematically builds a repertoire of needed performances.

Acquisition → Generalization & Incorporation

Behavior does not occur in a vacuum; writers of instructional programs generally specify the conditions under which each newly learned behavior will be performed. Two types can be distinguished:

- **Concurrent conditions (related to immediate task performance):**
    - Location and setting
    - Materials presented
    - Prompts used
    - Reinforcement contingency

- Error correction strategy
- Competing contingencies

- **Sequential conditions (related to the relationship of the task performance to *other* events):**
    - Occurrence of the target behavior relative to the prior or subsequent occurrence of other tasks, events, and contingencies in the environment

For example, a difficult handwriting program to teach writing one's name may specify several relatively concurrent conditions related to the task or target performance such as: *sits at a desk with 1:1 instructor, uses pencil, stays within lines that are ½ inch apart, performs with an initial verbal instruction*, and *reinforced with one check for each correct repetition*. Sequential conditions that may be in effect are related to the relationship of the task to other events:

- The task is presented relatively early in the morning
- No difficult tasks are presented in the morning before the handwriting task
- A coloring task precedes writing to "warm up" the student
- The student puts away his materials after writing
- An easy gross motor program follows writing

The conditions of performance listed above represent two separate and important aspects of task conditions. *Concurrent conditions* are more commonly enumerated and discussed than those in the second category, *sequential conditions*, but both types usually become established during the course of acquisition, whether by design or by chance. Both types of conditions are relevant when moving skills into natural environments and both are an equal part of the complex context controlling the performance of an acquired target behavior. New environments for acquired skills may not exhibit the entire array of conditions that has come to control target behavior and, therefore, a student may be entering an environment that is antagonistic to continued performance. Programming effort is required that analyzes target settings and implements procedures to address the continuum of differing conditions encountered:

- The term "generalization" describes when a target behavior is performed under circumstances that are different from those that existed during the original acquisition. Programming for generalization entails a variety of strategies that addresses *both* types of conditions (concurrent and sequential) described above.

- The term "incorporation" refers to the establishment of sequential conditions of skill performances, a topic related to *task interspersal*.

"Task interspersal" refers to the juxtaposition of two or more instructional programs, such as performing trials of matching followed by trials of receptive identification. Task interspersal is employed to create interaction effects between programs including facilitation of responding within the set of interspersed programs. It is a particularly useful methodology that we will discuss extensively later in this chapter[2].

A general plan may approach the generalization and incorporation of a skill into a new environment in stages such as those outlined in the protocol below:

Promoting Transference of Skills to New Environments and Conditions

Strategy Stages	Description
1. Performance in Highly Controlled Setting	Teach explicitly in a carefully controlled, distraction-free environment, with careful individualized programming to encourage initial acquisition of the skill under specific conditions
2. Generalization and Incorporation in Highly Controlled Setting	In the highly controlled setting, contrive opportunities to generalize and incorporate, extending the occurrence of the target performance to new teachers, new areas, varying instructional conditions and routines, new reinforcement contingencies approximating those in the target environment
3. Performance in Natural Target Setting	Set up a controlled, distraction-free environment in the target setting. Teach explicitly, establishing the occurrence of the target performance under limited conditions in the target setting, approximating those of the highly controlled setting

---

[2] Terminologically, while "task interspersal" is an accurate procedural description, it does not carry connotations that identify it necessarily with the creation of functional routines in the natural environment. Therefore, while we will refer to the procedure of task interspersal, the general goal of interspersal in this chapter will be called *incorporation*.

4. Generalization and Incorporation in Natural Target Setting	Gradually increase participation in target setting routines once the student is able to perform limited routines in the target setting and simulations of the new, target routines in the limited setting

Adopting a basic outline or continuum of generalization and incorporation steps focuses inclusion on defined functional outcomes, a crucial initial step. Next, the methodological details must be described for individual students and effectively implemented. The following sections of this chapter will explore a number of issues, techniques, and methodologies concerning generalization and incorporation within three major headings:

1. **Ecological assessment – Task Analysis of Natural Environment Activities**: natural environments are the target settings for developing skills and specify the topographies and conditions under which skills are reinforced. A thorough analysis of the target environment provides program planners with the ultimate goals of instruction

2. **Generalization Issues and Methods**: generalization strategies provide an important and useful technology for increasing the probability that skills will occur in target settings, one that should be built into every program plan

3. **Incorporation Issues and Methods**: functional skills are often multi-step processes. The relationship of one step to another determines how the entire sequence will operate

Task Analysis of Natural Environment Activities

Children spend much of their days in natural environments like home, school, and community settings. Therefore, the identification of target settings within the natural environment and an analysis of the skills and conditions required for competence in the settings, sometimes referred to as an "ecological assessment," is of paramount importance. For children with special needs, school is a major early target. Instruction in classrooms starting in preschool and continuing through the early grades takes many forms—circle activities, arts and crafts, story time, morning meetings, science demonstrations, mathematics games, physical education lessons, and a myriad of other events where students must give their collective attention to the teacher and engage in a variety of target behaviors. Kindergarten is often an entry point for a student's first structured classroom experience. In a typical kindergarten classroom, the teacher leads a group of 10-15 students. Students sit in groups on the floor, at tables, or at desks in front of display boards and tables where the teacher has placed materials for presentation and discussion. The teacher stands 3-5 feet or more away from the group, clearly visible, and in proximity to the materials to be used. The duration of the activities usually ranges from 5 minutes to 30 minutes or more.

Sample Kindergarten Observation

The following is an example of a circle group taken directly from an observation in a kindergarten class during the month of December. The activity was done every day at the same time. All questions asked by the teacher required students to raise their hands before suggesting an answer. The teacher called only on students who raised their hands. Note that some of the discussion, comments, and transition statements made by the teacher are left out for the sake of space. The activities are described in the left column and the skills required are noted at the right.

Description of Activity	Skills Required
1. Teacher softly blows a flute-like whistle and gives an instruction to call students to circle area.. Students interrupt present activity, walk to circle area, and sit on carpet, facing display wall. In order to prompt students to sit cross-legged on the floor, the teacher repeats "Criss-cross, applesauce" a few times.	Following group instructions Following special signals e.g., "crisscross, applesauce" (sit down cross-legged on the floor)
2. Students talk to each other as they wait for teacher to start. Teacher allows students to mingle for 1-2 minutes, then starts.	Spontaneous language Interaction with peers
3. Teacher: "Good Morning, everyone." Students in group: "Good Morning, Mrs. Smith"	Choral response to greeting
4. Teacher: "Let's start with the news. Does anyone have any news?"	Talking about past and future events
5. Student raises hand, waits to be called on, and states an event that happened or that will happen to him/her. ("I'm going to…" or "I _____ed")	Raising hand before answering. Listening/responding to speaker
6. When finished, the teacher says, "Let's say hello to our friends" and leads the children in a rhyme that greets the students around them. Starts rhyme, "Hey there, neighbor" and students recite rhyme together.	"Choral" recitation of rhymes and songs.

7.	Discussion of calendar: Students answer questions on what day, what month, what year, while looking at calendar. Teacher throws in some questions on related things like "What letter does Wednesday start with?"	Wh-questions about calendar. General information questions.
8.	Teacher has already highlighted some of the days of the month in a different color so that the days alternate between red and white boxes. The teacher points out the pattern on the chart and asks what kind of pattern it is.	Labeling A-B patterns
9.	Teacher starts singing and students follow. Students sing days of the week and months of the year songs.	Choral recitation of Days of Week song and Months of Year song
10.	Teacher asks, "What kind of weather is it outside?" Students look outside and suggest answers. Teacher points to words on the chalkboard and students read words aloud together.	Describing weather; Sight-reading in group with materials at a distance
11.	Discussion of more/less. Teacher: "Let's count the number of [counters] together." "How many?" "Which one is more? Which is less?"	Counting in a group (choral). Counting objects at a distance. More/less.
12.	Reading the schedule. Teacher leads children in reading the things that she has placed on the display board (simple sentences about the things discussed so far in circle like weather, activities, etc.) Children answer questions about what the activities will be during the day.	Sight reading aloud in group Answering questions based on past events.
13.	"Can you see a word that begins with "P" on our schedule? Let's count the p's. What p-thing did we do yesterday?"	Following abstract instructions. Recalling past events.
14.	Activity preview: Teacher introduces activity materials and asks questions about them. "How many potatoes are in this container? Guess. That's called estimating. How many children think that there are 8 potatoes? Raise your hand. Later, when you come back from gym you'll make potato pattern pictures."	Following instruction.
15.	"Now I'm going to read *The Painter*. But first we need to take a break. Ready, everyone stand up." Teacher-aide starts music and students perform the movement game Head, Shoulders, Knees, and Toes for one minute singing the song while they do the actions.	Following movement song with actions and singing.
16.	Teacher reads story of 8 pages with one sentence to each page. Intersperses questions, explanations,, and comments.	Answering questions based on multi-page story.

End of activity. Duration: 42 minutes

Analysis of Skills Required for Participation:

- Listening comprehension of natural language, multiple sentence presentations and sequences of instructions

- Coordinate behavior with the group (choral recitation, movements)

- Follow instructions directed at the group

- Respond to questions directed at the group including past events, abstract concepts

- Follow basic rules of a group (raise hand, don't interrupt, look at the speaker, etc.)

- Follow instructions involving performances and materials at a distance

- Interact with group members about group topic (asking for and giving information, addressing students by name, etc.)

- Sustain attention for long durations

Even brief observation in a regular classroom is enough to reveal major differences between the methods of presentation of instructional material in discrete trial formats and group instruction. In any individualized teaching setting the student is expected to wait only inconsequential periods of time, responding frequently to the material. Prompts and the difficulty of material are instantly adjusted to the student's needs, and reinforcers are tailored to the student's tastes. In group situations, the student is often expected to observe other student responses, waiting for a turn to respond. Students need to observe the teacher or speaker as well, respond to instructions given generally to the group by a teacher who is 5-10 feet distant (using materials that are equally distant), respond to complex language with instructions embedded inside several sentences, and to be motivated by intermittent praise or other secondary sources of reinforcement. The exact conditions of instruction found in any particular lesson are determined by an amalgam of factors including:

- Learning objectives for each classroom activity

- Constraints of the available materials and setting

- Size of the group of students

- Needs and learning styles of students

- Preferences and professional experience of the teacher

- Policies, procedures, protocols, and traditions of the school

Nevertheless, several instructional formats spanning a variety of typical activities are common to many classrooms:

- ***Demonstrations/explorations:*** students first observe the teacher's actions (usually with accompanying materials), listen to information presented about the activity or materials, and then engage in target activities based on the presentation. Examples: science experiments, arts & crafts.

- ***Presentations:*** the teacher engages in verbal narratives like stories in which the student listens for an extended period of time and answers questions based on the material presented. Examples: story time, presentation and discussion on specific informational topics.

- ***Group Interactive Activities:*** the teacher leads an activity or discussion in which, primarily, participants take turns engaging in the discussion or activity. Examples: morning meeting, discussing student reactions to current events.

At each grade level, teaching formats present increasingly complex demands for skills including sustaining attention, listening and responding, memory, abstract concepts, and group interactions. Each skill requirement is accompanied by a number of conditions and rules that builds on previously established conditions and rules. If a student is to actively participate in such groups, he or she must possess some specific abilities relevant to the format.

Demonstrations/Explorations

Examples: Science experiments, arts & crafts, operating a computer, playing a new game.

Description: This format often involves actions with materials or equipment that are usually present and displayed. Students may be seated in a group or standing (as during a physical education activity). The teacher may display materials on a table, hold them up, or show pictures/movies of the materials. During the display, the teacher talks about the materials in various ways. The teacher may:

- Exhibit and name materials and/or component parts

- Describe/demonstrate features of materials. This includes color, form, size, location, quantity, position, orientation,

- Describe/demonstrate the function of materials. This includes actions (verbs), cause and effect

- Describe/demonstrate operation of materials. This includes actions, sequence, position, orientation

During the activity and after completion the student is often expected to be able to follow multi-step instructions to complete activities involving the topic.

Sequential or Exploratory: The activity may be presented in one of two ways: *sequentially*, with a set order of presentation of information and controlled student input or *exploratory*, with more immediate student engagement with materials and teacher input and questions interlaced throughout. Each sub-format evokes a different set of experiences for the students.

Sample Exploratory Activity

The following activity is adapted from *Sandbox Scientist, Real Science Activities for Little Kids,* by Michael Ross.

Water Droppers (Duration: approximately 15 minutes)

Materials

- Plastic water droppers
- Large paper clips with one end straightened
- Pebbles, erasers, and other objects such as sticks or leaves
- Small plastic containers

General Instructions

Place sets of materials on student tables. Fill containers with water. Explain to children why they should not drink the water or poke the droppers in eyes, ears, or nostrils. Show the group the various materials. Ask them to experiment with dripping water on the various objects. Teacher reacts to students' experimentation by encouraging them to describe what is happening. Students are encouraged to show each other what they have discovered or to copy what others are doing.

Sample Teacher Interactions (only if students need further direction):

- "What is this called (holds up dropper)?" (Answer: a dropper.)
- "How do you get water in the dropper?" (Answer: put it in water and squeeze the top)
- "How can you make the water come out?" (Answer: take the dropper out of the water and squeeze the top)
- "What happens to the water when you drip it on things?" (Answer: It falls off, it goes inside, it makes the rock wet, etc.)
- "Make just *one* drop come out of the dropper."
- "Drip water on the dirty rock. What happens?" (Answer: The dirt comes off.)
- "Press hard on the dropper. What happens? (Answer: the water comes out faster and goes farther.)
- "What sound does the water make when it comes out?"
- "Try squeezing air from the dropper back into the container of water to make bubbles."
- "Try putting the paper clip into the dropper and squeezing fast. What happens?" (Answer: the paper clip shoots out.)

Discussion of Activity

This activity relies on the natural curiosity of children and their innate tendency to explore. Given the eye droppers and water they may not need much encouragement to engage and interact. However, some children may need a few prompts or guidance. Of course, this guidance should be as minimal as possible since the point of the exercise is to encourage self-initiated exploration. On the language side, children should be encouraged to label what they see if they do not do so spontaneously. This may occur in the form of excited comments to neighboring peers. Without stifling spontaneous commenting, the teacher should try and help students expand their verbal descriptions of what is going on, ask questions about the processes, share information with peers, and discover as many fun and interesting aspects of using droppers and water as possible.

Sample Sequential Demonstration

Arts & Crafts – Making Butterflies (Adapted from *Crafts for Young Children* by Jill Norris). *Please note*: this description is included to illustrate the format of sequential demonstrations. Descriptions of materials for conducting the activity such as templates and step-by-step illustrations are omitted because they are not essential to understanding the organization and structure of the format.

Preparation and General Instructions:

Cover a table with a plastic cloth. Put newspaper on the floor under the painting table. Pour a different color of paint into several flat Styrofoam meat trays and place them in the middle of the activity table. Put a pile of large white paper and colored construction paper in the middle of the table. Next to the piles place a number of 3 inch lengths of string, 4 pieces for each participant, a box of child-safe scissors, a box of pencils, glue sticks, and a box of 6 inch pieces of colored yarn, one for each participant. Construct a template in the shape of a butterfly for each table.

Have students sit at activity tables in groups of no more than 4 children, wearing smocks to protect clothing. Introduce the activity by describing what is going to be done and showing a finished example of the craft. This activity may require some adult assistance.

Sequence of Actions:

1. Take a large white sheet of paper and fold it in half.
2. Unfold the paper and lay it front of you.
3. Dip a piece of string into one color of paint. Make sure it is well coated.
4. Lift the string from the tray and lay it on just the right side of the white paper with the end sticking out over the edge of the paper

5. Do the same thing with several pieces of string dipped in different colors

6. Fold the paper over the strings

7. Press down on the paper with one hand and pull the strings out with the other hand

8. Open the paper and let it dry

9. Fold the paper again. Put the butterfly template so that the straight edge is against the fold and trace around it with a pencil.

10. Cut out the butterfly with scissors.

11. Take a piece of colored paper and lay the butterfly on top of it

12. Glue the butterfly to the paper with the glue sticks

13. Draw a line on the colored paper ½ inch away from the butterfly all the way around.

14. Cut along the line on the colored paper to cut out the butterfly.

15. Punch a hole in the top of the butterfly and thread a piece of yarn into the hole about halfway.

16. Tie a knot in the yarn.

17. Hang the butterfly

Discussion of Activity

This activity is a long series of mini-activities involving folding, dipping the strings, tracing, cutting, punching holes, threading yarn, tying yarn, and hanging up the product. The student must follow each instruction in sequence and be able to perform the individual motor actions. The child must perform the actions as part of a group, making his actions and materials correspond to the actions and materials of the teacher or other group members. Advanced receptive language skills are required involving a large number of individual and combined words and phrases.

- **receptive labels** for each of the materials, actions, and pieces of equipment ("white paper," "colored paper," "string," "paint," "butterfly," "template," "pencil," "scissors," "glue stick," "yarn," "hole," "knot'")

- **receptive actions** ("take," "fold," "unfold," "lay," "dip," "lift," "Do the same thing," "press down," "pull out," "open," "cut," "glue," "draw a line," "punch a hole," "thread," "tie")

- **receptive orientation** ("in half," "in front of you," "into," "right side," "with end sticking out," "over the strings," "against," "around," "on top," "away from," "all the way around")

Wherever the child does not understand or misses an instruction, she must observe the teacher's demonstration or the actions of a peer. If the child cannot accomplish the task she must ask for help. In early grades, teachers may rely on adult helpers at each student table to repeat instructions, demonstrate actions, or help complete the steps.

Presentations

Examples: Informational topics such as weather, holidays, animals, geography; reading stories aloud.

Description: This format is illustrated when the teacher is the primary presenter of information and the information is primarily verbal. Several sentences or even paragraphs may occur before individual members of the group are given the opportunity to overtly respond. Responses are often prompted by specific questions while spontaneous comments may be ignored as inappropriate, depending on the rules of the group. Students may be encouraged to indicate willingness to respond by raising their hand requiring the teacher to distribute the opportunity to respond among all of the participants, thus decreasing any one individual's overt responses. Sometimes verbal responses are choral; other times an individual may be required to leave his seat and interact with materials near the teacher. Students may be seated in groups, tables, or individual desks, depending on the topic. The teacher may:

- Describe events, processes, or read stories

- Describe persons, objects, and actions involved

- Describe features of the topic, including color, form, size, location, quantity, position, orientation, functions

- Describe rules or lessons generalized from the presentation

During the activity and after completion, the student is often expected to be able to expressively name and/or receptively identify certain objects, attributes, functions, and processes involving the topic (what, when, where). Other desired responses may involve cause and effect (why), sequences, compare and contrast (same/different), talking about past events, getting and giving information to the group, and relating relevant personal experiences.

Sample Presentation – Reading a Story

The teacher gathers students in the "Story Corner" by announcing to the group, "It's time for library, boys and girls. Finish up what you are doing and meet me in the Story Corner." The teacher moves to her chair in the area and positions a book on an easel, closed to show the illustration on the cover. The students spend 1-2 minutes gathering in the area, each sitting on an individual carpet square, and talking to their neighbors. The teacher gives a signal to the class to become quiet by rhythmically clapping, a prearranged signal with the class to give their attention to the teacher.

[The teacher picks up the book and points to the cover] "Today, boys and girls, we're going to read a story called *The Cat in the Hat* by Dr. Seuss. Does anyone know this story? [She looks around, several children say, "oh" and "yes"] That's great, I'm sure you are all going to like it. It's funny! [Opens book and starts reading first page, finishes page] Look at the way the cat is dressed. What's he wearing? [Everyone calls out, the teacher calls on a girl with her hand raised and the girl says, "A big striped hat"] That's right, Jennifer! But do cats usually wear hats? [Noooo, everyone calls out] Now, everyone, if you want to make a comment or answer a question, remember, raise your hand or I'll have to stop reading. [Turns page and reads the next four pages] What's happening here? Who is the cat? What is he going to do?"

Throughout the story the teacher continues to read several pages at a time, stopping to ask various questions of the students. Typical questions include the following:

- "What did he do?"
- "Why did he do it?"

- "What is that (pointing to an object)?"
- "Who did that?"
- "What's wrong with that?"
- "What is that like?"
- "Did that ever happen to you?"
- "What will happen next?"

After the story the teacher may review the action by asking students to retell parts of the story and their reaction to it:

- "What part did you like best?"
- "What did you think when the Cat dropped the things he was balancing?"
- "Did you ever make a mess like that?"
- "How would you like to have to clean up all that mess?"

Additionally, the teacher may try and extrapolate a rule or moral from the story:

- "Should we let strange cats in our house? How about people we don't know?"

Discussion of Activity

This kind of activity requires sustained attention from participants. The degree of compliance from students (active listening and participation) is usually related to the pacing, number of opportunities to respond, and intrinsic interest of the presentation. However, the degree of difficulty of the language presented (vocabulary, length of sentences, number of sentences per page) is also an important factor. Obviously, some wh-questions must be mastered in order to participate in the activity. However, student must also become accustomed to more advanced phrasing and questions including questions that are embedded in statements:

"O.K., class, I want you to pay attention to the next few pages because there is something really special in this story. Everybody put on your listening ears and sit up straight. Do you know what a rainbow is? It comes after a rainstorm. Look for the rainbow on this page. *What do you see underneath the rainbow?"*

The students' only overt opportunity to respond to the previous statements of the teacher is prompted by the question at the end of the paragraph ("What do you see underneath the rainbow?") However, the students must monitor the *entire* series of sentences for directions in order to respond correctly. Other important skills in this format include:

- Following multi-page stories read in a group at a distance
- Advanced wh-questions (why)
- Predicting the outcome
- Relating a sequence of events (retelling story)

Variation: Learning about President's Day

In this variation of the presentation format, several activities are centered on the theme of presidents, but the responses required from students are still primarily verbal. Students are invited to a section of the classroom where the teacher has set up a large easel with a flannel board, a blackboard, and an auxiliary table with a pile of handouts. With the students gathered together the teacher introduces the activity and hands out a "Weekly Reader" with a picture of Abraham Lincoln and George Washington on the cover.

"Well now, boys and girls, do you know who our president is? [Answer: Barack Obama]. "Yes, that's right, Barack Obama is our president. He's the President of the United States; of our country. This week we are celebrating President's Day. What's that?" [Answer: the birthday of the president] "Well, yes, that's right. We are celebrating the birthdays of two famous presidents. Look at your papers. Who can tell me who this is?" [Answer: Abraham Lincoln] "Right! Abraham Lincoln, our 13th president. And, who is this?" [Answer: George Washington.] "Right! George Washington, our 1st president. When were George Washington and Abraham Lincoln the president, now or a long time ago?

The presentation continues by reading a story about Abraham Lincoln and telling a legend about George Washington. Then coins and paper money are passed around to show the students other pictures of Washington and Lincoln, with the teacher pointing to large drawings of the various coins and bills posted on the easel. After 30 minutes, the teacher sends the students to their work tables to complete some worksheets related to the presentation. In order to complete the worksheets the students must:

- Match a picture of the presidents (Washington, Lincoln, and Obama) with their printed name

- Complete the sentences, "George Washington was our country's __ president" and "Abraham Lincoln was our country's __ president."

- Color the pictures of the presidents

- Circle the date of Washington's birthday and Lincoln's birthday on a calendar

Discussion of Activity

Groups vary in their response to this kind of activity. Often a number of children have been previously exposed to the information and eagerly attempt to answer all of the questions while others are silent. For some children, there are not enough opportunities to rehearse the information during the presentation and it is often necessary to reinforce key concepts in the presentation with additional questions while students are completing their worksheets. Pre-teaching the material, combined with additional practice after the presentation, may be necessary for students having difficulty.

Group Interaction Activities

Examples: Discussing student reactions to an important current event, planning classroom activities, making group decisions, expressing attitudes and feelings, discussing problem situations, and relating past personal events.

Description: In this activity format, the teacher guides students into discussing specific questions presented by the teacher. Students take turns speaking on the subject and must remain on topic, addressing the last point (or at least a recent point) made by a speaker. The teacher encourages appropriate verbal behavior exhibited by students through specific reactions, such as reflecting emotions, paraphrasing, and non-verbal behavior such as head nodding and short encouraging comments ("o.k.," "uh-huh," "right," etc.). When the conversation lags or gets off topic the teacher intervenes to move the discussion forward. The student is expected to exhibit several specific skills including:

- Looking at the speaker when listening and looking at the group when speaking
- Making statements of personal preferences and opinions
- Answering questions involving personal preferences and opinions
- Asking clarifying questions of group members
- Recalling or inferring information about topics of discussion and/or group members

Sample Group Interactive Activity – Morning Meeting

Morning meetings often take place at the beginning of the day and usually involve a mixture of semi-structured discussion topics, some routine and some new. The purpose of the activity is sometimes described as "preparing" students for the schedule of the day, "processing" occurrences or events, or "sharing" with the group. Specific activities contained within a morning meeting vary considerably, but examples include talking about the past weekend's activities, recognizing birthdays and special individual events, show-and-tell, talking about problems within the group, talking about upcoming field trips, and talking about the day's schedule.

The teacher begins the morning meeting by giving an instruction to the group to move to a specific area of the classroom. The group often sits on the floor or in chairs, close together, in a semi-circle around the teacher so that each student can see all members of the group. The teacher greets the group and introduces the first topic:

"Hello and good morning everyone. I hope you had a good weekend. What are some special things that you did on Saturday or Sunday?" Children raise their hands and the teacher calls on one student. The group listens to the student relate a story about a visit from his grandparents over the weekend and where they went to have fun. The teacher uses open-ended questions to help the student expand the descriptions of the events and use as many descriptors and full sentences as possible. The teacher then invites other children to react and ask questions. Some spontaneous comments or questions are tolerated, but the teacher reminds the students to raise their hands to ask questions. The student speaker calls on other students and answers their questions for 4-5 minutes. At times, the teacher intervenes to ask the group for a reaction to a certain aspect of the student's presentation like, "Did you ever go on a picnic like Danny and his family?" After the allotted time is up, the teacher moves on to the next student. Four students present in this way before the teacher transitions into the next topic.

"You all sound like you had a great weekend. Now we need to discuss what we are going to do today. Remember that Mrs. Bean is going to come in and help us do our cooking. We are going to follow a recipe and make pudding just before snack. [Teacher puts a small sign that says *Cooking* on the schedule board.] But before that, since it is Monday, we're going to the library. Did you remember to bring in your books from last week?" [Teacher puts *Library* sign on schedule board. The teacher continues describing the day's coming events until all of the time slots are filled—about 8 different activities. She dismisses children from the group by telling them to line up for library according to tables.] "O.K., table 3 first on line; now, table 1; table 2; table 4."

Discussion of Activity

Full participation in this activity requires more advanced conversational skills such as describing past events, asking and answering questions about student presentations, and observing and attending to others in the group. Fairly sophisticated receptive language skills are a must. Students should be able to separate out instructions and key bits of information that are embedded in multiple sentences, sometimes a difficult task when the operative parts of sentences are surrounded by a great deal of verbiage that is extraneous to the activity. The student must be familiar with prefaces to sentences like "O.K., now, I want you to…" and other natural language fillers and expressions that populate common speech. Secondly, students should practice following longer *sequences* of instructions expressed in natural language. Gradually, the complexity and variety of language and required responses can be increased as the student learns to stay with the activity and be more fully engaged for longer periods of time.

Since verbal responses in a group are usually performed one participant at a time, opportunities to respond for an included student may need to be manipulated, initially, in order to provide adequate reinforcement to establish a strong, consistent performance. The student may need to specifically practice turn taking and attending to other speakers in a simulated group where the frequency of being called on is gradually thinned to levels seen in the classroom. Once in the classroom a transition period may be necessary during which the teacher calls on the target student more frequently.

Summary

Analysis of performance conditions and response requirements in target settings such as those found in instructional formats is an essential component of preparing students to use their skills in new environments. Common formats such as demonstrations, exploratories, presentations, and group interactive experiences require specific skills and present new contingencies to the student that must be understood by program authors in detail so that functional and pivotal behavior related to each may be explicitly developed.

Connecting with a Standards-Based Curriculum

While ABA curriculum creation in schools may sometimes start at a relatively microscopic level, concerned with highly specific performances, such performances should be part of an overall long-range plan. For students in a given community, a "curriculum" of target skills is chosen according to their perceived value in helping the student to independently live, work, play, and interact with others. Creating programs that address the "big picture" allows for continuity of services and coordination of progress over the long-term.

A recent project completed by the author and an ABA teacher illustrates the process of connecting the creation of highly individualized teaching programs with broader, standards-based curriculum frameworks. Based on the abilities of a group of four students with autism in her ABA classroom, the teacher consulted a functional skills curriculum adopted by her district and chose a set of performances from one area of science described for first grade. From among the topics/essential questions listed, the teacher chose those that best suited the abilities of her students:

General Curriculum Area: Science

Topic: Plants

Scope of the Topic/Essential Questions:

1. Name the parts of a plant

2. Name several types of plants

3. Describe attributes of plants

4. What do plants do?

5. What do we do with plants?

6. Describe, illustrate, and predict plant growth

7. Describe and perform care of plants

The next part of the teacher's task was to elaborate the essential questions into highly specific target behaviors that could be included in individualized and small group program plans of the type typically required in ABA classrooms. To a large extent, the specific vocabulary of the topic (plants) provided the targets. Straightforward identification, classification, attributes, and functions were target performances similar to those that her students had previously worked on in other contexts. In addition, performances involved stating the steps of several processes ("How does a plant grow?" "How do we get our food?" "How do we prepare food?"). Finally, for these students, some simple functional performances related to the topic were included.

Defining Specific Target Performances

- **Parts**: stem, trunk. Leaves, flower, petals, branch, roots, twig, bark, bud, seed

- **Types**: flower, vegetable, bush, tree, grass, fruit, plant

- **Name/Identify 5 different flowers**: rose, daisy, tulip, sunflower, dandelions

- **Name/Identify 5 fruits**: banana, pear, strawberry, apple, grapes, watermelon, lemon, pineapple, peach

- **Name/Identify vegetables** (picture on plant): cucumber, squash, broccoli, corn, carrots, peas, lettuce

- **Sort and classify non-identical bushes**: rhododendron, boxwood, hedges

- **Sort and classify non-identical trees**: apple, cherry, pine, oak

- **Name/Identify attributes of plants**: tall/short; big/little; thin/thick; rough/smooth; dead/alive; wet/dry; alike/different; colors, edible/inedible, smells (roses, tulips, apples, strawberries, lemon, pineapple, peach, grapes, cinnamon) edible, pretty, dirty

- **Name/Identify color of plants:** (11 colors)

- **What do plants do?**: grow, drink, bloom, die; receptively id pictures and live samples

- **What we do with plants**: eat, pick, smell, cook, cut/mow/trim, water, plant, put in vases

- **How do you eat?:** a banana, orange, strawberry, watermelon, apple, peach, grapes, pineapple

- **What parts do we eat? What parts don't we eat?**

- **How do plants grow? How tall? How big?**

- **Put pictures of plant growth in order**

- **Describe plant growth**: roots get bigger, shoots come up

- **Name/Identify:** seed, shoots, plant, flower; **how you make a plant grow?**: plant a seed, water it every day, give it sun, watch it grow

- **Where do we get our food?:** Get from grocery store

- **How do we prepare food from plants?** wash, cut up, cook

- **Match cooked dish to component vegetable or fruit ingredient**: mashed potatoes, apple pie, salad, French fries

- **Plant a flower seed and measure its growth**

- **Pull up weeds around a plant**

- **Water a plant on a schedule**

- **Pick flowers and make a bouquet for parent**

- **Pick apples at orchard**

Standards are provided to guide curriculum development of all kinds at all age levels. The choice of target performances is not random or isolated, but connected to the larger educational frameworks established for all students by the student's community at the local, state, and national levels.

Generalization

During acquisition, a student's behavior comes under the control of the instructional conditions presented. The particular arrangement of materials, directions given, or even the instructor's tone of voice eventually exerts a strong influence over whether behavior occurs or not. *Generalization* occurs when a target behavior is performed under circumstances that are different from those that existed during the original acquisition. As discussed previously, generalization is necessary for skills to be extended from highly controlled acquisition conditions to those found in more natural settings. However, generalization of skills to new conditions is limited by the degree of similarity of the new conditions to the original ones. As dissimilarity increases between the acquisition setting and the natural setting increases, the tendency of the target behavior to generalize decreases. Numerous conditions and contingencies vary from setting to setting for many target skills including:

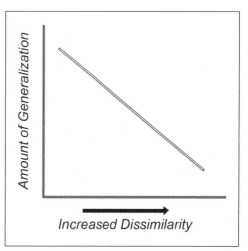

Stimulus Generalization Gradient. As stimulus dissimilarity increases generalization decreases

- **Target Setting, General Conditions**
    - Time of day
    - Location of performance
    - Size of group in which performance occurs
    - Seating arrangement
    - Persons present
    - Visual and auditory distractions

- **Target Setting, Task Conditions**
    o Nature of directions given
    o Type of instructional procedures used (prompts, error correction, etc.)
    o Materials used
- **Target Setting, Contingencies**
    o Reinforcement schedule
    o Performance criterion (frequency, duration, magnitude, topography, latency)
    o Contingencies/events preceding and following the target behavior
    o Concurrently available contingencies (required ancillary behavior, competing reinforcers)

When factors like those above are the source of significant divergence between natural environments and the original conditions of skill acquisition, intervention strategies to facilitate generalization of skills are essential. Stokes and Baer (1977) described nine general categories of intervention:

1. Train and Hope

Train and hope refers to the delivery of training under one set of conditions and hoping that, once acquired, the target behavior will occur in the target setting without any further intervention.

2. Sequential Modification

If generalization to new target conditions does not occur after acquisition training, explicit training is undertaken for each problem area. For example, if the student participates in successful acquisition training with one instructor but does not respond to a second instructor, explicit training with the second instructor is implemented. If the target skill is exhibited in one group activity but not a second, direct instruction is begun with the second activity. With sequential modification, direct, systematic teaching is individually completed for each target condition identified as relevant.

3. Introduce to Natural Maintaining Contingencies

Some target settings and activities provide naturally occurring reinforcement contingencies that are unavailable or different from those provided during acquisition. In this case, generalization is enhanced if the student is guided through the new activity or conditions so that he can experience the natural reinforcement. For example, playing with toys alone in a resource room may provides a degree of intrinsic reinforcement as well as praise from instructors. However, in a classroom of other students, play can produce highly reinforcing social interaction. Initially guiding the student through play in the classroom and ensuring that he experiences the pleasant social interaction is often sufficient to establish classroom play without further prompting.

4. Train Sufficient Exemplars

Successful acquisition of a skill may produce a student capable of responding only under limited conditions. For example: students learn to follow a series of directions from one adult instructor who initially conducted sessions with them but then fail to respond to other adults. Using the principle of training sufficient exemplars, additional training trials would be scheduled with a succession of adults. As responding expands to each new adult, the student's tendency to generalize to all adults (e.g., novel ones) is increased. The principle can be employed to increase responding under a wide variety of important stimulus conditions such as similar but not identical materials, different locations of instruction, and different forms of the same instruction ("Show me…" vs. "Point to…" vs. "Where is…").

5. Train Loosely

Implementers work hard to achieve consistency in their presentation of instruction, thus improving the ability of the student to discriminate contingencies and achieve the target performance. Once acquisition has occurred however, the same level of consistency may actually prevent students from generalizing by limiting their exposure to variability in tone of voice, facial expressions, positions of materials, etc. "Train loosely" refers to the deliberate inclusion of small amounts of variability in the presentation and structure of activities to help students learn to persist in their performance of the target behaviors in spite of inconsistency.

6. Use Indiscriminable Contingencies

Predictable reinforcement schedules are sometimes detrimental to generalization once acquisition has occurred. While continuous or fixed reinforcement schedules effectively produce consistent behavior in highly controlled settings, natural environments may not offer students such regular access to reinforcement. Therefore, interruptions and irregularities should become the rule in contingencies designed to enhance generalization. This will inoculate students against confusion caused by the inevitable disruptions of some environments.

7. Program Common Stimuli

Since individuals inevitably become accustomed to the paraphernalia of activities, generalization improves when materials follow into the target setting. Familiar task materials used during acquisition should be designed to be portable and reused, thus preserving and enabling strong stimulus control elements to elicit the target performance under new conditions.

8. Mediate Generalization

A response is mediated when an *extra* behavior occurs between the original stimulus and the final response that facilitates the occurrence of the final response. For example, imagine that a student hears a series of six numbers (original stimulus) and writes them down on a piece of paper. In 30 minutes, a teacher asks him to recall the numbers (final response), which is easily accomplished by taking out the paper and reading the numbers. The student's verbal response to the teacher is mediated by writing them down on a piece of paper and reading. Alternatively, the student might repeat the numbers frequently during the interval. Then, when asked to name them, the verbal repetition mediates. In both cases, hearing the original auditory stimulus is not the operative discriminative stimulus directly. Verbal and visual mediators like speaking, writing, and graphics can help students generalize behavior. Students can use a schedule, calendar, or agenda to prepare for upcoming activities or keep track of how much work they have accomplished. Unobtrusive icons or check sheets remind students of reward contingencies across settings. Learning the "rules" of the class and repeating them before each activity helps increase corresponding appropriate behavior during the intervening time periods.

9. Train "To Generalize"

Essentially, training students to generalize means explicitly reinforcing variability. For example, students taught to get adult attention by saying, "Look what I did" may also engage in a variety of related behaviors such as holding out their work, making eye contact, approaching adults, tapping adults on the shoulder, or other things. All of the behaviors can be defined as members of a category or "functional class," meaning that they accomplish the same result (getting the attention of an adult) and receive reinforcement. Defining and reinforcing a functional class increases the occurrence of all behaviors within the class, even those that are not performed as often as others. Functional classes that are commonly reinforced in classrooms include being "kind" (saying nice things to others, not getting angry, using polite words), "helpful" (sharing, solving problems with others) and "responsible" (putting away materials, following classroom rules).

Sample Intervention

Strategies such as those described above can be used alone or in combination to encourage generalization of key skills in a variety of areas. Consider the following example. The instructional format of discrete trials is not appropriate for many tasks in the classroom and the ability to follow directions in a highly structured setting must generalize to a classroom environment. Observation and analysis suggests that at least five conditions can be relevant to student success in following classroom directions:

1. The location of the student

2. The location of the teacher

3. The location and type of presentation of materials

4. The type of prompts used

5. The location of the student performance

The plan on Page 211 systematically combines the strategies of *sequential modification, program common stimuli, train sufficient exemplars, train loosely,* and *train to generalize* to gradually establish instruction following under conditions common to a classroom. The training occurs in a regular classroom that is empty of other students until Step 5 (*program common stimuli*). Prior to training the student has exhibited good instructional control in a discrete-trial format, conducted in a corner of the classroom. The student sits in his regular seat (*program common stimuli*) but is turned towards the front of the classroom with the instructor seated opposite (facing the student and between the student and the front of the classroom). In the first few phases of instruction, directions are given to a student with the teacher gradually moving apart from the student, assuming a standing position and referring to materials that vary in location and stretch around the student's whole visual field (*sequential modification*). Then the student's performance location gradually expands to include various places in the room (*train sufficient exemplars*).

Examples:

- "Count the pumpkins on the felt board" (next to the teacher)
- "Point to the number 20 on the calendar" (attached to the chalkboard behind teacher)
- "Get the red book" from the teacher's desk

As the student adapts to the changing location of the teacher, materials, and performance, he also must become accustomed to the use of more natural language (*train loosely*). Simplified language is important for the student when initially learning the meaning of an instruction. However, alternate/equivalent forms of the instruction that vary in wording and length must also be learned. After learning to follow the instruction "Give me the ball," the student learns "Touch the ball," "Pick up the ball," and "Please get me the ball" (*train sufficient exemplars*). As the student progresses, the instructions become longer and more natural sounding. When the student readily responds to single sentences containing natural language, additional non-instructional sentences can be inserted. "What's this, Brian? Right, a ball! In fact, there are two balls here—a green one and a blue one. **Point to the blue one**."

In the classroom environment, the student needs to listen to each sentence in a natural language presentation and decide whether it contains an instruction or not. This requires more sustained attention and receptive language skill than simply listening to a single sentence. Sufficient time and training is required to assist the student in gradually

Moving from Discrete Trials to an Inclusion Setting

Table: Sample Teaching Steps
(Bold type indicates changes from the preceding step)

More Structured (1:1)	Step 2	Step 3	Step 4	Step 5	Step 6	Less Structured (typical classroom)
Student sits at desk Teacher sits next to student Teacher presents materials on student desk Teacher prompts with simple verbal and physical prompts, as necessary Student makes responses at desk	Student sits at desk **Teacher sits 1 foot from desk facing student** **Teacher presents materials on easel or another table/desk within reach of student** **Teacher prompts with more complex verbal prompts and gestures** **Student makes occasional responses away from desk**	Student sits at desk **Teacher sits 3 feet from desk facing student, occasionally stands** Teacher presents materials on easel or another table/desk next to teacher **Teacher prompts with simple, natural language prompts** **Student makes responses at desk, while standing, and when next to teacher**	Student sits at desk **Teacher stands or sits 5 feet from desk, facing student.** Teacher presents materials on boards, easels, tables Teacher uses prompts with simple natural language Student makes responses at desk, while standing, away from desk, and wjem next to teacher	Student sits at desk Teacher stands 5 feet from desk facing student Teacher presents materials on boards, easels, tables **Teacher uses natural language instructions directed at group** Student makes responses at desk, while standing, away from desk, and wjem next to teacher	**Student sits at desk in group of 2 or 3.** **Teacher stands 5-10 feet from desks facing students** Teacher presents materials on boards, easels, tables Teacher uses natural language instructions directed at group Student makes responses at desk, while standing, away from desk, and wjem next to teacher	Student sits at desk in group of other students Teacher stands 5-10 feet from desks facing students Teacher presents materials on boards, easels, tables easily visible by students **Teacher uses natural language prompts, embeds instructions in multi-part sentences, directed at group** **Student makes responses any place in classroom**

developing the ability to discriminate between operative and non-operative sentences (*train sufficient exemplars*).

When students are placed in groups, they must respond to instructions that are given to the group rather than directly to them. Instead of looking at the student and saying, "Bobby, go sit down at your desk," the implementer looks around the room and says, "Everyone, please sit at your desks." When necessary, students are specifically taught to respond to group instructions; to maximize instructional control, group instructions can be practiced without the group before adding a small number of students and then progressing to a whole class (*sequential modification, train sufficient exemplars*).

Following instructions often involves answering questions. "Wh-questions" (what, who, where, when, why) and "how" questions are often the heart of teacher-led group presentations. Students should be able to answer wh- and how questions in order to participate fully; include them as drills when preparing the student for classroom groups (*program common stimuli*). There are dozens of forms of verbal or written instructions common to classrooms and worksheets, books, etc. that are candidates for pre-teaching. Include them systematically as part of efforts to prepare students for classrooms and other natural school settings.[3]

Incorporation of Programs - Sequences

Following generalization strategies like those described above directly addresses the conditions we called *concurrent conditions* in the beginning of the chapter – those conditions that describe the immediate task performance, separate from the occurrence of other skills. Some target performances are exhibited within a group of skills as part of a *process* or other more complex performance arrangement. In this case, the nature of each skill performance and its relationship to other performances (or *sequence conditions*) is very important. In the rest of this chapter we will discuss how, when skills are incorporated into performance chains, sequence conditions may be manipulated to facilitate performances and expand the student's functional repertoire in natural environments.

Several types of sequential arrangements of skills operate commonly in natural environments:

---

[3] Refer to the end of the chapter for a list of over one hundred instructions that are commonly used on worksheets.

- **Homogeneous response chains**: single skill chains that require repetition of the same behavior and do not involve inclusion of other performances within the routine

- **Fixed-sequence chains**: fixed-sequence chains employ more than one performance topography and function, placed in an order that does not vary

- **Variable-sequence chains**: variable-sequence chains are collections of skills that have more than one possible performance sequence

Natural environments are full of simple and complex sequences of skill performances that are assembled from such components. For example:

- A **handwashing "sequence"** is comprised of a *fixed-order* set of basic motor responses, usually acquired prior to their incorporation in the handwashing chain, such as turning or twisting a handle (turning water on and off), rubbing hands together, and dropping objects into receptacles (throwing out a paper towel). The routine is a relatively simple chain that is generally performed once in its entirety

- An **arrival sequence** involves *variable-sequence* chain components nested within *fixed-order* chain components: the student dismounts the bus, walks into school, navigates to the classroom, and walks to the coat area. Then, in any order, the student puts away her coat and lunch bag. Before putting away her back pack, the student takes out (in any order) her books, note books, and pencil box. Finally, the student walks into the classroom and takes her seat

- A presentation sequence on the **habitats of animals** is led by the teacher. Students listen and imitate the teacher when she turns a page (*fixed-sequence*), following along in a book. After the book is completed the teacher asks for a variety of responses from students, randomly working through wh-questions, matching activities, and writing activities (*fixed-sequence activities nested within a variable-sequence component*)

Function of Sequence Components

Each sequence component functions in a particular way within the sequence. Many sequences found in natural environments and those that are intentionally arranged as part of instructional programs contain performances that work together to:

- Facilitate generalization of performances to new conditions
- Produce a specific outcome
- Facilitate the occurrence of other performances

Arbitrary sequences – those with no intended relationship between components – can also occur. Arbitrary sequences come about when collections of drills occur in an order that is customary, traditional, or when program designers are unconcerned with the succession of tasks and allow them to take any order. For example, music may occur at 1:15 PM in the sequence of afternoon activities because of the scheduling needs of the music teacher. The Pledge of Allegiance occurs first thing in the morning because it is customary to do so in many schools. Customary or practical administrative issues exist within all ABA programs.

In other cases, arbitrary sequences occur because implementers do not plan for the employment of sequence effects or under-utilize them in the scheduling of activities and programs. This could occur early in implementation or when extensive changes are being made to a student's curriculum, when program authors are busy. Sometimes failure to employ sequence strategies occurs because planners do not appreciate the potential benefit to the student. Regardless of the reason, programmers certainly have a choice between intentional planning and allowing unplanned and "arbitrary" sequences of educational activities. In truth, while the order of activities may be arbitrary from the perspective of the planner, the student experiences the interaction of each schedule component with others, unintentionally programmed or not, and reacts accordingly. Thus, after an unplanned sequence is implemented, unforeseen consequences may be discovered: the student does well first thing in the morning but deteriorates as the day progresses; he dislikes attending music after snack or works surprisingly well on addition problems after working on the computer in reading. Regardless of planning, any interactive effects between program components that exist will affect the student.

Strategies to Facilitate Generalization of Performances

Incorporation strategies can facilitate generalization of mastered skills employing the concepts of "mediated generalization" from Stokes and Baer (1977). Simple task arrangements require a student to produce familiar discriminative stimuli that, in turn, set the occasion for the performance of a second task:

A student uses a marker to highlight the number next to addition problems that should be completed on a worksheet.

- A student lays out implements or tools to be used in a task
- A student names all the items that need to be put away
- A student names or reads all the days of the week prior to asking her to name today
- A student draws a tree before naming the parts

Consider a further example: a teacher would like a student to write down the names of two planets that are named in a presentation. Since the presentation is done fairly quickly and the student is a slow writer, the teacher asks the student to circle the names of each planet printed on a worksheet that contains pictures of all nine planets. Then after the presentation has been completed, the student copies the results to write the names of the planets:

- If a student is able to place cards inside a template of square outlines and has a history of working with arrays, another generalization strategy (program common stimuli) can be used to help the student independently complete the proper number of items of a language arts task. A sequence of skills is arranged starting with the student choosing printed words from an array:

- Student chooses words for a large array of word cards placed face down
- Student places each card inside one of the five outlined squares until all squares are filled
- Student reads and types each word into the computer until there are no words left on the squares

Combining Programs to Establish General Routines

Analysis of routines found in the natural environment provides an important part of the curriculum for incorporation and sequences. Program authors can deliberately incorporate tasks into a variety of routines and conditions that mimic the real world. In natural settings routines exist for just about everything from visiting the bathroom to visiting the library. Play is followed by clean-up and transition to another activity; math proceeds from review to presentation of new material to questions, discussion, and worksheets. Classroom routines for each aspect of a student's overall schedule may be identified, broken down into component sequences, explicitly practiced, both in isolation and in the natural setting, and then gradually reassembled to achieve successful intact performances that stretch over long periods of time.

It is particularly important to strengthen and lengthen sequences by increasing the variety, scope, and duration of tasks. While students may have had adequate exposure to some of the central components of a natural environment sequence, they could have difficulty with other components. **Preparation, clean-up and transition** are sometimes trouble spots that requires additional practice:

- Before reading, "Turn to page __"
- Before writing, "Get out your pencils"
- Before working on worksheets, "Come up and get a worksheet"
- After cutting out several shapes, cleans work area of scraps that clutter the area
- After completing a problem, raises hand to volunteer answer
- After putting away math materials, follows directions to the next instructional location
- Before looking for a new book in the library, sits at the table and waits for the teacher's instructions

Social and language performances are typically embedded in most group routines that occur in natural environments and also present challenges for some students:

- Asks questions about material presented

- Locates missing materials
- Obtains permission to start or stop
- Finds space to sit down at group table
- Supplies information to participant
- Coordinates actions to accomplish task step
- Recruits reinforcement
- Gives compliment

Long routines of tasks sometimes pose an especially difficult problem for students who are not used to sustaining their efforts. Recall the sample observation of the kindergarten morning meeting that lasted 45 minutes. Effective establishment of long routines relies on putting together routines from previously well-established components and adjusting both the difficulty and reinforcement schedule. Extremely long routines are generally not well-tolerated by most students and teachers may want to rethink the need for some. Nevertheless, both the length and number of routine components can successfully be programmed when careful selection and motivation strategies are employed. Discussion of motivation and manipulation of the relationships between sequence components to facilitate performances, including difficult or long performances, will occur in the final section of this chapter.

Combination of Skills to Create an Outcome or Product

Countless sequences of skills are commonly employed in natural environments to produce simple and complex target results including solving calculations, written and verbal communications, retrieving information, assembling materials, organizing, self-care, and other processes with specific, observable effects on the environment. Such multi-step routines are similar to other types of chains but contain some additional attributes whose operation within the components makes them unique. Like sequences in general, "process" sequences can include elements that have a fixed or variable order but only to the extent that they successfully function in a cause and effect manner; that is, the order of individual elements varies as long as the end result is the creation of a target effect. Effects may be intermediate or final products. For example, solving a simple mathematical word problem necessitates identification of the quantities involved, addition of the quantities, and, finally, writing the sum on a worksheet. The basic operations are divided into stages. Identification of the quantities is accomplished by (a) scanning the text with a finger until a number is encountered and (b) circling the number. Addition is accomplished by (a) writing each number into a template, (b) piling up small manipulatives to represent each quantity, and (c) counting up both quantities. Each operation produces intermediate products used by the next operation in the chain:

1. Circled numbers in the text control their entry into the template

2. Each number in the completed template controls the placement of manipulatives

3. The groups of manipulatives control counting

4. Verbalization of the final counted number controls writing that number into the template as the answer

Frequently, intermediate products involve the use of common materials among the sequence components. In the example above, the student was presented with a set of materials (word problem text and equation template) that was consistent throughout the progression of steps. Interactions between behavior and common materials early in the sequence promote later steps by establishing a central focal point associated with reinforcement.[4]

The individual steps of a process sequence are eventually consolidated when the student becomes more skilled. Scanning with a finger and circling is discarded in favor of looking at the whole text and writing numbers directly into the template. Use of manipulatives is substituted when the student learns to count on from the first number. Eventually, numbers are recalled rather than written into templates. Finally, students simply recall memorized sums (i.e. using addition "tables") of any two given numbers. When observing proficient students performing a process, consolidation of the steps can make it appear simpler than it really is. This misimpression frequently results in creation of a program that correctly identifies the main components of the process but fails to include enough individual steps. Necessarily, program designers must sufficiently analyze how each intermediate product leads to the next and combines to create a final product.

---

[4] Behavior analysts might discuss such a focal point as a "discriminative stimulus."

Facilitating Performance of Sequence Components and Motivation

Sequences may be simple or complex assemblies of skills acquired under carefully structured conditions. As with any behavior, motivation is always a concern. While the construction of sequences is designed to create performances that match the requirements of normal life, the effort required of an extended schedule of activities puts a premium on the ability of the program to maintain performances and propel the student forward from hour-to-hour and day-to-day. Effective strategies that facilitate the completion of sequence steps are invaluable in this endeavor.

To achieve an effect, motivational strategies manipulate the *order* of skill programs within sequences according to their *probability of occurrence*[5]. Arrangement takes one of two forms:

- Low-probability (Low-P) task followed by high-probability (High-P) task
- High-probability (High-P) task followed by low-probability (Low-P) task

Low-P followed by High-P

Commonly called the "Premack Principle" (Premack, 1959) – sometimes called "Grandma's Rule," this strategy arranges a high-p activity to follow a low-p activity. When successful, the high-probability task reinforces the occurrence of the low-probability task. For example, starting a class with something difficult and, after completion, progressing to something easier would qualify as a low-p/high-p intervention. High-p tasks consist of any relatively preferred educational task but often include mastered tasks. Scheduling high-p tasks after low-p tasks increases the duration of sustained work (low-p + high-p activities) without undue fear of contingency failure due to lack of reinforcement. Certainly, there are limits to using this strategy related to satiation of the high-p activity. Konarski, Johnson, Crowell, and Whitman (1980) found that a student will not work for any more access to a preferred activity than they usually like to have. Also, there are constraints on the effectiveness of high-p tasks as reinforcers. The most effective contingencies arrange

---

[5] Probability of occurrence refers to a student's relative likelihood of engaging in a particular educational task compared to all other educational tasks. Probability of occurrence is measured in a manner identical to preference. The term probability is used to be consistent with the literature reviewed in this chapter. For the purposes of this discussion, high probability means that the activity was chosen 66% or more of the time while low probability means that the activity was chosen less than 34% of the time.

the highest high-p tasks to follow moderately low-p tasks. Extremely low probability tasks will probably occasion strong escape behavior regardless of the promised reward (Carbone, Morgenstern, Zecchin-Tirri & Kolberg, 2007). In such cases, duration, difficulty, required rate of behavior, and other factors related to the effort required for reinforcement make the probability of occurrence of some behavior nearly zero.

The facilitation effect of the low-p/high-p structure depends somewhat on the ability of the student to discriminate when a succession of components will occur. In the laboratory, well-established discriminative stimuli are required to produce clear effects of one schedule component on the preceding component (Ferster and Skinner, 1957). If a switch to a new task is predictable to the student, it is, potentially, more reinforcing (Krägeloh, Elliffe, and Davidson, 2006; Fantino, 1977). Tasks with poorly specified criteria for completion, unscheduled delays, non-reinforced ancillary tasks, and indistinct transitions provide an inconsistent progression to the preferred task and may interfere with the effectiveness of the contingency.

High-P followed by Low-P

While perhaps counter-intuitive, presenting a high-probability task first followed by one that is of lower probability can increase responding on the low-p activity under the right circumstances. Use of this strategy is fairly common in typical educational settings:

High Probability Activity Low Probability Activity
• Beginning a class with a learning game or by presenting a high interest series of stories concerning a topic of study, followed by more typical exercises (questions, worksheets, etc.) with the material to be learned.
• Starting with a "warm up" where students engage in easy forms of a relevant target behavior and gradually take on more difficult versions
• Conducting a "content review" where the teacher reviews previous lessons first. Students answer questions about previously mastered lessons before moving on to new material
• "Scaffolding" where easy, more basic questions are presented and correctly answered before more complex and difficult questions.

Much of the supporting scientific study of high-p/low-p strategies is based on the work of Mace and his colleagues (Hock & Mace, 1986; Mace, Hock, Lalli, West, Belfiore, Pinter, & Brown, 1988) who developed a procedure called a "high-p request sequence" (Cooper, Heron, & Heward, 2007). In experiments with non-compliant students, a subject's willingness or unwillingness to perform a series of simple requests was evaluated. Based on the evaluation, each request was then categorized as high-p or low-p. According to Mace (1996), in order to increase the "persistence of compliant behavior…" several requests for high-p behavior (e.g. high-fives, etc.) were delivered followed by a low-p request (e.g. "Come here", "stand up"). Experimenters found that, during the treatment condition, mean compliance with low-p instructions increased from 40 – 50% to over 90%.

The facilitation effect of low-p behavior following a series of high-p requests has been well established (Sprague & Horner, 1990; Mace & Belfiore, 1990) and applied to a variety of behaviors including spelling (Neef, Iwata, & Page, 1990), social interaction (Davis, Brady, Hamilton, McEvoy, & Williams (1992), food acceptance (Patel, 2002), and academic behavior (single-digit multiplication problems followed by three-digit multiplication problems (Belfiore, Lee, Vargas, & Skinner, 1997).

Mace's intention to increase the "persistence of compliant behavior" references work by Nevin et al. (1983) suggesting that behavior with a strong history of reinforcement (i.e. high-p) develops "response strength" similar in principle to *mass* in physics, that could be called *behavioral momentum*. Just as heavy objects in motion are more difficult to stop than lighter ones, behaviors that have high "response strength" tend to persist, even during interference from distractions, changes in tasks, or weak reinforcement schedules. Persistence has been shown to occur in humans during visual discriminations (Dube & McIlvane, 2001), household chores (Mace, Mauro, Boyajian, & Eckert, 1997), stereotypy (Ahearn, Clark, Gardenier, Chung, & Dube, 2003), and sports (Roane & Kelly, 2004).

To summarize the high-p/low-p research: in a number of studies spanning a variety of behaviors, a series of high-probability behavior requests were followed by a low-probability behavior requirement. Facilitation of the low-p behavior was reported and may represent a phenomenon related to high response strength behavior called *persistence* or *behavioral momentum*.

Additional practical questions have also been discussed in related research concerning the parameters of producing a facilitation effect in high-p/low-p strategies:

Are all high-p and low-p behaviors equivalent when it comes to the facilitation effect?

- Studies of high-p request series ranked high- and low-p behaviors and found the best facilitation effects to occur when the highest probability behaviors were requested and performed first

Specifically, which high and low probability tasks have been paired in studies?

Some successful pairings have included:

- Simple social requests (high-fives) followed by household chores
- Single-digit math problems followed by three-digit math problems
- Receptively identification of preferred items followed by instructions to interact socially
- Eating bites of preferred foods followed by bites of non-preferred foods
- Mastered spelling words followed by non-mastered spelling words

How long should the high-p behavior occur before switching to a low-p request?

- Hock & Mace (1986) scheduled three-four high-p requests before a single low-p request
- Neef et al. (1990) alternated known and unknown spelling words
- Belfiore et al. (1997) scheduled three easy multiplication tasks before one hard multiplication task
- Eckert, Boyajian, & Mace (1995) found that more frequent high-p trials preceding the switch to low-p requests resulted in greater facilitation of low-p requests

How close together must the high-p and low-p behaviors occur?

- Mace et al., 1988 stress the necessity of contiguity of the high-p behavior to the low-p behavior. Houlihan, Jacobson, & Brandon (1996) found that five second delays in switching to the low-p request were more effective than 20 second delays

How long can the low-p behavior occur before a return to high-p behavior is necessary?

- Cohen (1998) reported that the strength of the behavioral momentum effect is localized and gradually tapers off the longer the low-p behavior is repeated

Must low-p and high-p behaviors be similar?

- Maybe, to some degree. Mace suggests that the occurrence of high-p behavior facilitated the occurrence of low-p behaviors in part because they were part of the same *response class*. For example, "Give me a high-five" and "Come here and sit" are both classified as *requests*. Through implementation of the procedure, requests by instructors for high-p behavior become discriminative stimuli for successful responding and reinforcement. When some (or several) of these conditions continue into a second task immediately following, the student may generalize (continue to respond) even though some of the stimuli have changed. In a low-p request following a high-p request situation, usually most stimuli (reinforcement, setting, personnel, etc.) would be identical except for the nature of the requested behavior. According to Killu et al (1998), some degree of stimulus control may be transferred from the high-p request to the low-p request through the inclusion of common features of the task that accounts for the resulting improved low-p behavior. Nevertheless, in *all* of the current studies the topography of the low-p behavior differed to some extent. In the author's experience, response topographies may differ considerably without interfering with the facilitative effect. Possibly, reinforcement delivery is more critical than response class. Mace et al. (1998) found that one of the most important variables in effectiveness of the procedure depended on the rate of reinforcer delivery with rapid, very short latency reinforcer delivery the most effective. Therefore, if rapid reinforcer delivery rate is maintained, interspersal of mastered spelling words with non-preferred math problems may work as well as interspersing mastered and non-mastered spelling problems or mastered matching may be effectively interspersed with non-mastered receptive identification.

There are probably some practical limits. As Cohen (1998) reported, the effects of facilitation are local and limited in time. Switching between a task that is located at a classroom table and a task performed in the next room five minutes later is unlikely to create much momentum. Program authors should design high-p/low-p sequences with low-p tasks that are similar to high-p tasks in key ways. For example, a student is asked to play a simplified "Concentration" game where he easily matches words. Following every third successful match, he is requested to read the last word

Are there any other factors to keep in mind when designing high-p/low-p sequences?

- Yes, there is one more design consideration worth mentioning. Facilitation of the low-p behavior may also result if the student simply fails to discriminate a changeover from the high-p to the low-p behavior. In the game of *Simon Says*, a rapid rate of responding results, over a period of trials, in the subject being less attentive to a change in instructions. This effect could occur if responses come under partial control of aspects of the task such as the inter-trial interval. A student responding rapidly, several times in a row to the same instruction eventually responds less to the instruction and more to the particular rhythm of responding, thereby becoming less sensitive to a subtle change in the instruction. Indeed, the aim of the player calling the instructions in *Simon Says* is to entice another player to make errors by encouraging a transfer of stimulus control *away* from the instruction, "Simon says do this." This is achieved by establishing a rapid rate of responding combined with an extended fixed rhythm of correct responding before abruptly switching to "Do this", strongly inviting an error in discrimination.

    Interfering with the student's ability to discriminate between high and low-p behavior requests requires establishing a momentum of high-p behavior that absorbs the student so completely that he fails to perceive a change in response requirements. With time and practice, one might expect that a person could improve in their ability to detect changes, especially if reinforcement is strong enough. This occurs with very low-p behaviors where motivation is high to avoid them. However, with well-designed sequences where the low-p task is well integrated into the action of high-p behavior, the participant is likely to perform it without even thinking (like a computer game that rapidly presents simple, attractive and exciting (high-p) response opportunities for several minutes before requiring the participant to engage in a short, difficult (low-p) task before continuing).

Sample Sequences

When constructing program sequences based on the foregoing analysis and principles, program authors address three major goals:

- Improve sustained engagement during multi-step performances
- Improve motivation and facilitate completion of complex tasks
- Create approximations of functionally relevant natural environment tasks

Each sequence author is free to place instructional programs together in a nearly endless number of combinations as long as the end result successfully addresses the needs of the student. Many early learning performances are good candidates for simple sequences. For example, students in discrete-trial instruction often establish a repertoire of early to intermediate-level skills that includes some or all of the following:

- Manipulating objects and materials
- Matching
- Identifying pictures based on spoken words
- Naming pictures
- Counting items
- Drawing figures
- Writing letters
- Naming features, functions, or classes of items
- Sorting
- Reading words
- Sequencing

Skill sequences are built from combinations of these and other performances that greatly extend and enhance the student's capabilities and satisfy all three major goals of sequence writing. Writing programs that are based on sequences, therefore, is often of great benefit from almost the very beginning of programming. The length, complexity, and difficulty of sequences increases as the student is able to incorporate additional individual skills. In the following sequence examples, a number of possible combinations of skill programs are listed that illustrate relatively simple sequence designs that may function effectively for students, depending on their skill repertoires, learning styles, and history of reinforcement. These designs are intended as samples and should be considered as a starting point for program designers.

Turn Page → Label → Check Off

Step	Target Performance		Step Attribute
1	Turn Page	Receptive Instructions: Turn page ("Turn the page") [3-ring binder with 5-10 pages inside sheet protectors; words or sentence printed on pages]	Mastered, High-P
2	Label	Expressive Labels, Features, Functions Class, etc.: (Wh-question)	Not Mastered
3	Check Off	Writing: Makes check mark with dry erase marker	Mastered, High-P
Comments			
• Opening book and turning page makes a good initial observing response to engage the student • Adjust number of pages to length of task • Can mix wh-questions. If the labeling instruction is the same for all pages, direction can be faded. Mixed mastered and non-mastered pages generate good responding momentum • Check mark should be accompanied by praise. Student should independently turn the page immediately after making the check mark			

Select → Verb → Location

Step	Target Performance		Step Attribute
1	Select	Receptive Instruction: Pick an object from a large array ("Pick one")	Mastered, High-P
2	Verb	Receptive Instruction: Performs unusual or silly action with object ("[Verb] it")	Mastered, High-P

3	Location	Receptive Instruction: Puts object in unusual or silly location ("Put it [location]")	Mastered, High-P
Comments			

- Simple combination of receptive mastered activities

- Chain repeated several times

- Fun actions ("Put it on your head", "Make it fly") motivate the student; they may be alternated with more routine actions

- Putting in a location also functions to clear the area for the next repetition of the chain

Select → Count → Write

Step		Target Performance	Step Attribute
1	Select	Receptive Instructions: Picks item from large facedown array of cards ("Pick one")	Mastered, High-P
2	Count	Quantitative Concepts: Count up to 10 items ("Count these")	Not-mastered, Low-P
3	Write	Writing: Writes numeral just counted ("Now write that number on your paper.")	Mastered, High-P
Comments			

- Short, simple sequence to practice counting and 1:1 correspondence

- Selecting the item enhances choice and attention/engagement

- Counting is followed by writing the number; this should be a mastered task if it is to reinforce counting.

- The sequence interposes two steps (Writing and Selected) between counting trials, which may enhance attention for some students

- Step 1 could be replaced by presenting a worksheet with varying numbers of identical figures, objects, or shapes. The student would circle all examples of a given shape before proceeding to count them in Step 2.

Select → Read → Match → Copy → Type

Step		Target Performance	Step Attribute
1	Select	Receptive Instructions: Picks sample from facedown array of cards ("Pick one") and turns over	Mastered, High-P
2	Read	Reading Words: Reads word printed on card ("Read")	Mastered, High-P
3	Match	Matching: Match word on sample card to picture on second multi-choice array placed face up	Mastered, High-P
4	Copy	Copy printed word on lined paper with pencil	Mastered, Low-P
5	Type	Stand up, move to computer and type word into document, press enter key to move to next line, return to desk	Preferred, High-P
Comments			

- Reading is followed by a comprehension match

- Writing is a task that is frequently non-preferred by students. In this sequence it is sandwiched between two high-p tasks

- The final step involves a highly preferred task, typing into the computer. It is a good opportunity to ask the student to independently move to a separate desk to accomplish this step and then move back to his original seat

Select → Name → Match → Put Away → Record

Step		Target Performance	Step Attribute
1	Select	Receptive Instructions: Picks sample from facedown array of cards ("Pick one") and turns over	Mastered, High P
2	Name	Expressive Labels: Names item, attribute, part, function, etc. ("What ___?")	Mastered, High P
3	Match	Matching: Match sample to identical item within second multi-choice array placed face up	Mastered, High P
4	Put Away	Place pair of cards in done bin	Mastered, High P

5	Record	Check off/cross out number of trial on clipboard	Mastered, High P

[Instructor replaces cards in both arrays]

Comments

- This sequence simply arranges mastered steps into a more complex arrangement. Naming and matching are the core performances but the addition of selecting, putting cards away, and checking off a trial counter with a pencil, adds some common housekeeping elements.

- Step 2 can be any wh-question, depending on the skill of the student

Select → Name → Name Feature → Name Function → Name Parts → Put Away

Step		Target Performance	Step Attribute
1	Select	Receptive Instructions: Picks item from large array ("Pick one")	Mastered, High P
2	Name	Expressive Labels: Names picture of item ("What is it?")	Mastered, High P
3	Name Feature	Expressive Labels: Names color ("What color?")	Mastered, High P
4	Name Function	Functions: Expressive naming of function ("What does it do?", "What do you do with it?", "What does it say?") for tools, vehicles, animals	Mastered, High P
5	Name Parts	Attributes: Names two parts of tool, vehicle, or animal ("Name two parts of it.")	Mastered, High P
6	Put Away	Receptive Instructions Verbs- Puts card into a bucket ("Ok, make it slide away", "Make it hop away", "Make it fly away.")	Mastered, High P

Comments

- This sequence requires the student to listen carefully to the wh-questions. Steps 2-5 should NOT be presented in a fixed order to encourage the student to listen carefully to the wh-question. This part of the sequence can be shorted from 4 steps to 1 or 2 steps initially to develop a solid conditional discrimination between wh-questions

- The last step is designed to end with some fun but still require listening

Addition: Select → Match Quantity → Select → Match Quantity → Count → Count On → Write → Type

Step		Target Performance	Step Attribute
1	Select	Receptive Instructions: Chooses numeral card from array ("Get a card")	Mastered, High P
2	Match Quantity	Match Quantity: Select matching quantity card from second array ("Match how many")	Mastered, High P
3	Select	Receptive Instructions: Chooses numeral card from array ("Get another card")	Mastered, High P
4	Match Quantity	Match Quantity: Select matching quantity card from second array ("Match how many")	Mastered, High P
5	Count	Quantitative Concepts: Count up to 10 items ("Count these")	Mastered, High P
6	Count On	Quantitative Concepts: Counts second quantity. Counts on from previous number ("Now count on" while indicating the second card)	Mastered, High P
7	Write	Writing: Writes total amount just counted ("Now write that number on your paper.")	Mastered, High P
8	Type	Writing: Type the quantity into computer ("Okay, type it")	High-P, Preferred Activity

Comments
• All steps are mastered in isolation but may not be mastered as part of the overall chain for target students
• Matching numeral to quantity simplifies the discrimination. An alternate arrangement might require the student to make a matching number of marks below the numeral
• Saying and writing the total number just counted can sometimes be difficult for a student. Practice in isolation if necessary
• Typing can be omitted as a step if the sequence needs to be shortened but it may be a satisfactory motivational step for a student

Read → Match → Repeat → Retell

Step		Target Performance	Step Attribute
1	Read	Reading: Reads sentence printed on card	Mastered, High P
2	Match	Reading Comprehension: Matches printed card to card illustrating action in sentence. Places picture cards in left-to-right sequence. (Puts sentence card away).	Mastered, High P
3	Repeat	Repeat Steps 2-5 times	
4	Retell	Reading Comprehension: Student retells story in sequence using pictures – one sentence for each picture	Not Mastered
Comments			

- Pictures provide intermediate product that helps retell.
- As a fading step, retell can be done without looking at cards or by looking at cards only when necessary
- Wh-questions can be added to sequence after retell

Select → Name → Spell → Write

Step		Target Performance	Step Attribute
1	Select	Receptive Instructions: Chooses card with picture of an object from array ("Get a card")	Mastered, High P
2	Name	Expressive Language: Names object on card	Mastered, High P
3	Spell	Spelling: Spells (orally) name of object	Not Mastered
4	Write	Writing: Writes name of object on worksheet	Not Mastered
Comments			

- Selection can be omitted if a more traditional spelling sequence is desired, similar to a spelling test. In that case, the teacher dictates the word instead of providing a card
- Spelling followed by writing may be too difficult or laborious for some students. If so, omit writing until spelling is easier

Find Place → Greet → Unpack → Listen → Perform 1 → Perform 2 → Pack → Move

Step		Target Performance	Step Attribute
1	Find Place	Student takes box with markers and paper to table, selects empty seat and sits	Not Mastered
2	Greet	Student says "Hello" to person on right and left	Not Mastered
3	Unpack	Student takes materials out of box and puts them on table. Places box out of the way	Mastered, High P
4	Listen	Student looks at teacher/group leader and waits quietly	Mastered, High P
5	Perform 1	Student follows direction with materials	Mastered, High P
6	Perform 2	Student follows second direction with materials	Mastered, High P
7	Pack	Student places materials back in box	Mastered, High P
8	Move	Student moves to next table	Not Mastered

Comments

- Sometimes group performances are mastered once the student has made a transition but the transition itself is not mastered. This sequence can be done with a small group or even a whole class that needs to learn to move in an orderly fashion. It is often worth the investment early in the year. Provide enough adults to avoid confusion. Move from step to step in a deliberate fashion

- Repeat movement 3-4 times

- Actions with materials should be simple (e.g. "Draw a circle", "Print your name", "Color the square red")

Listen → Repeat → Add

Step		Target Performance	Step Attribute
1	Listen	Receptive Labels: Look at object or listen to word presented; listen to person describe one attribute	Mastered, High P
2	Repeat	Repeat attribute last stated	Mastered, High P
3	Add	Describe attribute of object not previously stated	Not Mastered
Comments			

- Classroom discussion requires listening to peer and responding to topic, which can be very challenging to those with attentional issues. This sequence gives a simple structure to a class "discussion" that can be learned relatively quickly

- Can start by naming members of a given category before progressing to describing different attributes (e.g. "Tell me the name of a color."). Write down names as they are mentioned

- Participating students should already be able to describe objects in multiple ways. For example:
    - What is it called?
    - What color?
    - What parts?
    - What function?
    - What attributes (size, shape, long, short, tall)?
    - What is it made of?
    - Where do you find it?

- As a visual prompt, a list of words or icons can be displayed representing possible attributes. Cross out the word or icon as it is mentioned

- Can start in partnership with one adult and expand to two partners, then three, etc.

Manipulate → Report → Repeat

Step		Target Performance	Step Attribute
1	Manipulate	Receptive Instructions: Object Manipulation: Manipulate exploratory object according to instructions of an instructor. For example: "Pick up and look." "Turn over." "Hold like this." "Put in, on, under…" "Put a drop of water on it."	
2	Report	Expanding Language: Describes object or result of actions: Subject-Attribute ("The rock is green.") Modifier-Object ("Green rock.") Names parts ("Leaf, stem, flower.") Counts parts ("3 leaves.")	
3	Repeat	Repeat	

Comments

- Instructor is at head of class; student is at table with object to be explored and all needed materials

- Establish student performance individually and at a distance before joining small or whole class groups. When done with remote student performance, ensure that necessary prompts and reinforcement can be delivered if necessary

Chapter Appendix: Common Kindergarten Worksheet Instructions

- Color each picture red
- Color the _____ red
- Color the one that is different red
- Color the one that is the same red
- Circle the blue picture in each row
- Draw a picture of something else green
- Color the picture
- Color each picture the same color as the crayon above it
- Color the fruits and vegetables
- Cut out the shapes and glue them in the correct color box
- Trace the circle below. Then draw a line under the circle in each row
- Circles can be different sizes. Trace the circles below. Then color the pictures
- Draw an X on the pictures that have the shape of a circle
- Squares have four sides of the same length. Help Sue get home. Color the path that has only squares
- Trace and color each shape. Draw and color two more of each shape
- Look at the shapes in the picture. Color the circles blue. Color the squares red. Color the triangles green
- Cut out the shapes and glue them on paper to make a picture
- Help Jim get to the kite shop. Color the path that has only diamonds
- Draw a line to the matching pictures
- Trace the star below. Then draw a line under the star in each row
- Connect the dots in order to make your own stars
- Color the stars. How many stars?
- Look at the shapes. How many white shapes? How many blue stars?
- Draw a line from each shape to the basket it belongs in
- Bob is looking for stars. Help him find them. Color all the stars blue
- Listen to the riddle and tell me the answer:
    - I can move
    - You can ride in me
    - I have four circles

- My seat belts keep you safe
- What am I?
- Draw an X on the shapes in each row that are different from the first shape
- Color the shape in each row that looks the same as the first shape
- Draw an X on the picture in each box that is different
- Color the pictures in each row that go together. Draw an X on the one that does not belong
- Cut out the boxes below. Match the pictures that go together
- Opposites are things that are different in every way. Draw a line to match the opposites
- Draw a picture of the opposite
- Look at the pictures in each box. Circle the pictures that are big
- Look at the pictures in each box. Circle the pictures that are small
- Color the small pictures in each box orange. Color the big pictures purple
- Cut out the boxes below. Put the animals in order from smallest to biggest
- Circle the thing in each box that is long
- Circle the thing in each box that is short
- Circle the picture in each box that has something short
- Cut out the measuring stick at the bottom of the page. Measure each pencil below. How many boxes long is this pencil?
- Draw an X on the shorter pencil. Circle the longer pencil
- Use the measuring stick to measure these pencils
- Circle the picture that is taller. Draw an X on the picture that is shorter
- Circle the full container. Draw an X on the empty container
- Look at the picture. The sun is above the bird. Circle the pictures above the bird
- Look at the picture. The car is below the bird. Draw an X on the pictures below the bird
- Circle the picture that is above the others. Draw an X on the picture that is below the others
- Color the pictures above the clouds first. Then color the pictures below the clouds
- Trace and color the cat that is between the other cats. Color the mouse that is between the other mice
- Color the shape that is between the other shapes
- Draw a line from the top picture to the bottom picture
- Color the pictures on the left blue. Color the pictures on the right red
- Draw a line from the picture on the left to the picture on the right
- Names are special. We use capital letters to set them apart from other words. Circle the capital

letters in the names below
- Write your name. Circle the capital letter
- Write your name. Draw a picture of yourself doing something you like
- Write your house number on the house
- Write your address. Draw a picture to show where you live
- Write your phone number. Practice dialing it using the phone below
- Trace and write the letter A. Start at the dot. Say the sound the letter makes as you write it
- Circle the letters in each row that match the first letter
- Look at the letter each insect is holding. Circle the same letter below
- Trace and write the letter D. Start at the dot. Say the sound the letter makes as you write it
- Look at the uppercase letter in each row. Color each picture with a matching lowercase letter
- Draw a line from each uppercase letter to its matching lowercase letter
- Help the walrus get back to the sea by following the letters in ABC order
- Find out what the elves are making. Draw a line to connect the dots in ABC order
- Draw a line from each uppercase letter to its matching lowercase letter. Then color the pictures
- Help Adam get to the playground. Follow the letters in ABC order
- Color each fish that has an uppercase and lowercase letter that match
- Color all the letters red. Color all the numbers blue. Write the letter message below
- Color the spaces with the J sound blue. Color the other spaces yellow
- Help the birds find their nest. Follow the path with the pictures whose names begin with the same sound as nest
- Short Oo is the sound at the beginning of the word octopus. Say each picture name. Color the socks that have the short Oo sound. Does this octopus have enough colored socks?
- Say each picture name. Say each word. Draw a line from each picture to the word that names the picture
- Say each picture name. Cut out the words. Glue each word where it belongs
- Say the sound the letters make. Circle the pictures in each row that begin with the letter shown
- Pam only picks things whose names begin with the same sound as panda. Say the picture names. Circle each picture whose name begins with the same sound as Pam and Panda
- Look at the pictures on the quilt below. Say each picture name. If the picture begins with the same sound as quilt, color the square yellow. Color the other squares purple
- Look at the letter in each column. Cut out each picture and glue it under the correct beginning sound

What's Next?

***Put this chapter to work*: GENERALIZATION AND INCORPORATION**

Adopt the four strategy stages in the table *Promoting Transference of Skills to New Environments and Conditions:*

- o Discuss the table with program staff and identify target environments

- o Identify pivotal skills to generalize and incorporate

- o Identify concurrent and sequential conditions of task performance that are most important to your students

- o Identify other staff whose cooperation will be necessary when moving skills to new target environments

- Perform an ecological assessment for important target settings:

    - o Analyze the relevant conditions and contingencies of performance in the target setting

    - o Identify complex performance arrangements and break down into sequence components

- Connect all individualized programs with common core curriculum standards

- Build generalization strategies into ALL individualized student programs directed at the student's prioritized target environments:

    - o Sequential Modification

    - o Introduce to Natural Maintaining Contingencies

    - o Train Sufficient Exemplars

    - o Train Loosely

    - o Use Indiscriminable Contingencies

    - o Program Common Stimuli

    - o Mediate Generalization

    - o Train "To Generalize"

- Create a sequence library: programs with incorporated routines and conditions that function in natural environments:

    o Increase a student's duration of sustained on-task activity using multi-step sequences

    o Add functional ancillary steps to educational tasks (preparation, clean-up, etc.)

    o Teach a student to perform a multi-step "process"

    o Use low-p/high-p strategies to facilitate sequence performance

    o Use high-p/low-p strategies to facilitate sequence performance

Chapter 9

Data-Based Decision Making

Data-based decision making (DBDM) has been front and center in the field of education for some time. The No Child Left Behind Act of 2001 and current special education law require accountability of the instructional process in the form of objective measurement of results. Instructional "technologies" such as individualized programs and curricula, based on research methodologies and scientific principles are most effective when the result of their application is quantified and evaluated under unbiased and controlled conditions.[1] Objective measurement allows implementers to form a precise representation of behavior change, centered on the individual student, to guide the learning process through the course of inevitable and necessary program adjustments. Frequent student-centered progress measurement can provide the most accurate and definitive basis for such program adaptation in real-time – that is, in time to minimize errors and increase effectiveness of acquisition of the target skill.

---

[1] Baer, Risley, & Wolf, (1968) identified "technological" as one of the seven defining characteristics of Applied Behavior Analysis.

Results-driven corrections are a frequent part of daily life. For example, when operating a moving car, movements of the gas pedal, brake, and steering wheel are coordinated to maintain course. If the road turns left, the direction of the car is corrected with the steering wheel; if the car moves too rapidly, the brake is applied to correct the speed. Correction relies on the employment of precise feedback. A clear, unobstructed visual field, vestibular sensation, speedometers, and a variety of road markings and signs instantly informs the driver as to heading and velocity and allows for timely course revisions. So, too, with instruction; measurement of a student's response provides information on which the implementer acts. When interventions are "blind," barriers to learning cannot be avoided and, ultimately, the student is adversely affected.

This chapter is concerned with the measurement and analysis of the results of instruction for individuals in Applied Behavior Analysis. The science of Applied Behavior Analysis is rather unique in its focus on evaluation and control of the behavior of single individuals that makes it ideal for DBDM purposes in educational settings, where individualized instruction is paramount. Three sections are presented:

- Creation of measureable instructional objectives

- Systematic data collection and graphing

- Using measurements to identify instructional barriers and make decisions on revision of instruction

Creation of Measureable Instructional Objectives

"Progress" measures the process of acquisition of a target behavior. Targets are specified in a manner that must respect the validity of the desired behavior. Thus objectives must include:

1. An objective, observable, and measurable definition of the behavior

2. Specification of performance conditions

3. Specification of performance criteria

Observing and Describing Behavior

According to a prominent textbook on behavior analysis, a behavior is:

"...an organism's interaction with its environment that is characterized by detectable [movement] in space through time of some part of the organism ...that results in a measurable change in the environment" (Johnston and Pennypacker, 1993, p. 23).

From the standpoint of behavior analysis and teaching, descriptions of behavior that contain the most useful information use words that are objective, observable and measurable. Everyday language is filled with imprecise speech that often leads to incorrect interpretations and confusion about behavior. We might report that a person was "unhappy" earlier in the day even though all that was observed was an intense look on the person's face during a study time. A child who has tantrums might be described as "angry" at his teachers or "rebellious." When motives or internal emotional states are assigned to behavior, a biased interpretation of facts is imposed on those exposed only to the conclusions of the person reporting the behavior, not the raw facts. Furthermore, such descriptions are difficult to talk about consistently. How often is the student "unhappy?" Even a close observer may not consistently identify behavior described so imprecisely.

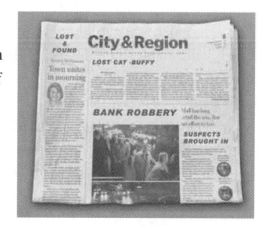

For example, recently an item appeared in the fictitious newspaper, *The Non-Behavioral Daily Times*. On the first page of the City & Region section under "Lost & Found," a notice seeking the return of a lost cat read, "Please look out for Buffy, our family cat. She was lost yesterday. She is loving, playful, curious, and a real rascal. If found, please call 456-8934." On the same page a headline reads: "Bank Robbery" and follows with: "The State Bank was robbed yesterday by five men who got away with $50,000. Witnesses described the men as suspicious-acting, fearful, aggressive, hostile, cruel, and unintelligent. Police are investigating."

Such imprecise descriptions are open to interpretation. Behavior, along with lost cats and bank robbers, is most usefully described in *objective* terms, using words that describe observable actions or qualities of the behavior and avoiding interpretations or *inferred mental states*.

Characteristics of Behavior

Using action words is the first big step towards the scientific study of behavior. If the behavior is objectively described its occurrence can be measured. Six aspects of the occurrence of behavior are especially useful in crafting even more precise definitions:

- **Topography** refers to the shape or form of the behavior
- **Frequency** refers to the number of times a behavior occurs during a particular time period
- **Duration** refers to how long a particular behavior lasts
- **Latency** refers to how much time passes between a prompt or initial event of some kind and the occurrence of the behavior
- **Inter-response time** refers to the amount of time elapsed between responses
- **Magnitude** refers to the force with which a behavior occurs

Many baseball fans seem to be obsessed with the details of behavior of all types. They describe the *topography* of a swing. They measure the *frequency* of pitches thrown, strikes, balls, singles, doubles, home runs, wins, and losses. Sports fans also measure the *duration* of the game or even the duration of the "hang time" of a curve (length of time in the air). *Latency* measures how much time elapses between gaining possession of the ball and scoring (football). *Magnitude* could be measured in the force of a punch (boxing) or the loudness of a noise. Sometimes magnitude is estimated or inferred from the results of the behavior like measuring the distance of travel of the baseball off the bat (a "hard" hit) or the speed of the baseball thrown (a "fast" ball).

Behavioral Definitions and Objectives

When behavior change is important, precise behavioral definitions are indispensable. Language needs to help ensure that observers will *consistently* and *reliably* identify the occurrence of a behavior. In other words, a single observer will identify each time Behavior X occurs *and* at least one more observer will agree. Behavioral definitions are especially useful when creating objectives for instruction and, as listed previously, contain three components that work together:

Component 1: Behavior

Component 2: Conditions of occurrence

Component 3: Criteria

Component 1, specification of the *behavior*, is limited to action words ensuring observability. Components 2 and 3 are designed to improve precision. The *conditions* of occurrence describe the exact context of the performance while the *criteria* of the performance identify measurable parameters of relevant behavior characteristics.

Behavior	Conditions	Criteria
The student will **place** a picture card on top of an identical card	Within a field of 3 choices, when given an identical card and the direction, "Match"	Novel pictures, 90% of trials, 2 consecutive sessions
The student will **name** an object	When an object is displayed at eye level within 2 feet and given the direction, "What is this?"	10 objects, 85% of trials, 2 consecutive sessions
The student will **copy** a word	Using a marker and white board, when shown an index card with the word printed and given the direction, "Write this word"	15 new words, forming letters of any size but conformed to the shape of the sample, letters equal size, spaced evenly and close together, and bottoms within ¼ inch of line drawn on the board. All letters match sample, 2 consecutive sessions

The three objectives defined in the table above contain the three components listed for three common target performances. The verb in each specification of behavior is shown in bold type. By itself, the specification of the behavior makes it possible for the reader to picture a student engaging in the behavior, but the conditions and criteria add the precision necessary to decide whether a performance has occurred exactly as the objective author intends. From the earlier discussion of performance conditions in the previous chapter, it should be apparent that any number of conditions could be specified for a particular target and, in the present examples, additional conditions could be included. For example, conditions related to the setting and instructional format are less detailed; it is not clear whether instruction will occur in discrete trials, a small group, at a table, in music, etc. Sometimes, such conditions are specified outside of the objective in an attempt to avoid long and unwieldy definitions. Nevertheless, many programs require attention to more involved specifications of conditions, such as when generalization to new environments is part of the objective or if the performance will be incorporated into more complex routines:

- ...when directed in a small group

- ...as part of the morning meeting routine

- ...when asked by a peer during a free play activity

- ...using a notebook with lined paper and pen

- ...in a show and tell group activity

Criteria of the performance offer an additional opportunity to add performance specifications, especially those relating to the characteristics of behavior including topography, frequency, duration, latency, or magnitude. Measures of the accuracy of the performance within a session are sometimes accompanied by a measure of the durability of the performance across time. For example: "90% correct for 2 consecutive sessions" combines accuracy ("90% correct") and durability ("for 2 consecutive sessions") to specify when a performance is considered mastered. Depending on the nature of the desired behavior, other criteria may be important to specify. For example, writing goals, like the sample goal above for copying a word, provides several criteria related to the topography of the performance including how letters should be formed, spaced, sized, and positioned. Without this information, it would be difficult to discriminate between how the objective author intended to define the "correct" and "incorrect" formation of letters. Criteria vary considerably among performances and can involve each of the characteristics of behavior:

- ...five times per minute
- ...within five seconds
- ...for 20 seconds or more
- ...loud enough to hear from across the room
- ...pausing less than 1 second between actions
- ...including subject, verb, and object

Learning Sets

Criteria for objectives also include a specification of the set of performances comprising the target behavior. For example, if a student is learning to name objects, a specific set of objects should be defined in the criterion (or separately), including the identity, number and nature of the objects such as: "20 objects commonly found in a classroom (pencil, book, stapler, marker...)." The set, sometimes called a *learning set*, varies with the nature of the performance. Learning sets for discrimination tasks, behavior chains, and "shape to criterion" tasks are common:

- **Discrimination tasks** generally involve conditionally performing an action dependant on the presence of a particular discriminative stimulus. Learning sets for discrimination tasks are comprised of individual targets included within the stimulus class associated with the discrimination:

Sample Discrimination Tasks and Learning Sets

Stimulus Class	Discriminative Stimuli	Conditional Performance	Individual Targets (Learning Set)
Pictures of Objects	Array of 3 cards, each with different picture of object. Card presented to student with picture of a target matching one of the cards. Direction: "Match"	Student places sample card on matching card in array	Car, bus, block, marker, spoon, cup, dog, house, etc.

Objects	Presenting object and direction: "What is this?"	Student names object corresponding to direction	Pencil, fork, string, penny, doll, truck, etc.
Auditory Instructions to perform motor actions	Spoken direction: "[Verb]"	Student performs motor action corresponding to direction	Stand up, turn around, wave, clap, "come here," etc.
Color cards	Presenting colored card and direction: "What color?"	Student names color corresponding to card presented	Blue, red, green, yellow, orange, purple, black, white, pink, grey, brown
Printed letters	Pencil, paper, direction: "Write [letter]"	Student writes letter on paper corresponding to direction	a-z; A-Z
Wh-Questions	Picture of object in photograph depicting multiple attributes; direction: "[What color? vs. What doing? vs. Where? vs. Who?]"	Student names attribute in picture corresponding to question	Any combination of 11 colors, 5 locations, 7 occupations, 10 actions (each listed)

Some discrimination performances are not limited to a particular set of stimuli but are intended to *generalize* to all items, including novel ones, within a stimulus class. For example, the skills of identical matching and imitation are not limited to a specific set of items, pictures, or actions, but eventually generalize to *all* items, pictures, or actions, even those that the student has not seen before. Individual target performances within discrimination tasks are generally added a little at a time as items are mastered, leading, in some cases, to very large, unwieldy numbers. Therefore, during some instructional sessions, only a portion of the mastered set is presented. This requires implementers to implement strategies to maintain mastery of items of the set included in sessions only occasionally.

- **Behavior Chain** learning sets are comprised of the steps of a task that are done in a particular order. For example, a handwashing learning set includes a list of 12 steps required to successfully wash hands. The invariable order of completion of the steps is a defining aspect of this type of learning set. In addition, as opposed to discrimination learning sets, all items of the learning set are generally performed during a session – prompts may be temporarily used to assist with those that are not independently performed:[2]

---

[2] See Chapter 5: *Prompts and Prompt Hierarchies*.

Sample Learning Set for Behavior Chain Tasks

Skill	Discriminative Stimuli	Conditional Performance	Individual Targets (Learning Set)
Handwashing	Presence of sink, soap, towel; direction: "Wash your hands"	Student performs all steps of directed task. The completion of each step produces discriminative stimuli that set the occasion for the next step	1. Approach sink 2. Turn on water 3. Wet hands 4. Get soap on hands 5. Rub palms together 6. Rub backs of hands 7. Rinse hand under water 8. Turn off water 9. Take towel 10. Rub towel on palms 11. Rub towel on backs 12. Throw away towel

- **Shape to Criterion** learning sets are comprised of performances whose *conditions* and *criteria* vary but whose general topography does *not* vary. For example, a student is given a direction to retrieve a remote object from a shelf or other location across the classroom. At the beginning of the program the student retrieves any of a set of objects from a small table in front of him (within one foot) but is not successful if the objects are placed farther away. The performance goal, therefore, maintains the topography of the behavior (retrieving a named object) while establishing a learning set composed of increasing distances of retrieval. Shape to criterion learning sets follow an established order of increasing difficulty or complexity:

Sample Learning Set for Shape to Criterion Tasks

Skill	Discriminative Stimuli	Conditional Performance	Individual Targets (Learning Set)
Retrieving remote objects	In classroom, with familiar object in sight; direction: "Get the [object] and come back"	Student retrieves object and returns to seat vs. performing another action	1. Retrieves known object from table – 2 feet 2. Retrieves known object from table – 3 feet 3. Retrieves known object from table – 5 feet 4. Retrieves known object from table – 8 feet 5. Retrieves known object from table – 12 feet 6. Retrieves known object from table – 20 feet

Complex Sets

Learning sets encompass all of the individual performances, behavior components, conditions, or criteria subsumed under the established objective. A learning set for a given objective can include an array of topographies, conditions, and criteria. For example, a discrimination task could be presented to the student that defines ten individual targets under identification of animals as well as three performance conditions and two criteria:

Skill	Discriminative Stimuli	Conditional Performance	Individual Targets (Learning Set)
Naming pictures of animals	In classroom, when shown picture of animal; direction: "What animal is this?"	Student names animal displayed in picture	Tiger, lion, cat, dog, raccoon, mouse, fox, elephant, skunk, deer 1. When shown at desk 2. When shown at small group table 3. When shown in whole class group, sitting at desk, teacher in front of class 10 feet away • Names within 5 seconds • Names within 2 seconds

Management of Learning Sets

Program plans address the acquisition of individual learning targets within learning sets according to the needs of the student, the nature of the performance, and the characteristics of the sets. Task analysis and errorless teaching techniques are applied as appropriate. Frequent performance opportunities are essential in achieving an appropriately intensive learning environment. In addition, protocols are established to govern the details of common decisions regarding the progress of an individual through the elements of the various learning sets from initial presentation through mastery of the terminal performance. Such protocols are centered on the performances specified in the learning set and comprised of highly defined practical procedures that control every important aspect of program implementation.[3]

Program protocols take a variety of specific forms but, essentially, accomplish the same set of indispensable tasks:

- Initial measurement of the student's performance with respect to the new objective
- Composition of the initial presentation of learning set items
- Measurement of ongoing student performance on the learning set
- Determination of mastery of learning set items
- Conditions and procedures for adding additional targets
- Procedures for assessing and maintaining previously acquired targets
- Procedures for identification of barriers to progress
- Criteria for revision of protocol or procedures based on student performance
- Procedures for ensuring program integrity (accuracy and consistency of implementation of procedures)

---

[3] Applied research is, of course, a primary source for information about protocols. Don't miss the free searchable database of (over 2.7 million articles and 1272 journals) the US National Library of Medicine (National Institutes of Health) at http://www.ncbi.nlm.nih.gov/pmc/

Initial Measurement

Objectives are added to a student's plan when assessment has determined that the student has *not mastered* the target performance within the parameters specified by the objective (behavior, conditions, and criteria). Program protocols specify appropriate procedures to initially measure the performance of the student with respect to each terminal performance considered for inclusion. Sometimes called "initial probes," or "cold probes," a version of the instructional program is presented to the student under specific evaluation conditions to assess whether the student can already engage in the terminal performance partially or completely. During initial probes the program is typically presented in the same manner as during instruction, using the terminal conditions, criteria, and learning set. In contrast to instructional sessions, initial probe sessions usually do not offer prompts, reinforcement, or error correction since any of the three would tend to influence the performance of the student and, thereby, interfere with an impartial assessment. After the student responds to the presentation of the trial, minimal feedback is offered (when necessary, a neutral comment like "good try" or "okay" is inserted before presenting the next stimulus) and the next trial is presented.

> **THREE NOs:**
> **Initial Data Probes**
> - No prompts
> - No reinforcement
> - No error correction

Learning set items for discrimination tasks are probed in randomly presented trials. To ensure adequate confidence in measurement, probe sessions for discrimination tasks are conducted with a *minimum number of trials* for presentation of each item, which may be exceeded with students but not reduced. For evaluation purposes, the more trials conducted without serious degradation in student effort, the more assurance that a performance is a true measure of the student's ability. However, accommodations could be necessary to keep the overall number of trials within the student's capabilities. For example, if a new program has 40 words in its learning set, a probe may be broken up over two sessions. Alternately, evaluation of the second 20 words might be postponed until after the first 20 are learned.

Minimum Trials Presented During Probes – Discrimination Tasks
New Items
3 trials per item

For shape to criterion tasks, probes start at either end of the learning set: the terminal performance condition may be immediately presented in a session or the entire series of performance conditions may be presented starting from the easiest and working towards the hardest. If the student is suspected of having some ability but it is clear that he cannot complete the final performance, the second option (starting with the easiest step) will work better to identify the point where the student begins to fail. As with discriminations, repetition of the probe conditions helps in establishing a consistent result. With shape to criterion tasks, however, the entire probe is repeated at a later time rather than presenting multiple trials at once.

With behavior chains, performance of the entire learning set is completed within one session. After giving the initial direction, the evaluator assesses whether or not each step of the chain is performed independently. Since performance of elements of the chain produce effects that are prerequisite to completing later steps, a mechanism is required that allows the individual to continue responding, even after a failed performance earlier in the chain. For example, when a student is evaluated on a chain of handwashing steps and cannot turn on the water, the chain is interrupted and later steps will not be evaluated. Therefore, probe procedures stipulate that if the student fails to perform part of the chain, assistance is given to the student until he completes the failed step and progresses to the next portion of the chain where evaluation resumes. The session continues similarly until the chain is completed. As with shape to criteria tasks, sessions are repeated only after sufficient time has elapsed to obtain a consistent finding; with some chains, especially longer ones, immediate repetition is avoided.

Sample Protocol - Initial Probes		
The **initial probe** is designed to provide a baseline on a new skill (all learning set items)		
For **BEHAVIOR CHAINS**, the student performs all steps of the chain. Provide prompts only if the student fails to correctly complete a step and only help enough to get the student past that step.	For **DISCRIMINATION LEARNING TASKS**, present the items of the learning set at least three times each, randomized throughout the session.	For **SHAPING TO CRITERIA TASKS**, have the student perform the task starting with the easiest criterion and then gradually work through the harder criteria as the student is successful.
PROBE CONDITIONS: Except as noted above, DO NOT reinforce correct performances, prompt, or use error correction for incorrect performances. Move from one trial to the next with a generic encouragement like "Okay" or "Thanks, here's the next one."		
Record a **plus** or **minus** for a trial or step that is independently correct (+) or incorrect (-).		
Mark a + for each step independently performed **in the correct order**. Repeat the probe two times on consecutive days. Consider steps with a + on both sessions to have "passed" the probe.	If the percent correct of a learning set item is 100%, mark the item as "passing" the probe. Continue probe sessions until all learning set items are assessed.	Mark the highest step performed to the stated criteria with a + and consider that step as "passing" the probe.

Additional Considerations for Conducting Data Probes

Ending Probes Early. Even though efforts are made to disguise whether a student responds correctly or incorrectly on a series of trials, the student may be aware that she is not performing a task adequately. At times the student might not respond at all to a probe trial. At the very least, with no reinforcement available, some students may find it difficult to continue probe trials for an extended period. If a student repeatedly responds incorrectly, fails to respond, or exhibits frustration during a probe, the instructor can consider ending the session early and resuming at a later time or designating the target performance *not mastered*.

Keeping Students Motivated. Although no reinforcement, prompting, or error correction is customarily provided during data probes, it is still important to maintain student motivation. When serious probing difficulties are encountered, it helps to intersperse trials of the probe with trials of mastered tasks. The mastered tasks receive reinforcement when the correct response is given but the probe trials do not. Effectively, the two programs are run concurrently with two different schedules of reinforcement. For example, a student's probe on receptive identification of colors could be run simultaneously with gross motor imitation, which is mastered. The session begins with three trials of imitation followed by two probe trials, followed by one trial of imitation, two more probe trials, etc.

Despite implementation of the procedures above, there are still students who are extremely sensitive to the absence of reinforcement and tend to underperform during initial probes. Underperformance results in failure of the probe and, therefore, at worst, the student will receive additional practice in a task that may actually be mastered. While this is not overtly harmful, it tends to slow down the learning process. For such students, implementers could depart somewhat from the protocol and offer reinforcement for correct responding on probe trials. (When this variation is employed, prompts and error correction are still not used during the probe trials.) Interpretation of the initial probe results implemented with reinforcement should consider that learning may have occurred during the probes.

Condition Sets

Probes of learning sets provide a baseline for decisions about target performances in an instructional program. Mastered set items are documented and additional targets are chosen that extend, combine with, intersperse with, or follow mastered performances and comprise the program's new list of targets. The illustration on the next page[4] shows a sample learning set for a program that teaches receptive identification of body parts. Below the program information are listed nine specific learning set items. Two were marked as mastered after an initial probe.

The entire learning set – all nine items – comprises the full list of individual targets selected for the program. They represent the final list which, when mastered, satisfies the terminal performance. When initiating the program, implementers using errorless

---

[4] This screen shot comes from the ABA curriculum development software program called *The ABA Program Companion 3.0 (ABA-PC3)* included with this book.

methodologies, usually present items a little at a time, gradually developing the student's repertoire and maximizing success. Therefore, a subset of the entire learning set is created, called in this protocol a "condition set." The condition set, depicted to the right of the full learning set contains both mastered items (head, nose) and three additional non-mastered items (belly, ears, chest). The condition set items encompass the acquisition and maintenance targets that are presented in the current teaching sessions. In this protocol, the condition set is given a unique name ("body parts") that is applied to all data collected on the set and displayed on graphs:

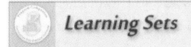

Student: Andrew G

General Area: Receptive Labels

Program: Body Parts - Receptive

Target Performance: Student locates specific body parts when requested.

Item Description	Type	Mastered	Current Condition: body parts
head	Maintain	04/09/13	head
nose	Maintain	04/09/13	nose
belly	Target		belly
chest	Target		ears
ears	Target		chest
hand	Target		
foot	Target		
mouth	Target		
chest	Target		

Managing Progress on the Learning Set

The criteria for mastery of items on the condition/learning sets is set by program designers to ensure a fluent and durable performance that is maintained when the performance is combined with additional performances and generalized to new settings. Some ABA programs find it convenient to include a standard or default accuracy and durability criterion for mastery that applies to many or all instructional programs, unless otherwise specified. For example, percent of items correct (accuracy) exhibited in a specified number of consecutive sessions (durability) are two criteria frequently applied to discrimination tasks, as illustrated in the condition set below:

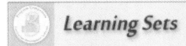

Student: Andrew G

General Area: Receptive Labels

Program: Body Parts - Receptive

Target Performance: Student locates specific body parts when requested.

Item Description	Type	Mastered	Current Condition: body parts
head	Maintain	04/09/13	head
nose	Maintain	04/09/13	nose
belly	Target		belly
chest	Target		ears
ears	Target		chest
hand	Target		90% of trials
foot	Target		2 consecutive sessions
mouth	Target		
chest	Target		
90% of trials	Criterion		
2 consecutive sessions	Criterion		

Mastery criteria are the subject of much discussion in Applied Behavior Analysis. Some practitioners[5] strongly advocate for fluency criteria that specify *rate of responding* in addition to, or instead of, percent correct. They argue that rate is a more sensitive and valid measure and that setting a high *rate of performance* criteria results in better generalization (Pennypacker, Gutierrez, & Lindsley, 2003; Kubina & Yurich, 2012).

---

[5] See the Kubina and Yurich (2012) book for an excellent overview of the area of behavior analysis called "Precision Teaching."

In addition to criteria, the conditions of performance of the task may enter into the specification of the condition set. As previously discussed, generalization and incorporation conditions are extremely relevant to acquisition of skills and, therefore, should be explicitly listed. For example, the setting and instructor variables could be specifically identified in a condition set:

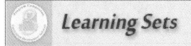

Student: Andrew G

General Area: Receptive Labels

Program: Body Parts - Receptive

Target Performance: Student locates specific body parts when requested.

Item Description	Type	Mastered	Current Condition: body parts
head	Maintain	04/09/13	head
nose	Maintain	04/09/13	nose
belly	Target		belly
chest	Target		ears
ears	Target		chest
hand	Target		90% of trials
foot	Target		2 consecutive sessions
mouth	Target		2 different instructors
chest	Target		at individual desk
90% of trials	Criterion		at table in common area
2 consecutive sessions	Criterion		
2 different instructors	Criterion		
at individual desk	Criterion		
at table in common area	Criterion		

Conditions and criteria included in mastery standards distinctly influence interpretation of student performance data; protocols should ensure that data displayed in graphs and tables are clearly identified and associated with the proper set specifications.

Prompts as Conditions of Performance

The previous chapter, "Prompts and Prompt Hierarchies," explored using instructor actions or environmental manipulations to assist students. When used, such assistance constitutes conditions of performance in themselves. Some learning sets specify prompts as items within condition sets. This is no different in principle from the inclusion of other conditions. For example:

Goal: The student will match a vehicle card to an identical card

- In a field of 5 cards
- When given a pile of 20 vehicle cards
- At his desk, in Room 5
- *When the instructor immediately points to the correct card in the field*

Prompt conditions are additional conditions on which student performance is based. The validity of measurements made under prompting conditions relies on the consistency of the prompting conditions. Prompts and prompt fading procedures present challenges to consistent specification of instructional conditions because they frequently change. Measurements made during one set of prompting conditions is not strictly comparable to measurements made during a different set. Protocols can address this problem by always attaching specific information on prompting conditions to the data set. For example, data collected with full physical prompts must be segregated from data collected with touch prompts or pointing prompts. Alternately, data from *all* prompted performance could be distinguished from data from independent performances. This topic will be a subject of discussion later in the chapter.

Measurement of Dependent vs. Independent Variables

Prompting protocols vary the prompts used according to student behavior. Decisions about the type of prompting to use are made according to a variety of criteria specified within the prompting protocol. Measurements of performance, therefore, may reflect instructor behavior rather than student behavior. It is difficult to pinpoint exactly what controls instructor actions from moment to moment when prompts are employed but accuracy and reliability of prompt application may be a problem. Protocols should objectively describe implementation conditions and follow practices that improve consistency:

- Specify a prompting condition that does not vary *within* a session and is not dependent on the student's behavior *during* the session. Set a mastery criterion that specifies when the prompting condition will be faded to the next lower condition *between* sessions. For example, define a prompting condition as:

    o Use partial physical guidance to assist a student to place a card on another card

    o Fade after 10 accurate performances to the next lower level of prompting

- Use stimulus prompts instead of instructor-based response prompts, which can be more objectively defined and faded

- Avoid data collection of prompted performances entirely in favor of intermittent probes where prompts are not used. Schedule intermittent probes every 3-5 sessions (or sooner) and follow the probe procedure described previously. Do not take data on regular teaching sessions. Graph probe session data. (See sample protocol for intermittent data collection in the following section)

Data Collection

Once target performances, conditions, and criteria are defined and highly structured into the equivalent of learning and condition sets, data collection issues center on the format and logistics of actual measurement. The nature of the learning sets and methodology of instruction contribute to the design of a data collection system. For example, Chapter 5 illustrates data collection grids for behavior chains and prompt hierarchies in addition to providing protocols for taking data on forward and back-chaining procedures. With discrimination tasks, learning sets become differentiated into targets that are mastered vs. those that are actively taught, requiring separate rows on a data sheet.

At any given moment, data collection should be capable of answering two questions:
- What progress is being made with respect to the acquisition of the active target item(s)?

- What is the present state of performance of the mastered item(s)?

The illustration below presents a sample data sheet for a discrimination task with two mastered items (designated "Maintain") and three active target items (designated "Target"). Each set item is placed within a grid on a separate row, with boxes for performance data to the right of each item. The separate collection of performance data for mastered and target items allows separate assessment of maintenance and acquisition, facilitating a more detailed analysis of progress and, especially, allowing problem items to be pinpointed should errors occur.

Grids like those above are convenient for the collection of trial-by-trial data in sessions. The results of each trial are noted for each learning opportunity according to data codes displayed above the grid. In the illustration, a simple plus or minus for "correct" and "incorrect" is provided but, as noted in Chapter 5, codes representing prompt hierarchy steps may be used).

A grid arrangement may be convenient for recording other common behavior characteristics such as rate of occurrence:

Prompt Hierarchy/Data Codes:

1	Occurrence	+ (plus)

Set/Condition: Sort Rate 1

Set timer for one minute and start. Record a plus in the appropriate box for each card correctly sorted;

Type	Item													
Target	Sort head - 1 min. sample													
Target	Sort nose - 1 min sample													
Target	Sort ears - 1 min sample													

Data Collection for Multiple Performances (Sequences)

When skills are performed in a pre-determined order as part of a multi-step process or program sequence, single skill data sheets become less desirable. A collection of pages, each with a single grid for program data requires awkward paper-shuffling. Placing the sequence of programs together, one after another, on the same page (or a short series of pages) minimizes the number of pages while maintaining the proper presentation order. A sample data sheet with this type of data collection arrangement is illustrated on the next page.

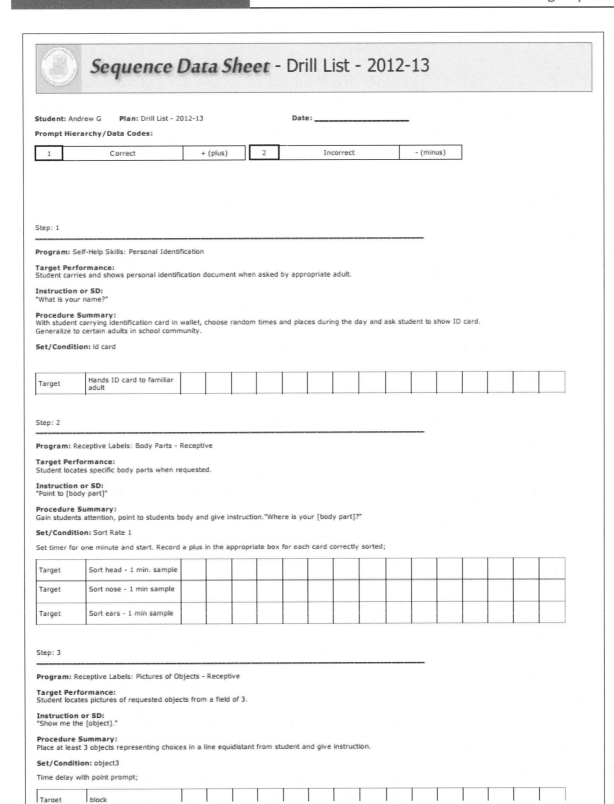

Facilitating or Streamlining Data Collection

Data collection is an indispensible tool for objective evaluation of student performance but it is sometimes criticized as intrusive, distracting, and even deleterious to effective instruction. Finding time for documentation of student performance may be challenging when instruction entails intensive, multi-step procedures, simultaneous manipulation of materials and split-second decisions to ensure a successful trial. But, needless to say, elimination of data collection is not a serious option if the integrity of the implementation is to be preserved, since all capacity to evaluate program effectiveness and student progress would be lost. At the same time, nothing is gained when performance measurement is preserved at the cost of procedural integrity. If implementation collapses, documentation becomes a moot point. Therefore, the methodology of data collection must adjust to the requirements and resources of the situation and accomplish its task without impinging upon the ability of the implementer to deliver accurate and effective instruction. In other words, data collection must be effective but do-able.

For data collection as well as most other aspects of well-designed individualized instruction, rehearsal and familiarity with procedures plays the most important role in easing strain. Many experienced teachers compare teaching to a ballet where each movement is choreographed and practiced until it is smooth and becomes second nature. Yet, even with practice there are situations that remain difficult and there is no reason why program designers should not employ every means possible to ensure that data collection does not entail unnecessary effort:

- **Device-Facilitated Data Collection:** laboratory-based procedures often use automated apparatus for measuring behavior, a kind of "Holy Grail" for those working in applied settings. True automatic (unattended) data collection is still a thing of the future, but device-facilitated data collection is becoming a reality. As of this writing, several software programs are available for tablets and smart phones that allow the user to set up convenient portable systems of data collection. While such systems require briefly looking away from the student and some degree of tapping buttons, navigating between screens, etc., they still simplify and speed up data collection. At the present time, most are not completely integrated with the student's curriculum and require time to set up and transfer information. Nevertheless, further development in this area holds great promise for the future.

- **Sampling and Intermittent Data Collection**: intermittent data collection in probes or samples can be relatively accurate (and even approaching the accuracy of continuous data collection) while leaving instructors free from data collection responsibilities during intervening teaching sessions. In addition, as discussed previously, data taken in probes may avoid measurement of instructor behavior since data is not collected for prompted performances. A sample protocol for conducting intermittent data probes is illustrated below:

Sample Protocol Intermittent Data Collection – P1 and P2 Probes		
P1 and P2 Probes are used to test whether, after teaching, a new stimulus has been learned to criterion and if the student should move on. They are also used to check on the **maintenance of progress** on the other items in the learning set (if applicable) and to **document** the student's progress.		
PROBE CONDITIONS: Except as noted above, DO NOT reinforce correct performances, prompt, or use error correction for incorrect performances. Move from one trial to the next with a generic encouragement like "ok" or "thanks, here's the next one."		
Default Criterion for Passing Probe 1 — For **BEHAVIOR CHAINS**, all steps that are independently performed during the probe are marked as passing the first probe.	For **DISCRIMINATION LEARNING TASKS**, if the percent correct of the target stimulus by itself is 100% AND the overall student performance on the trials is at least 90% the student has passed the first criterion.	For **SHAPING TO CRITERIA TASKS**, the target criteria is marked as passing the first probe if it is performed independently by the student
Data Probe 2 — If the first probe is passed, a **second** data probe is scheduled on the following day to test the durability of the performance gain and to help ensure that the student really is ready to move on. Whenever possible the second data probe should be performed with a different implementer.		
Passing Probe 2 — The steps that have passed the second probe are marked as mastered.	If the criterion is met (see above), the stimulus is marked mastered	The criterion that has passed the second probe is marked as mastered.
Resume Teaching — Resume teaching after the data probe(s), adding a new target stimulus if both probes were passed. Target stimuli that were not correctly performed in both Probe 1 and Probe 2 retain a designation of TARGET when teaching sessions are resumed.		

Compilation of Data

Individualized instructional programs present multiple opportunities for the student to respond to conditions and contingencies of instruction. Each performance is reduced to a single value linked to the condition set and performance conditions. For example, a single target performance is specified as follows:

Condition Set	Performance conditions	More Performance Conditions
Given that a random set of three objects...	...is presented in a field of three and a question is asked of the student, "What is this?"...	...at a desk, with a 1:1 instructor, with extrinsic reinforcers available ...

Performance Representation (Data Point)
<ul><li>...a "correct" response is counted with a plus if the student speaks the name of the object...</li><li>...an "incorrect" response is counted with a minus if the student does not speak the name of the object...</li><li>...a "fluent" response is counted with two plus signs if the student speaks the name of the object...</li></ul>

Performance Criteria
<ul><li>Within five seconds</li><li>Within two seconds (fluent)</li><li>Without assistance</li></ul>

A data point or "performance representation" is a simplified but valid delineation of the full performance. It does not communicate all information possible about the event – just the limited information meaningful in the context of the other information specified. Abstractions and simplifications of performances are quite helpful for comparing multiple measurements of one performance over time:

- **Correct vs. Incorrect**: target behavior is exhibited (or not exhibited) under specified conditions and criteria during one learning opportunity

- **Accurate**: target behavior is exhibited under specified conditions and criteria during one learning opportunity, *with or without prompts*

- **Independent**: target behavior is exhibited under specified conditions and criteria during one learning opportunity *without prompts*

- **Fluent**: A correct performance that occurs *at a specified rate*

Once data is collected, it is compiled into forms that facilitate analysis of the current status of the performance in comparison with all other points. Depending on the nature of the measurements, the forms usually include tables, statistics, and graphs. Tables of data may present the raw information about each performance sequentially for inspection by an evaluator, such as when implementers look through the grids on raw data sheets from day to day. Tables can also contain statistical transformations of raw data compiled for specified groupings of data. "Transformation" refers to a wide array of computations made on a set of data. Simple transformations include calculating sums or averaging and are commonplace in many ABA programs. More complicated transformations include sophisticated statistical analyses rarely employed outside of research.

Measurements of student performance can be grouped to focus on specific targets of inquiry. For example:

- **Individual Program Performance Grouped by Time:**
    - All trials within a session
    - All sessions within a day, week, month
- **All Program Performances Grouped by Time:**
    - All sessions within a day, week, month
- **Individual Program Performance Grouped by Implementer**
    - All sessions within a day, week, month
- **All Program Performances Grouped by Implementer**
    - All sessions within a day, week, month
- **Individual Program Performance Grouped by Trials**
    - Number of trials needed to reach a specified criterion

Data set groupings can also be created for caseloads, sequences, or whatever factors exist within the raw data. The most frequently seen data set is possibly compiled from all trials within a session for an individual program. For example, the result (correct or incorrect) of each of 10 trials completed during a short session is combined and transformed into the percentage of trials correct for the session using the formula:

Percent Correct = Number of Trials Correct/Total Trials x 100

Another often computed statistic is the frequency of occurrence of a target performance per unit of time (also called *rate*). For example, the rate of requesting by a student during a six-hour day is computed using the formula:

Rate of Occurrence = Total frequency of requests/six hours

Data for high frequency behavior that does not occur just within trials or sessions may be more conveniently collected using a system called "partial-interval recording." In this system, the day (or smaller time period) is divided into equal intervals. If a target behavior occurs one or more times, the corresponding interval is checked once. At the end of the day (or other designated time period), the number of intervals of occurrence of a target are summed and divided by the total number of intervals to calculate the percent of intervals of occurrence:

Percent of intervals of occurrence =
Sum of intervals of occurrence of target behavior/Total intervals x 100

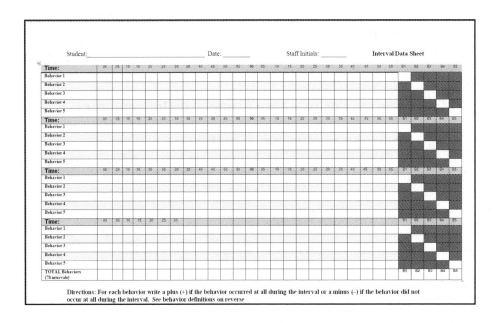

Sample Interval Data Sheet. Form divides a six-hour school day into 78 five-minute intervals for up to five target behaviors.

Graphing

Data is the abstraction of information about behavior, made possible by objective definitions and collected as a means of scientifically evaluating the results of instruction. Grouping and transformation of raw data into simple statistics, like those discussed above, is helpful in the process but an additional dimension of analysis is attained when data sets are displayed visually in graphs. While raw data and statistics reduce events to a series of separate numbered values, graphs visually display values in a spatial relationship where multiple bits of information are packed into a single point.

Construction of Graphs

Graphs for evaluating behavior generally consist of two *axes* that intersect at a single point (the *origin*) and extend vertically (*y-axis*) and horizontally (*x-axis*). Graphs with two axes are called two-dimensional because each event depicted on the graph (*data point*) contains two values, one for each axis. Two-dimensional graphs can represent many different phenomena. When data are related to learning, the change in value of a behavioral characteristic over time is often the most relevant representation. Therefore, a time value is often chosen for the x-axis while the numerical measurement of a characteristic of behavior (frequency, duration, magnitude, latency*)* is usually chosen for the y-axis. Sometimes, instead of a direct measurement of a behavior characteristic, a statistical transformation like *percent correct, frequency-per-hour, or percent of intervals* is chosen for the y-axis.

Simple two-dimensional graphs are drawn by placing the point of origin in the lower left hand corner of the graphing space and extending the two axis lines upwards and to the right. The length of one axis relative to the other is somewhat important for proper display. Recommendations for y:x proportions vary (1:1, 1:2, 3:5, 5:7) but in many implementation settings, an appropriate display can be made from a single sheet of 8.5 x 11 paper placed in landscape orientation which will accommodate an x (horizontal) axis that is roughly twice as long as the y (vertical) axis (1:2):

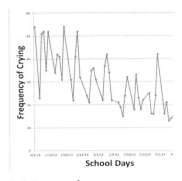
1:1 Proportion

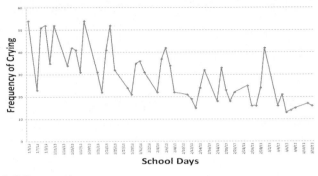
1:2 Proportion

A more critical determination for implementers constructing graphs is the scale adopted for each axis. The y-axis scale displays the value of the dependent variable – that is, the behavior of the student. The x-axis scale displays the value of independent variables. In an instructional setting this generally refers to instruction – the setting, materials, and methodology of teaching, or just the date of teaching sessions.

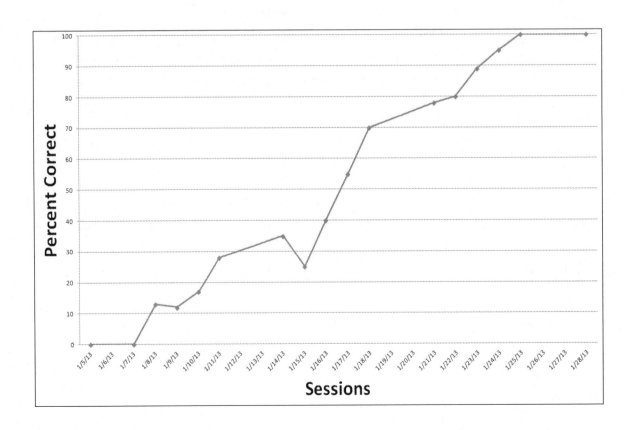

In the illustration on the preceding page, the y-axis depicts the percent correct for each of the session dates listed on the x-axis. Other variables that might be displayed on an x-axis include:

- Trials

- Locations (Cafeteria, Hallway, Classroom, Library, Gym)

- School personnel (Mrs. Smith, Mr. Brown, Principal Jones)

- Activities (Free Play, Group, Individual Instruction)

Sessions and trials occur within a time range and are said to represent a *continuous* set of data. Locations, school personnel, and activities represent discrete and separate sets of data that are called "discontinuous." Both continuous and discontinuous data labels are equally spaced along the x-axis with enough room to easily isolate one value from the next. The space between session dates or trial numbers is typically adjusted to display a meaningful range when evaluating the graph.

Values on the y-axis are determined to some extent by the expected range and variability of the data. In the example above, percent correct values vary between 0–100 and ten axis divisions (10, 20, 30, 40, 50, 60, 70, 80, 90, 100) are reasonable. Alternatively, if the *frequency of approaches to peers* during recess was expected to vary between 0-25, axis divisions might be set at 5, 10, 15, 20, and 25. Of course, there is no certainty that expectations of values will be met and, "outliers" (values that fall outside the established axis limits) may occur from time to time. If this occurs, the scale may be adjusted to encompass the broader range. With a computer assisted graphing program, redefinition of the scale is simple. With manually constructed graphs, a point is marked at the topmost position of the y-axis, below where the point should be located, with an arrow pointing upwards and the number value of the point noted in parentheses.

The maximum scale value of the y-axis affects the vertical position of data points and, hence, the visual impression conveyed by the graph as a whole. Consider the following four graphs. The first three display the same data set with different maximum y-scale values. The fourth graph displays the same data set with a different proportional length of x-axis to y-axis:

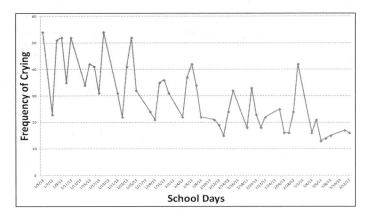

1:2 Proportion, 0-60 Y Scale

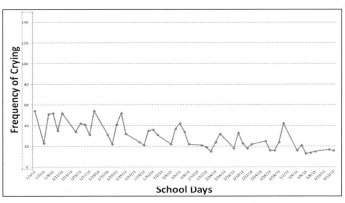

1:2 Proportion, 0-140 Y Scale

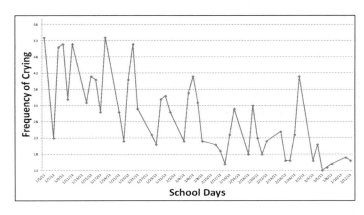

1:2 Proportion, 13-60 Y Scale

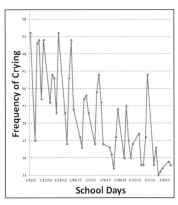

1:1 Proportion, 13-60 Y Scale

The y-axis scale in the graphs depicted above is divided into equal intervals meaning that the amount of distance between each division (10, 20, 30, etc.) is equal. Therefore, equal variations in the value of each data point on the graph are represented in the same manner regardless of value. For example, a data point with a y value of 4 is one vertical unit higher on the y-axis than a data point with the value of 3, just as a data point with the value of 3004 is one vertical unit higher than a data point with the value of 3003. The 1:1 ratio of value to height in equal interval graphs is not accepted as ideal by all behavior analysts. Some argue that a change in value from 3 - 4 should result in a *greater* change in y-axis height on the graph than a change in value from 3003 – 3004 because it is proportionally greater (33% is added to 3 to get 4 while only 3.3% is added to 3003 to get 3004). To correct for this, some program designers prefer to construct y-axis scales with logarithmic intervals such as the one illustrated below:

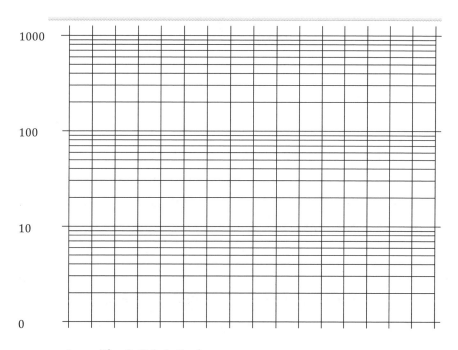

Logarithmic Y-Axis Scale

With logarithmic scales, the vertical distance between points *decreases* exponentially as the value *increases*. Therefore, the distance between the y-values 0 and 1 is the same as the distance between the values of 10 and 20, 100 and 200, and 1000 and 2000. Such scales are especially appropriate for displaying measurements of target behaviors that vary considerably in frequency (for example, between 10 and 1000).[6]

---

[6] For more information on semi-logarithmic graphs see Pennypacker, Gutierrez, & Lindsley (2003).

Plotting Data

Values from data collection sheets need to be collated by their x-axis value (usually dates) prior to entry onto a graph. Some degree of summarization or transformation may be required. For example, if each x-axis value is a single date, all data for that date need to be aggregated. A data summary table helps with this intermediate process:

Date (X Value)	Raw Data	Aggregated Y Value
3/14/13	10 Total Trials, 8 independently correct	80%
3/15/13	20 Total Trials, 15 independently correct	75%
3/16/13	10 Total Trials, 9 independently correct	90%

A marker for each *data point* (typically a dot) is placed on the graph at the intersection of the point's x and y values. For continuous data, a line is drawn connecting the dots creating a *data path*. More than one set of data may be placed on the same graph creating *multiple data paths* and providing an even denser concentration of information. When more than one set of data is displayed, the shape, color, or fill pattern of data markers and the lines of data paths should be adjusted to help distinguish one data set from another. In this case, a small box (called a *legend*) with samples of each point/line style attached to a data set label is placed at an inconspicuous location on the graph.

Analysis of Data

Line graphs like those pictured above are simple to construct but, still, powerful analytical tools that fulfill vital functions required of data used in educational settings. They assemble multiple measurements of a behavior over time in one place and, by permitting easy and immediate visual inspection of data, facilitate documentation, comparisons, and decision-making.

Conventions are typically followed when constructing graphs of performance that assist in analysis:

- No more than four separate data paths are usually placed on a single graph. When deciding to place more than one data path on a graph, take care to ensure that the lines do not cluster or obscure each other

- Significant events like procedure changes, medication changes, long absences, or changes in personnel that occur during the time span covered by the graph are labeled, the data path line is broken, and a line separating conditions is drawn between the last point of one condition and the first point of the next

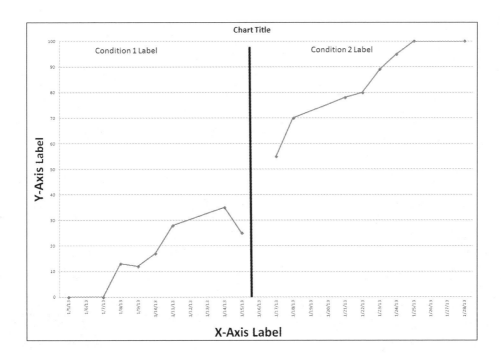

Variations in this traditional scheme may occur for instructional situations where frequent changes in condition occur. For example, the following graph does not break the data path line or draw a vertical condition change bar. Instead, a simple change in label is attached to the first data point after the change occurred to illustrate condition changes. Two data paths are displayed on the graph, each labeled with three conditions. The leftmost label (*RecBody1* for "receptive identification of body parts") is applied to both data paths on the same date, changing to *RecBody2* and, finally, to *RecBody3*. A legend in the

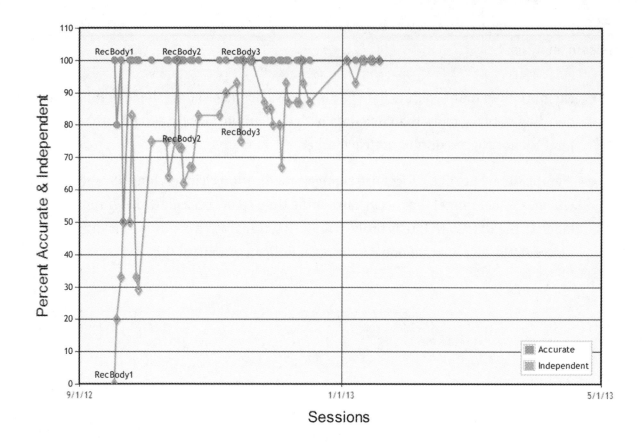

lower right corner of the graph contains labels and a sample of the color of the line. (The shape of the data point marker also varies for each data path.)

Analysis of line graphs generally involves a comparison of the height of data points individually or as a group. Since any two data points are connected by a line, the slope of the line represents the change in value between the two points. Slope may be positive or negative over time and may be determined for any group or sub-group of points, including the data set as a whole. The analysis of the slope of a group of data points is called "trend analysis." For example, the data set in the graph above may be fitted with a mathematically calculated line that depicts the trend of the data path labeled "Independent:"

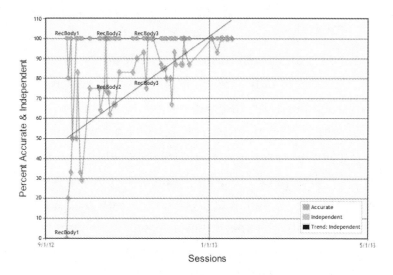

An increasing global trend (positive slope) is depicted, despite some short-lived local decreasing runs.

Trend lines like the line fitted to the data above portray the change in value of data over time as constant but other trend forms are possible. For example, a mild increasing trend may occur for five points followed by a more rapid increase (increased slope) for six points, followed by an even more rapid increase for four points.

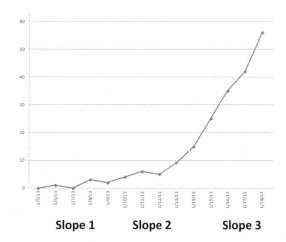

Slope 1   **Slope 2**   **Slope 3**

In the case of the data above, the *slope* of the data path increases over time. While a global trend line might correctly identify a positive trend, it would not identify that the slope itself is following an increasing trend, called *acceleration*. Increases or decreases in slope over time (acceleration or deceleration) require close inspection of local trends in data.

Variability and Systematic Evaluation of Instructional Procedures

Identification of trends and acceleration/deceleration assesses the *variability* of data values on a graph. Fundamentally, behavior analysis is deterministic and assumes that each value is an approximate but valid measurement of a behavioral event controlled by the conditions under which it occurred. As such, there are reasons for variability from point-to-point (or measurement to measurement), even if, at times, such reasons may be obscure. Logical principles are applied to graphic display of information to help account for variability and assist practitioners in making decisions about the effectiveness of applied procedures. Based on single-subject experimental research designs, they function by establishing a reference point of comparison between the application of a procedure and the measurement of a subsequent change in behavior.

For example, suppose that a new instructional program has begun and data on the student's performance is collected and graphed. Further suppose that the performance data does not show rapid acquisition and that percent correct bounces between 0 and 30%. After reviewing the data and observing the implementation of the procedure, a teacher makes some changes in the presentation of the materials of the task. A review of the graph following the procedural change now shows that the student's performance is approaching 100%:

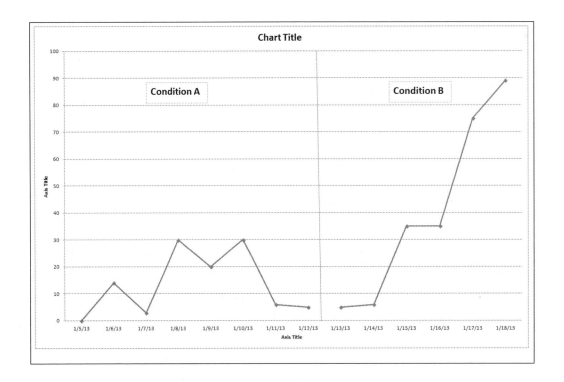

It may be tempting to immediately accept that the procedural change resulted in the change in the student's performance, but we should first pause for a bit of deliberation. It is important to assess what we actually know:

1. Before the procedural change, a stable, weak performance with no upward (improving) trend was established (there is actually a downward trend in the last five points). Based on this assessment of the variability of the data, it would be logical to expect that *future* student performance would be in the range of 0 – 30 percent

2. The first two data points of Condition B are relatively close in value to the last data point of Condition A. These Condition B points are in the closest temporal proximity to the condition change

3. After the second data point of Condition B there is a rapid increase in performance

Since the variability in the data of Condition A allows evaluators to reasonably predict future performance, the data that is received *immediately after* a change in conditions is the most valuable in assessing the effects of the change. Unfortunately, the first two points are not dramatically different from those of the previous condition. Nevertheless, as the new condition continues, a more rapid change does occur, lending some support for concluding that the switch is responsible.

Strong evidence of causality is necessary when decisions with extensive and critical ramifications are made. For example, we decide to reduce the number of choice items presented in an array from four items to three in a program and observe improved performance. While interesting, this may not be sufficient cause for reducing *all* choice arrays for the student and program supervisors may feel obliged to confirm that the effect is real. A relatively simple confirmation could be obtained by implementing a "reversal," that is, returning to the more complex four-choice array to observe the results, described as an A-B-A design.[7] Returning to the previously implemented condition provides an additional point of comparison between conditions when regarding the data:

---

[7] The brief discussion of the single-subject research designs in this section is intended to give the reader a sense of how a formal structure might be realistically applied to every-day clinical decision making. For more information see Johnston and Pennypacker (1993) *Strategies and Tactics of Behavioral Research*.

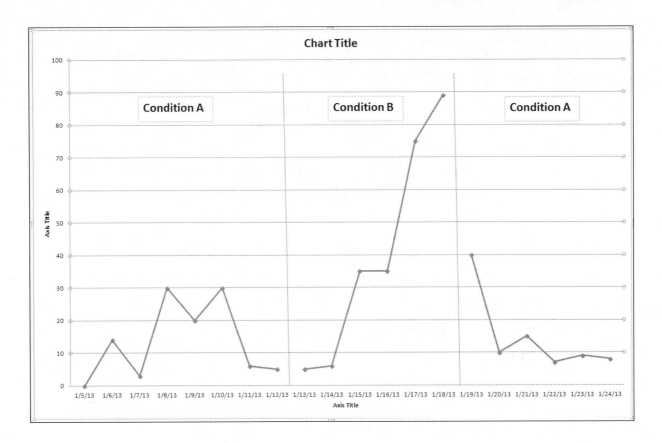

Reversals may be repeated (ABAB, ABABAB) to establish further points of comparison. Other designs arrange comparisons of conditions between different tasks, settings, or even students. For example, when considering the change in field size for a student, the change is applied first to Task 1, with the results documented and reviewed. Then, the change might be repeated with Task 2 and, subsequently Task 3. Alternatively, the change may be sequentially applied in Setting 1, followed by Setting 2 and Setting 3. Referred to as a "multiple-baseline design," each additional task or setting provides an additional point of comparison on which to base conclusions.

A third design, called an *alternating-treatments design* (Barlow & Hayes, 1979) randomly alternates conditions from session-to-session to provide frequent comparison points. While the reversal and multiple-baseline designs collect several data points after a single change in condition, the alternating-treatments design collects only a single data point before a condition change. This procedure potentially creates many comparison points.

Applying the Logic of Analysis to Real World Problems

The foregoing discussion has implications and applications for day-to-day work in ABA programs. As teachers and behavior analysts we constantly evaluate the effects of our interventions. Applying a certain amount of scientific rigor and logic to our thinking will clarify complex and ambiguous situations. It is important to develop careful, productive habits of approaching every clinical judgment, formal or informal, and assimilating the logic of scientific investigation into each appraisal of a graph, datasheet or student performance. Keep these underlying principles of analysis in mind:

- Changes in procedures that *closely* coincide with changes in performance strengthen the hypothesis that the first event caused the second

- When supporting evidence is lacking, intentionally and systematically manipulate the occurrence of conditions under study; this creates multiple points of comparison where the measured values of one condition are literally placed side by side with those of another condition, facilitating the identification of significant differences. Each repetition contributes evidence of the effect's validity and reliability

The Data-Based Revision Process

The scientific process of effective progress evaluation depends on:

- Objective definition of behavior, target conditions, and target criteria which allows measurement of performance

- Collection, summarization, transformation, and graphic visualization of data makes the results of instruction accessible

- Systematic manipulation and comparison of conditions under which data is collected; this increases confidence in the validity and reliability of the data

All in all, these measures represent a very powerful applied technology available for every-day application to instructional programs. Yet, progress evaluation is not an end in itself; rather, it is a means to make decisions regarding instructional programs. Progress evaluation allows implementers and program authors to determine the current status of instruction, including the identification of problems, in order to make adjustments if necessary, in a timely manner that keeps the student moving forward. Regular progress evaluation routinely integrated into the workflow of instruction and used as a basis for program revision has been associated with highly effective teaching (Ysseldyke, Thurlow, Grade, Wesson, Deno, & Algozinne, 1983).

Decision Rules

Carbone, Hagerty, and Sweeney-Kerwin (2007) implemented a protocol applying standardized decision rules to the review of student progress in a center-based program for children with autism. Measurements of student performance were graphed individually for each instructional program and monitored daily. If three data points without progress occurred, implementers were required to fill out a form detailing revisions to program procedures. If the changes did not result in a return to progress within three additional data points, a supervisory review was initiated, including observation of the implementation, supervisor initiated procedure changes, and follow-up. The protocol was successfully implemented during several occurrences of "lack of progress" – as defined by the protocol – leading to program revision, resolution of the problem, and return to progress.

Protocols for program review are instrumental in optimizing instructional procedures and overcoming the barriers to progress, inevitably encountered during implementation. The timeliness of the response to a lack of progress is critical and a decision-rule such as the one implemented in Carbone et al. (2007), when followed reliably, potentially minimizes student time spent with ineffective procedures. However, while decision-rules are a necessary first step, acceptable revision of ineffective procedures depends on the identification of the source of the problem and specification of a more effective replacement. In the Carbone et al. (2007) system, instructors directly working with students took the first crack at program revisions, documenting them on a *program change form*. The form was constructed to offer specific guidance in the selection of alternate procedures.

Designating an instructor as the first decision maker, allows the person most familiar with instruction to attempt to strategically intervene. Potentially, this saves time and effort. However, designing revisions to ineffective procedures is a complex activity with many variables and options. Therefore, training for implementers on how to successfully approach an instructional problem once a problem is identified is an important part of any protocol. Once lack of progress occurs, the implementer develops an alternate plan by engaging in four steps:

1. ***Examine*** the behavior, antecedents, and consequences in the instructional process that are relevant to errors and lack of progress. This can take several forms including direct observation, review of data, interviews, checklists, and brainstorming

2. ***Identify*** the events and factors that are the most likely elements of instruction responsible for errors and lack of progress. This involves starting with general, non-specific classes of problems and, through further investigation, refining one's understanding until a very specific focus is achieved, including a detailed definition of the problem event in behavioral terms

3. ***Classify*** the problem event(s) into recognized general categories using conceptually-systematic terminology from Applied Behavior Analysis

4. ***Select*** a procedural change associated with best practice and research and customize it to meet the needs of the student and situation

Pinpointing Instructional Barriers

Examination and identification of ineffective instructional programs assumes that specific factors exist within a procedure or the instructional environment that result in a failure of the student to make progress. These "barriers" to learning require identification and examination to pinpoint their precise method of functioning and interference with progress. The identification process could begin with a very narrow focus if it is clear where the problem lies. Otherwise, a more general assessment is required. An organized, logical approach considers the most frequent sources of potential difficulty at the outset and gradually proceeds to additional areas if early considerations are not significant. Protocols guide implementers through the process and take various forms, depending on the extent of assistance intended. As an initial step, simple screening tools or checklists can be useful; they cast a wide net, superficially examine a large number of potential factors, and help narrow down the field of focus rapidly.[8]

---

[8] Gina Corso and Amy LeQuire contributed to the development of the screens provided in the following pages.

Pinpointing Instructional Barriers

Student: _____   Date: _____

Instructor: _____   Program: _____

Screening Factors In or Out – Initial Screening Checklists

The first three screening checklists deal with overarching topics of concern: **procedural integrity** issues are prerequisite to the effective operation of every other aspect of instruction and must be examined before proceeding to other areas. If student errors occur due to inconsistent/incorrect implementation of the program, lack of student progress is a by-product of the behavior of the implementers and their supervisors/case managers. **Target and program selection** issues concern the validity of the goals of the instructional procedures. Each skill program depends on the prior establishment of appropriate prerequisite skills and individual targets to prevent placing unrealistic expectations on the student. Finally, unaddressed interference from **problem behavior** preempts and competes with the application of instructional procedures.

Identify items only if you think they have contributed **specifically, directly, and substantially** to the student's lack of progress

Procedural Integrity and Administration Checklist

- ☐ Y or ☐ N   Did I follow the program write-up? (I have reviewed the program write up and believe that I have implemented it as it was designed to be implemented)

- ☐ Y or ☐ N   Is the program write up complete and accurate/free from missing details, with the correct learning set, etc?

- ☐ Y or ☐ N   Have all implementers received training in implementing this program as designed?

- ☐ Y or ☐ N   Has the student had a sufficient number of teaching sessions delivered? Were these sessions delivered close together enough in time?

- ☐ Y or ☐ N   Has the student had consistent staffing (trained instructor or teacher)?

- ☐ Y or ☐ N   Has inter-observer agreement (IOA) been calculated and is it at an acceptable level?

- ☐ Y or ☐ N   Has necessary supervision or consultation been provided?

☐ Y or ☐ N   Are appropriate resources consistently available?

If you answered **NO** to any of the above questions, **do not** make a program change. Work with a program supervisor to ensure procedural integrity and administrative issues are resolved and continue to monitor.

Target Behavior Appropriateness Checklist

This screening checklist evaluates whether the target performance is appropriate – that is, whether the student is capable of learning the target behavior at the present time.

Answer no to any of the following questions where you think the problem or lack of progress is a direct result of the factors presented:

☐ Y or ☐ N   Student exhibits all necessary prerequisite performances?

☐ Y or ☐ N   Student understands the instructions?

☐ Y or ☐ N   Student can perform the target behavior and has no difficulties due to motor, visual, auditory, or memory limitations?

☐ Y or ☐ N   Student does exhibit important ancillary behavior required for instructional format (small group, whole-class group, community setting etc.) such as raising hand before answering, remaining seated in a group, attending when teacher gives instructions to group, staying with group in public areas, etc.?

If you answered no to any of the questions above, consult with the teacher or specialist responsible for the goal and discuss changing teaching pre-requisite behavior or changing the specifications or mastery criteria of the target performance.

Interfering Behavior Checklist

Answer YES to any of the following questions where you think the problem or lack of progress is a direct result of the factors presented:

☐ Y or ☐ N   Inappropriate or dangerous behavior significantly interferes with implementation of instruction?

☐ Y or ☐ N   Functional behavior assessment exists and applies to the instructional situation of concern?

☐ Y or ☐ N   Behavior intervention plan exists and adequately addresses the behavior?

☐ Y or ☐ N   Procedures in behavior plan allow for safe implementation of instruction?

If you answered **YES** to any of the questions above, contact the supervising teacher and/or the behavior analyst to consider revisions to functional assessments and behavior intervention plans.

Instructional Design Screening Checklists

Six additional lists are presented below for *setting and materials, attention and engagement, response prompts, task performance, reinforcement,* and *error correction*. Note that some questions may be similar to those in other sections to facilitate consideration of the factor in a different context.

Setting and Materials

☐ Y or ☐ N   Manipulates materials improperly or in a way unrelated to completion of task

☐ Y or ☐ N   Makes the same error with materials consistently

☐ Y or ☐ N   Selects answer based on position or other non-relevant dimension of the choice array or materials

☐ Y or ☐ N   Makes error after change in materials or presentation

☐ Y or ☐ N   Reacts to stimulus *other* than those relevant to instruction when instruction is given

☐ Y or ☐ N   Comparison stimuli in a field contain differences that are not systematic

☐ Y or ☐ N   Construction of materials not appropriate and needs redesign

☐ Y or ☐ N   Presentation of materials requires redesign

☐ Y or ☐ N   Setting is associated with a history of off-task interfering behavior such as stereotypy or hyperactive behavior

☐ Y or ☐ N   Stimulus prompts used (e.g. superimposition, redundant cues, etc.) are ineffective

☐ Y or ☐ N   Distracted by visual composition of setting (size, configuration, seating arrangement)

☐ Y or ☐ N   Distracted by noise

☐ Y or ☐ N Distracted by behavior of others

☐ Y or ☐ N Target performance negatively influenced by previous or following task; scheduled presentation of task not optimal

Attention and Engagement Checklist

☐ Y or ☐ N Is the student seated properly and oriented towards the instructor when the instruction is given and materials are presented?

☐ Y or ☐ N Does the student look at the materials adequately?

☐ Y or ☐ N Is the student engaged in a non-task related activity prior to responding or when you present the SD?

☐ Y or ☐ N Does the student make a response before you have finished presenting the instruction?

☐ Y or ☐ N Does the student use materials in a non-task related manner?

☐ Y or ☐ N Are extraneous environmental distractions present that attract the interest of the student?

☐ Y or ☐ N Does the student make random errors or guess?

☐ Y or ☐ N Does the student require frequent repetition of the SD or pause before responding?

Response Prompts

☐ Y or ☐ N Waits for prompts

☐ Y or ☐ N Defensive to touch/physical prompt

☐ Y or ☐ N Makes errors when prompts are attempted to be faded

Task Performance Errors or Factors

☐ Y or ☐ N Does the student frequently guess?

☐ Y or ☐ N Engages in scrolling (respond with one random answer after another)?

☐ Y or ☐ N Responds without attending to materials or instructions?

☐ Y or ☐ N   Makes errors late in session?

☐ Y or ☐ N   Makes errors on first trial?

☐ Y or ☐ N   Makes errors following errors?

☐ Y or ☐ N   Exhibits a performance that is too slow?

☐ Y or ☐ N   Exhibits a performance that is too rapid?

☐ Y or ☐ N   Exhibits a mastered performance in an isolated setting that fails to generalize to natural setting?

☐ Y or ☐ N   Exhibits a performance that is not persistent enough?

☐ Y or ☐ N   Exhibits a performance magnitude that is not sufficient?

☐ Y or ☐ N   Exhibits a performance duration that is not sufficient?

☐ Y or ☐ N   Exhibits a performance latency that is too long?

☐ Y or ☐ N   Exhibits a performance topography that is incorrect?

☐ Y or ☐ N   Repeats last reinforced performance, regardless of correct/incorrect?

☐ Y or ☐ N   Shows a position preference in array?

☐ Y or ☐ N   Always chooses the same stimulus?

Reinforcement

☐ Y or ☐ N   Student rejects reinforcement?

☐ Y or ☐ N   Student requests reinforcer not available?

☐ Y or ☐ N   Student constantly requests reinforcer?

☐ Y or ☐ N   Student resists surrendering reinforcer?

☐ Y or ☐ N   Student is inattentive, slow to respond or makes errors immediately after reinforcement?

☐ Y or ☐ N   Student does not look at the displayed reinforcer with excitement, does not respond to selection quickly, does not smile?

☐ Y or ☐ N Student seems disinterested in the conditioned reinforcer (token) i.e. does not look at the token when given or respond to delivery with some excitement (does not smile)?

☐ Y or ☐ N Student responds quickly at first but responds more slowly as trials continue?

☐ Y or ☐ N Student looks away from the instruction at a particular time or at the introduction of a particular stimulus?

☐ Y or ☐ N Student selects the same reinforcers over and over again?

☐ Y or ☐ N Student does not enjoy social or other commonly available reinforcers i.e. physical contact, praise, attention, playful behavior?

☐ Y or ☐ N Student engages in incorrect or substandard performance but is reinforced anyway (e.g. he can say "apple" but after some problem behavior staff begin to accept and reinforce "ap")?

☐ Y or ☐ N Satiation decreases potency of reinforcer offered (e.g. edible offered right after lunch)?

☐ Y or ☐ N Off-task behavior or non-compliance interferes significantly with task completion and reinforcement?

☐ Y or ☐ N Engages in significant task avoidance or escape?

☐ Y or ☐ N Frequently requests alternate activity?

Error Correction

☐ Y or ☐ N Student deliberately makes error to receive help?

☐ Y or ☐ N Student engages in problem behavior when corrected?

☐ Y or ☐ N Student repeats errors after correction?

☐ Y or ☐ N Student repeatedly self-corrects?

☐ Y or ☐ N Student scrolls?

Observation of Students

The focus of investigation can be narrowed significantly with the use of screening checklists to pinpoint issues or barriers involving particular aspects of instruction. In some cases they may provide sufficient information by themselves for immediate revision of the procedure. As an adjunct to the checklists, observation of the student during instruction provides opportunities to study the student's behavior in ways not otherwise possible. For example, independent observers can:

- Conduct an independent check of procedural integrity including reliability of data collection

- Focus attention and observation on specific instructional events of interest during the session and collect supplementary data

- Cooperate with the instructor to prototype new procedures and immediately examine their effects on instruction

Observations of students are an important part of the normal workflow of program development and, as such, require full integration into the revision process. Protocols can be created to systematize *when* and *how* observations occur as well as how resulting information and decisions are documented, compiled, and promulgated. In the PC3 curriculum development and implementation system, observations are documented in a series of six panels. Basic information like the name and position of the observer, default reason for observation, date of observation, and the name of the student is automatically recorded by the software. Narrative comments describing the events observed are recorded in the first panel followed by narrative comments on the changes and next steps determined. Observational information in narrative form can be helpful in documenting many details of the student's performance, procedural difficulties, and the general evolution of program revisions from observation to observation.

Screen captures of the Observation Tracking panels in ABA-PC3 Software

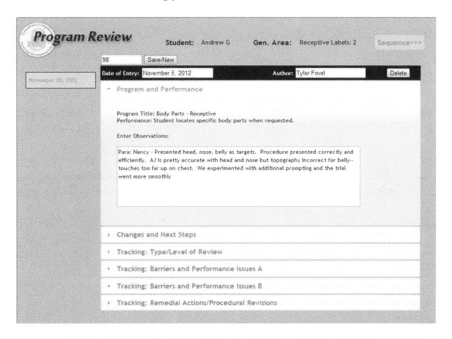

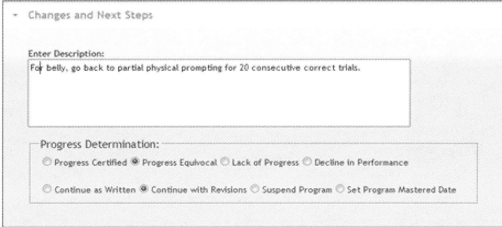

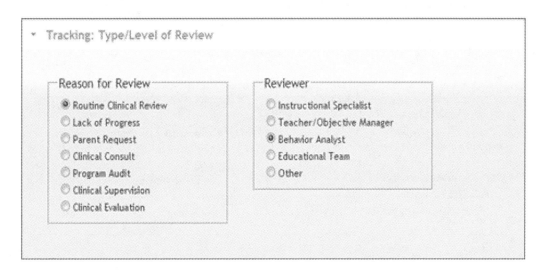

Tracking: Barriers and Performance Issues A

Inaccurate Response
- ☐ No response
- ☐ Too slow/fast
- ☐ Too weak/forceful
- ☐ Too frequent/infrequent
- ☑ Deficient topography
- ☐ Duration too short or long
- ☐ Latency too short or long
- ☐ Incorrect sequence
- ☐ Other response barrier

Conditional Performance
- ☐ Position preference
- ☐ Frequent 1st trial errors
- ☐ Scrolls or guesses
- ☐ Anticipates SD
- ☐ Responds to wrong SD
- ☐ Faulty or absent generalization
- ☐ Other conditional barrier

Interfering Behavior
- ☑ Protests/complains/refuses
- ☐ Property disruption
- ☐ Self-injurious behavior
- ☐ Stereotypy-self-stimulation
- ☐ Irrelevant behavior
- ☐ Aggression
- ☐ Attempts to leave
- ☐ Resists giving up reinforcer
- ☐ Other behavior barrier

Tracking: Remedial Actions/Procedural Revisions

Program Integrity
- ☐ Program integrity/data Check
- ☐ Repeat review
- ☐ Further implementer training
- ☐ Program meeting required
- ☐ Additional supervision
- ☐ Additional information required
- ☐ Change staffing resources

Revisions Required
- ☐ Materials
- ☐ Context, setting or location
- ☐ Reinforcement
- ☐ Attention/engagement procedures
- ☐ Error correction procedures
- ☑ Prompting procedures
- ☐ Learning set/target performance
- ☐ Mastery criteria

Tracking: Barriers and Performance Issues B

Target Appropriateness
- ☐ Target too hard
- ☐ Student lacks prerequisites
- ☐ Target non-functional

Procedure-Related Issues
- ☐ Faulty/absent scanning/referencing
- ☑ Frequent inattention
- ☐ Other attention/engagement barrier

- ☐ Rejects reinforcer
- ☐ Asks for unavailable reinforcer
- ☐ Other reinforcement barrier

- ☐ Repeats error
- ☐ Resists error correction
- ☐ Other error correction barrier

- ☐ Waits for prompt or prompt dependent
- ☐ Resist prompt
- ☐ Other response prompt barrier

The ABA-PC3 system uses observations to compile statistical information about implementation, which is compiled and available for analysis. In the first "Tracking" panel the software asks the observer to note:

- Whether or not progress has occurred up to and including the results of the observation

- Whether the program was mastered

- The disposition of the program after observation (continued, continued with revisions, suspended)

The observer is also asked to note the occurrence of instructional barriers and revisions required. Instructional barriers are identified within six categories:

- Inaccurate Response

- Conditional Performance

- Interfering Behavior

- Target Appropriateness

- Procedure-related Issues

- Program Integrity

When the data is pooled with other observations, statistics on the overall occurrence of any individual barrier may be accessed. Statistics allow analysis and tracking of global trends in implementation across observations, students, caseloads, and settings. For example, in the PC3 system, the following statistics can be compiled for students, caseloads, classrooms, sites, or the total organization:

- Percent of observations reporting progress?

- Percent of observations reporting interfering behavior?

- Percent of observations reporting procedural changes related to prompting?

- Percent of observations reporting problems with procedural integrity?

- Percent of observations reporting changes to reinforcement procedures?

- Percent of observations reporting problems with conditional discriminations?

- Percent of observations reporting revisions to learning sets?

ABA-PC3 Observation Summaries and Compiled Statistics

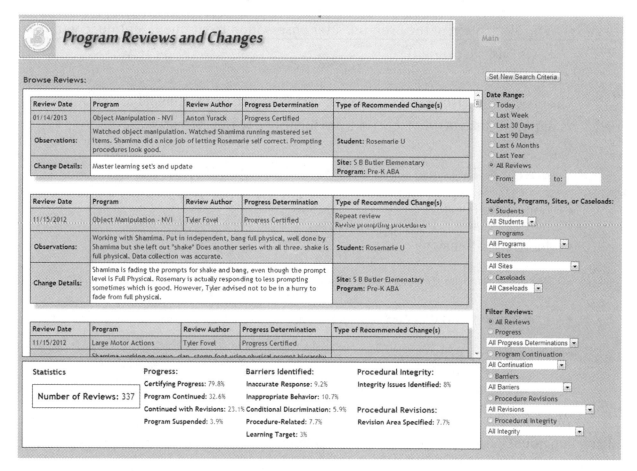

Classification of Learning Barriers

Once performance errors or procedural inconsistencies are identified, program (re)designers focus on classification. Classification refers to the process of defining attributes of a problem and associating them with scientifically-studied concepts and principles. Classification statements that also identify a dependent and independent variable are called *hypotheses*. Hypotheses are constructed as part of the error analysis process to assist in the identification of potential procedural revisions. The dependent variable describes the topography of the student error and the independent variable describes the antecedent conditions under which the error occurs. The language of the hypotheses is important in its effectiveness. Precision, comprehensiveness and use of recognized terminology is important. For example, consider the hypotheses below:

Hypothesis 1

Statement: "The student is randomly choosing from the choice array because he isn't motivated enough to pay close attention"		
Dependent Variable (Result)	**Independent Variable (Antecedents)**	**Scientific Literature Related to Hypothesis Statement**
The student is randomly choosing from the array	Because the student isn't motivated enough to pay close attention	• Preference Assessment • Token reinforcement • Motivating Operations • Reinforcement Schedules

Hypothesis 2

Statement: "The student doesn't look at the materials because they are too small"		
Dependent Variable (Result)	**Independent Variable (Antecedents)**	**Scientific Literature Related to Hypothesis Statement**
The student doesn't look at the materials	Because the stimulus materials are too small. Instead, he is looking at preferred objects that compete for his attention	• Stimulus Control • Reinforcement Contingencies • Competing Behavior

Hypothesis 3

Statement: "He always chooses the item on the right"		
Dependent Variable (Result)	**Independent Variable (Antecedents)**	**Scientific Literature Related to Hypothesis Statement**
The student always chooses the item on the right in the 3-choice matching array	Because he is ignoring the sample. The sample has not been established as a discriminative stimulus	• Stimulus Control • Conditional Discriminations • Matching-to-sample

Good hypotheses need not contain highly technical or formal language but they should clearly and comprehensively describe the topography and conditions of the student error, even though an analyst may be making some rough guesses. In order to facilitate association of the hypothesis with the most relevant evidence-based methodologies, the language of the hypothesis should refer as directly as possible to scientifically validated concepts of behavior change.

Hypotheses vary in precision and detail and, therefore, vary in their ability to suggest potential directions of further study or revision. The error "event" may require detailed study over time to identify relevant conditions. Ultimately, however, the analysis of learning barriers gives way to decisions about a specific course of remedial action. Within their protocol, Carbone et al. (2007) grouped common procedural changes into antecedents and consequences to facilitate selection. Checklists, such as the statements in the screening questionnaires, can assist in the formation of hypotheses and the selection of logical methodological revisions. Items describing error patterns may be matched with suggested changes to consider:

Signs of an Insufficient Reinforcement Strategy

- Attention and engagement difficulties
- Slow or weak performance
- Errors alternate with independent performance
- Highly distracted by non-instructional stimuli
- Proportionally high non-task related behavior
- Proportionally high escape-related behavior
- Rejection, lack of interest in reinforcer, asks for reinforcer not available
- Conditioned reinforcement lacks powerful backup reinforcers
- Preference assessment not completed regularly
- Potential reinforcers used repeatedly
- Potential reinforcers lack novelty and variety
- Schedule of reinforcement thin

Reinforcement Strategy Changes to Consider:

- Make reinforcer more salient
- Make work requirement more salient
- Schedule task to capitalize on or maximize MO's (deprivation)
- Use high interest (intrinsically motivating) materials in design of task
- Allow choice
- Decrease effort required
- Decrease duration required
- Use High-P Request Series
- Warm up/practice run
- Remind/exhibit reinforcer
- Use tokens (token train first)
- Display reinforcers before starting work
- Prime reinforcement (give a taste of the reinforcer before starting)
- Increase variety of reinforcement
- Increase novelty of reinforcement
- Increase magnitude of reinforcement
- Increase frequency of reinforcement

Summary

The final stage of data-based decision making is using the objective information gathered about students to make decisions. Protocols like decision-rules oblige us to adopt healthy decision-making habits. Tools like screening checklists and direct observation supplement data collection to assist in the identification of problem causes and potentially effective revisions.

What's Next?
Put this chapter to work: DATA-BASED DECISION MAKING

- Randomly sample your target behavior definitions including specification of the conditions and criteria
    - Would an ABA teacher unfamiliar with the student be able to recreate the program based on your definitions?
    - Are all learning set items included somewhere (either in the goal or on a separate sheet)?
    - Are the conditions and criteria actually followed?
- Develop a procedure for initial probes that covers all of the features discussed in the chapter. Make sure that implementers are consistent when performing probe procedures
- Assess your protocols for managing a student's progression through the items on the learning set
    - Do they adequately cover all types of learning sets?
    - Do they specify how to maintain mastered set items?
- Discuss the collection of student performance data with clinical staff
    - Consider the pros and cons to collecting data on implementation of prompts vs. intermittent probes
- Consider the present use of graphs within your program for evaluating student performance
    - Are graphs up-to-date?
    - Are they checked frequently?
- Establish a protocol for using performance data to trigger revisions to programs
- Establish a protocol for documenting regular observations of student programs and integrating the information into program revision
- Provide staff training on analyzing barriers to learning

Chapter 10

The Big Picture - ABA PROJECT MANAGEMENT
Controlling the *Workflow* of Program Creation and Implementation

An ABA project is a complex entity. Start with a myriad of implementers (teachers, instructors, related service personnel, behavior analysts, parents, administrators); add in a curriculum, materials, space, and a hundred other things.[1] *Whether your team serves one student or many; whether you are school-based, work in a private agency, or implement a home program; your organizational structures comprise a framework on which program implementation rests – one that affects every outcome for the life of the project.*

Effectively arranging and managing your team's actions and how they create and implement programs promotes success. It's easy to forget that every procedure and method is ultimately defined by what is done, rather than what is written. As discussed many times previously in this book, the quality and fidelity of implementer behavior constitutes the procedural integrity of the project. Behavior analysts know a thing or two about task analysis but can be surprisingly remiss

---

[1] You can find a list of many of those things in the New York State Department of Education Autism Program Quality Indicators (NYS Department of Education, 2001 or in the Program Audit Form included in the Appendix at the end of this book).

about applying what they know to managing their own behavior or the behavior of those around them not in the category of "student." In contrast, in the world of business and industry, where millions of dollars may be at stake, whole departments are devoted to the study of *workflow* and *human factors engineering*. Just as we analyze student tasks as part of the process of changing student behavior, we can study our own workflow in order to better organize, control and improve work behavior.

This chapter presents an overview of some of the concepts and structures related to developing and managing the complex chains of work behavior involved in program creation and implementation—with optimization of the team's workflow as the desired end result. Optimization of workflow means better work performance and, ultimately, better instruction for students.

The Concept of Workflow Applied to Instruction – Processes and Products

Try listing all the things you do in your job during the course of a week and you will have quite a list.[2] You may have experimented with ways to be more efficient or organized. In doing this, you are tinkering with your workflow. Is a different organization of the instructional space in order? Possibly, a different data sheet or picking an alternate response measure would increase reliability of data. Maybe just getting everyone a clipboard would improve things. The details involved in successfully creating and implementing an ABA program are voluminous. Fundamentally, however, efficient and effective workflow results from the intentional analysis of work behavior and the careful design/implementation of processes that produce specific results.

Products and Control Structures

The term "control structures" denotes all of the various meetings, written programs, data sheets, policies and procedures, training, diagrams, wall posters, and environmental designs—in short, everything that controls or affects the implementation of a program. Technically, the term refers to a collection of organizational *discriminative stimuli and contingencies* that control the behavior of employees. Among the many categories are:

---

[2] Try filling out the *Clinical Activity Log* in the Appendix.

Policies	Procedures	Trainings
Observations	Protocols	Programs
Reports	IEP Documents	Specialization of Roles
Curricula	Assessments and Evaluations	Meetings
Program Books	Data Sheets	Graphs
Supervision	Consultation	Notes
Functional Analyses	Computer Programs	Mastered Goal Lists
Current Program Lists	Communication Logs	Meeting Minutes

Considerable effort is involved in creating such structures. Even seemingly small details are found to play important roles. For example, I have found over and over that time to shop for preferred objects, snacks, and games must be placed on an explicit schedule if one is to avoid running out of effective reinforcers at a crucial time (usually due to satiation of over-used stimuli). Regardless of the nature or priority of the need, control structures address the myriad of details and problems involved in coordinating the complex entity of implementation. Consider the questions below:

Some Workflow Questions to Consider About Implementation:

1. *When* do implementers write detailed programs?

2. *When and how* do program supervisors provide supervision to programs?

3. *When* do implementers make written revisions?

4. *How* do program supervisors train others to implement plans that change often?

5. *When* do implementers engage in probing and evaluation to create new curriculum development ideas?

6. *How* do implementers establish strict programming across all of the student's environments?

7. *Where* do new ideas come from? *Whose* job is it to brainstorm and try new things? *How* often should it happen?

8. *Who* sees the big picture? *Who* checks that the goals are really addressing core needs or that enough progress is being made?

The answer to these and many other questions lies in the creation of control structures. Control structures provide detailed specifications of the mechanisms involved in directly engineering behavior change consistent with effective programming. These specifications include the same elements of behavior change common to student programs such as discriminative stimuli and contingencies.

The point is illustrated with a common control structure. In order to ensure consistency and completeness, an organization decides to specify a format to be followed when writing behavior or instructional programs. A written policy is established and all program authors are trained on the format requirements. The object of training is to ensure that future written programs will conform to the newly established format. The mechanisms that effect this change involve some fairly straightforward contingencies and learning histories: (1) the agency communicates to the author that they will be reinforced for compliance to the new standard or punished for non-compliance, (2) the author is presented with the standard, given examples, guided, shaped, etc. until he achieves a standards-compliant performance, and (3) the author participates in supervision that reviews his work and delivers reinforcement or punishment. In this system the contingencies of "supervision" are combined with various discriminative stimuli established in training (written headings and guidelines of the policy) to exert control over program writing. Adoption of a control structure like a program format results in better workflow for program writing and improves the speed of program development. Authors spend less time guessing about what to include or revising programs to suit the expectations of supervisors and supervisors spend less time revising and communicating their expectations to authors.

The Analysis of Workflow

Much like functional assessment, workflow issues, problems, and irregularities are approached through observation, data collection, and analysis. Consider this example: a program supervisor in a small ABA school recently attended a workshop on student evaluation methodologies and is concerned with her program's process of initially evaluating students. In order to understand how the current process is functioning, the supervisor observes the on-going evaluation of a new student, conducts interviews with the evaluators, and reviews some of the results:

- The teacher conducting the initial student evaluation phase chose direct and indirect assessment methods based on his preferences and familiarity with the materials

- One indirect skill assessment took over two weeks to complete and it is unclear how the results from the indirect skill assessment were used in creating target objectives

- Direct probing occurred for only a few skills that the teacher was interested in beginning right away

- Methods of probing carried out by the two instructors helping with the initial assessment were not consistent

The observations create a number of questions for the program supervisor:

- Is there a policy and procedure regarding assessment of students and stating when the assessment is to be done and by whom?

- What assessments can be used within the school? How are the results integrated into the creation of target objectives?

- Does the assessment procedure include specific guidelines for the scope of probing ?

- Does a training procedure exist for performing initial assessments and probes?

Measuring Workflow

Workflow measures are revealing. Cohen-Almeida (2005) proposed *number of learning trials presented by instructors* as the single most important component of programs identified as "intensive" interventions. In discrete trial programs, the dates that new stimuli are added to the program are indicative of program momentum. Long delays between added stimuli are telltale signs of stagnation. Some other informative numbers are outlined below:

Some Valuable Workflow Statistics to Know

At Student Level:

- Number of trials/learning opportunities presented per unit of time in each program setting
- Number or percentage of spontaneous language initiations reinforced by instructor
- Number or percentage of social initiations reinforced by instructor
- Percentage of 15 second intervals that an instructor is engaged with students
- Number of times per week that a particular program is presented
- Number of days between mastery of new steps of a program

At Program Level:

- Number of minutes of direct interaction/discussion (about programs) between supervising teacher and instructor
- Number of minutes of direct interaction between BCBA and teacher, BCBA and instructor
- Number of minutes of clinical meeting time for each student per month
- Number of minutes of program revision time for each student per month

Training:

- Number of new programs described and demonstrated to instructors per month
- Number of times instructors observed per month
- Amount of time devoted to training

Self-report methods are useful as part of an overall system of workflow data gathering and analysis. Clinicians record information about their activities retrospectively or contemporaneously from diaries, existing calendars, meeting minutes, training records, revision dates on programs, and files of observation and feedback forms.[3] From this information statistics are amassed on a variety of clinician activities that permit determinations such as the frequency and scope of program revisions and the relative amount of time spent in activities such as meetings, preparation, evaluation, and training.

A variety of other forms provide regular data on staff behavior related to implementation:[4]

- **Observation and feedback** forms provide significant information on a variety of staff behaviors related to specific instructor-student interactions

- **Program audits** provide structured inventories to comprehensively asses the presence or attributes of best practices at the level of the organization or project

- **Goal-/Process-control forms** may assist in objectively delineating large, amorphous tasks and keep track of progress towards agreed upon goals. Three sample forms are provided in the appendix. The *Consultation Plan* helps consultants and their clients define the scope, individual goals, and timelines for their projects. The *Inclusion Plan* is used to promote organization of inclusion experiences implemented in teams by defining goals, methods, resources, and settings. The *Project Management Grid* documents the current status of development for projects with multiple students and staff

While not forms, student performance indicators such as the VB-MAPP (Verbal Behavior Milestones Assessment and Placement Program, Sundberg, 2008) provide an indirect measure of implementer effectiveness when data is pooled for multiple students. The same can be said for standardized grade-level tests in reading, writing, mathematics, or other achievement tests.

---

[3] See the Appendix for a copy of the form illustrated.
[4] *Ibid*

The Standardization—Individualization Continuum

Control of implementer behavior requires well-defined procedures at every level. Standardization provides the opportunity to build in consistency and expertise, guiding less experienced personnel in the completion of common tasks. It can seem illogical to apply standard techniques to students who have idiosyncratic needs; the fields of special education and applied behavior analysis are strongly linked in their concern with individualization. Most research, therapeutic, and educational efforts are focused on the individual, from single-subject experimental designs in applied studies to individualized needs assessment and intervention. Reinforcers, prompts, and many other methodological decisions are based on individual differences. Yet, despite the value of individualization, students are commonly grouped into classes and reading groups, workers function on teams and departments, and businesses design products and services for general consumption.

Generic procedures and products save businesses money and time. They allow mass production of "standard" services that lower the cost for all consumers, while providing a highly consistent product. Whether you eat a "Quarter Pounder" in Ohio or a "Burger Royale" in Paris, they will taste the same. However, generic services and products have limitations, especially when it comes to education. It is difficult to motivate *all* students with praise or use the same prompt to teach hand washing to every student in the class. On the other hand, a picture schedule using a standard set of icons works well for most students. In general, a wise course in ABA program development is to try and standardize the *repetitive* aspects of the workflow while customizing the individual programs themselves. An artist may buy canvas and paints in bulk, stretch several canvasses on frames at once, or even quickly sketch out a number of ideas of a particular scene or subject before beginning a project. Yet, each painting is individual and unique. A teacher follows the same logic. The normal workflow of ABA programs has many opportunities for standardization:

Opportunities for Standardization in ABA Program Workflow

- Forms
- Graphing conventions

- Curriculum Assessment Checklists
- Program formats
- Preference assessment protocols
- Program book organization
- Bulk reinforcer purchases
- "Boilerplate" language for describing standard events

Standardization does *not* work well when developing and communicating precise technical details of teaching programs for learners who have complicated and varied needs. For example, we would not create standard programs to deal with interfering behavior because the effectiveness of the program procedure depends on the function that the behavior serves for the individual. The function of interfering behavior in one case may be to gain attention while in another case it happens to be escape from demands. Learners with autism are among the most challenging of students with constellations of learning needs that are as numerous and varied as the students themselves. The over-use of standardized programs with such students sends the wrong message to instructors:

- "All students will learn if you follow this prescription. These are tried and true recipes—they'll work with anyone"
- "If the student has trouble, keep it up—things will get better. After all, this is an approved procedure"
- "If the procedure is not working, it must be my fault. I need to try harder"

There is absolutely no guarantee of progress implied by using a particular procedure, even if it has worked with others. While perseverance is important and crucial in many cases, it is also true that ineffective strategies must be discontinued or revised because they will not work no matter how long or how hard they are tried. Analysis and objective measurement, not conformance to convention, should guide decision-making.

While our programs should not come "off the shelf," they can be built from common components. This is a bit like receiving directions to a destination from a computerized service like MapQuest or Google. The destination is specific but the path depends on our location at a given moment. Directions are made up of common components ("go right" on one street; "go left" on another street) that might be a part of *any* set of directions. It is the *unique combination* of directions based on our specific need that makes a particular set of directions appropriate for us.

The relationship between standardization and individualization is best described as a continuum on which programs fall. The point of placement of programs on the continuum (i.e., the balance of standardization vs. individualization appropriate to the student) must be carefully chosen. The standardization—individualization continuum has implications and opportunities for many aspects of implementation workflow. In the next section, we will explore recommendations for creating control structures, processes, and products that may improve consistency and order without limiting flexibility.

Recommendations for Control Structures, Processes, and Products
Workflow Recommendation #1

- **Empower a Core Team that is *In Touch* and *In Charge***

    o Designate a coordination team to lead the project with one or more experienced individuals who have a clear mandate and a realistic "master plan"

    o Ensure clear lines of communication, authority and responsibility between the coordination team and all other participants including schools, parents and family members, related service personnel, outside service providers, medical personnel, and others

    o Ensure that the coordination team has direct access to resource providers

    o The first priority of the coordination team is to establish a trust relationship with stakeholders

Leadership, vision, and coordination are qualities essential to all projects. When they do not exist, we work at cross-purposes, things fall through the cracks, quality plummets, stakeholders lose trust, and the project eventually fails. Without them, today's priority changes tomorrow and each day is spent putting out fires rather than moving forward with a plan. For work to focus properly on students, leaders must provide consistent direction with clearly established goals shared by all stakeholders as well as the resources required to enable action. In other words: a viable *master plan.*

Workflow Recommendation #2

- **Establish a Regular Cycle for Clinical Tasks**
    - Program review meetings
    - Student and instructor observations
    - Program housekeeping activities (filing, duplicating, scoring, graphing)
    - Preference assessment and reinforcer purchase
    - Curriculum development activities
    - Program audits

A mix of routine discussions, meetings, observations, and tasks pervade daily work life. Establishing a cycle for the occurrence of routine but important tasks ensures that they happen in a *timely* manner. Putting tasks on a schedule is more obvious for some activities than others. For example, it is typical for ABA programs to schedule regular student reviews but other tasks should be placed on the calendar as well, such as student observations. It is also extremely advisable (and worth repeating) for busy teachers and special education directors to allow for time to shop for toys and trinkets that will be used as reinforcers. A two-hour block once a month could profitably be allocated to this activity. Allowing 15-30 minutes per day on a scheduled basis for implementers to file old data sheets, score drills and enter the information into the computer is realistic and necessary. For supervisors and behavior analysts, regularly scheduled and specifically designated time for curriculum development activities is necessary. These clinicians can quickly find every day filled with on-site activities, leaving no time for writing. Finally, program audits (checklists and evaluations of program-wide service delivery during a particular time period) are a crucial but neglected activity in many programs that should be integrated into the schedule of regular clinical events.

Workflow Recommendation #3

- **Develop Forms, Formats, or Let the Computer Do It**

    o   Use consistent formats for functional assessments, behavior intervention plans, and skill acquisition programs

    o   Adopt a comprehensive curriculum and use prepared goals whenever possible with pre-written "starter" procedures and default learning sets from which to choose. Customize as needed

    o   Consider adopting a "core vocabulary" for the curriculum that is consistent between language drills[5]

    o   Establish an "approved" set of data sheets for discrete trials, incidental social and language, learning set lists, etc.

    o   Create and use forms for student objectives lists, mastered skills lists, schedules, etc.

    o   Make sure all forms are able to be completed on the computer, emailed, and saved electronically

    o   Provide laptop computers for teachers and clinicians with access to the internet and email so that they may work remotely when necessary

Word processors and spreadsheets are just the beginning of the technological tools that can improve accuracy and speed of completing repetitive tasks. A variety of forms can be quickly developed and re-used in different settings. Standardized checklists help keep assessments consistent and our memory intact. Digital collections of photos, icons,

---

[5] See Verbal Behavior Targets, A Tool to Teach Mands, Tacts and Intraverbals (2008) by Diana Luckevich.

programs, clip-art, and other resources prevent reinvention of the wheel. Templates can be developed for speeding the creation of behavior plans and functional assessments, including boilerplate text. I do recommend caution in re-using text—it is all too easy to cut and paste a standard paragraph from one evaluation to the next and forget to change the name of the student. Nevertheless, standard explanations of procedures and tests, headings, and other material that does not change from one document to the next can easily and legitimately be included in standard templates.

As technology improves, computer software has become increasingly helpful in program selection, organization, implementation, and evaluation. The ABA Program Companion 3.0 software (Fovel, 2013) included with this manual is one example. It simplifies goal selection and monitoring progress by providing a standard curriculum and interface to write and monitor implementation of skill acquisition programs, produce data sheets, graphs, and analyze results. Specialized software exists for data collection, graphing, ABA training, a variety of curriculum-related areas, and many other instructional topics.[6]

Workflow Recommendation #4

- **Establish Standard Protocols for Common Tasks**
    - Baseline curriculum assessments and periodic follow-up
    - Creating individualized student curricula
    - Setting up program books and materials
    - Meeting and training schedules
    - Preference assessments
    - Social skills assessment
    - Language assessment
    - Observing and giving performance feedback to instructors

---

[6] Rather than provide a resource that will be immediately out of date, I suggest that the reader search the internet using terms similar to "aba software" or "autism software."

- Entry/exit criteria for programs or classrooms
- Communication
- Professional behavior

Small programs do not have an abundance of people in support positions that can develop consistent policies and procedures and monitor performance of critical common tasks. This is unfortunate because good programs grow and, eventually, problems occur that might have been prevented by such practices. Many issues in the creation of ABA programs are foreseeable and program directors who intentionally put off developing "extra" procedures should continue to review the relevance and priority of their choices as their program grows to avoid falling into a reactive mind set.

Workflow Recommendation #4

- **Provide a Standard Set of Preferred Materials and Curriculum Resources for Programs**

    - Partitions, tables, chairs, bookcases, cabinets, individual storage space that match, fit the space and needs of the students

    - Organized "materials library" for common drills

    - Basic toys, games, gross motor equipment, computer(s) and software, and materials appropriate for age-group, developmental level

    - Provide a variety of materials for more advanced academic subjects like language arts, mathematics, and science, including appropriate curriculum kits, software, manipulatives and supplementary materials

- Become familiar with scripted curricula like SRA-Distar language, reading and mathematics programs and employ where appropriate

- Obtain a set of curriculum materials used in inclusion settings

- Hold trainings to familiarize all staff with materials

Schools and other educationally-oriented organizations set up classrooms and other activity spaces as a matter of course. There are no differences in some of the materials needed for ABA programs. However, there are many areas of departure as well. Manuals, journals, computer software, electronic devices, flashcards, and many other materials are required and sufficient resources should be allocated. Ordering enough materials at the outset will save much time later during the curriculum development process. It is particularly important for programs to possess a variety of curriculum resources since a single source is unlikely to be applicable to every student. Typically, individualized programs are created from multiple sources, taking the most relevant parts of each. Once obtained, staff should receive an orientation to all materials so that they are familiar with how to employ them before facing a student.

Creating standardized "learning sets" i.e. lists of the stimuli or steps that will be learned for each program, will increase efficiency and consistency in at least two ways:

1. The suggested sets provide a quick starting point for instructors

2. The learning sets can form part of an overall master list of learning targets that flow from one program to the next. For example, a large master list of nouns, verbs, modifiers, locations, categories, etc. can be chosen that reflect vocabulary needs during early childhood educational activities. Not only can the team work in a more coordinated fashion when they are working from one list but later programs can be developed that are based on the vocabulary developed in earlier programs

Finally, materials related to the specific learning sets should be available in a "library" that can be easily accessed by teachers and instructors. Some programs have used inexpensive plastic food storage containers to have the specific starting materials for programs ready and waiting, avoiding the inevitable scavenger hunt for materials that often precedes the start of new programs.

Workflow Recommendation #6

- **Develop Standardized Training Materials**
    - Provide new employees with a book of policies and procedures that describe all aspects of their job performance and agency function
    - Provide written description of training procedures and dates of training
    - Provide self-guided training materials (preferably with computer-based multimedia content) to train on basic concepts
    - Standardize content and outline for all training topics
    - Establish regular cycle for review of training
    - Establish ongoing effort to develop new training materials within agency

Lots of instructors, teachers, and behavior analysts are "naturals" to some extent but everyone struggles to become effective. Becoming competent in the development and delivery of instruction is a long process that may be helped or hindered by training. If we are committed to good teaching with students it is natural for us to extend our commitment to the individuals, both professional and paraprofessional, who will determine the success of programs. Training is a primary task that we must get right at all levels—orientation, classroom-based instruction, on-the-job training, professional development activities, and many other experiences designed to improve the skills of individuals and teams working with students. A thoughtful, organized, and comprehensive approach will pay dividends immediately and also down the road. Certainly, new employees must receive individual attention as they become familiar with the new organization, personnel, and students. Providing a book of policies and procedures and reviewing the crucial elements directly pertaining to the employee's job conveys a feeling of order and structure to most people and preempts the confusion that results from being told different things by different people. Done the right way, it can also be an exciting way to begin a job—the opportunity to join a project that is highly competent and good at changing the lives of students is a powerful incentive to attract and retain staff. Creating this perception is usually under our control. Largely, new employees will "imprint" (form durable attitudes about the agency or project) during the orientation process and first few weeks.

During that period, a clear summary of training should outline all aspects and goals of orientation. Standardized training outlines ensure that information given is consistent. However, a significant amount of time may be saved by using multimedia presentations to convey basic information. A number of computer-based software programs exist that are easy to use and allow integration of video, text, graphics, and sound to create presentations that are far more engaging than a simple lecture. With a little effort, in fact, presentations can be created that move at the pace of the user and even modify content based on the user's input.

Subsequent training should also be standardized as much as possible. For example, teachers should be trained to describe and demonstrate discrete trial programs to new instructors in a standardized, effective manner. Both the training for the instructors and the training for the teachers should have a specific written outline. Written outlines for *all* aspects of training should exist with schedules and documentation of implementation available for review during program audits. Finally, ongoing effort should be made to develop additional training materials and assess the effectiveness of present efforts.

Conclusion

Undoubtedly, readers have grappled with many of the concepts and challenges discussed in this chapter. We all have experienced an overburdened work schedule or lack of resources and felt frustrated in not being able to offer more to students. A high level of preparation and execution is required to provide customized programs, well-trained instructors, and on-going clinical support. Improving the efficiency of service delivery is likely to improve student outcomes as long as the services are effective. In Applied Behavior Analysis, our technology is solid and we, therefore, are equipped to succeed. The message of this chapter is that, by applying that same effective science of explicit measurement, analysis and specification to optimize efficient workflow in ABA projects, we seize the means to optimize beneficial outcomes for students.

What's Next?
***Put this chapter to work*: ABA PROJECT MANAGEMENT**

- Make a commitment to objectively study work performance issues. Choose a workflow analysis project that will address an issue that you've wanted to deal with:
    - Observe, define, and measure performance
    - Present the results
    - Discuss and implement policy and procedural changes that will improve performance
    - Continue to measure and revise until a satisfactory outcome is obtained
    - Apply the same process to additional issues
- Try listing all the things you do in your job during the course of a week using the clinical activity log:
    - Break down your work into categories
    - Prioritize the categories
    - Compare the amount of time you spent on each category with the relative priority of the category
    - What are your barriers to greater effectiveness?
- To what extent are unplanned "crises" taking precedence over priorities?:
    - Can you think of any new control structures that would eliminate these problems?
    - What can you do to streamline your work to concentrate more on priorities?
- Set aside a day or so to observe your program:
    - Complete the Program Audit form for your program (see Appendix)
    - Identify the bottlenecks in your workflow
- Consider how you will evaluate your program effectiveness on a regular basis

- Review the list of *Common Control Structures in Organizations Implementing ABA Programs* from the Appendix :

    o Identify important policies and procedures that your organization should develop

    o Get a group together to help develop the policies and procedures

    o Don't forget to objectively assess effectiveness of the new structures

- Review your training program:

    o How does each part contribute to a more effective employee?

    o Is there a balance between developing verbal skills and performance skills?

    o How often are implementers observed? How is feedback from observations documented?

    o How are professional staff members included in training? What are expectations for their professional growth?

- Review your leadership:

    o What can you do to improve communication of your vision of the program?

    o How can all stakeholders be included more in making decisions and determining future direction?

Appendix

Common Control Structures in Organizations Implementing ABA Programs

General Categories:

1. Program Structure
2. Personnel
3. Program Development Resources
4. Program Services
5. Training
6. Supervision
7. Communication

The following list pertains only to control structures directly related to service delivery and represents the author's recommendations for consideration as part of the written policies and procedures of the organization. The nature of the control structures—written information and descriptions of practices—should include direct references to the contingencies that control compliance with the policy such as required reports, supervision checks, audits, etc.

Program Structure

- Name of organization, address, contact information
- Mission and scope of services
- Populations(s) served
- Composition of organization (divisions, subsidiaries, departments, etc.)
- Method of governance, nature of legal entity

- Affiliations
- Director's name, address, phone, email
- Location and description of facilities
- Geographical area(s) served
- Entry and exit criteria for individuals served by program

Personnel

- Organizational chart
- Job descriptions and duties
- Qualifications, certifications, affiliations of personnel
- Caseloads

    Method of assignment, regular workload, limits

    Work hours

    Allocation of hours (on-site, meetings, direct work, preparation, travel, written work, research)

    Work Locations

    Supervision received and given

Program Development Resources

(Describe availability and procedure for accessing the following resources):

- Written curricula
- Curriculum resources
- Copying and printing
- Budget
- Supplies, office & educational
- Capital resources: tables, shelves, desks, partitions, etc.
- Computer resources including software
- Secretarial support
- Research support

- Professional books and journals
- Public and private research library access
- Conferences, courses, workshops for professional development
- Consultants and specialists
- Professional associations
- Local professional community and liaisons
- Community resources

Program Services

- Description of services
- Requirements of applicable laws, statues, and regulations governing delivery of services
- For the following procedures include a detailed description of procedures, timelines, responsible personnel, instruments used, format of products, reporting requirements.

    Acceptance and intake

    Baseline assessment

    Professional and paraprofessional services allocation (teacher, related services, BCABA, BCBA)

    Instructional settings and format determination (inclusion, 1:1; groups, community, etc.)

    Instructional program selection and creation

    Behavior program creation

    Daily progress assessment (daily data collection, graphs)

    Quality assurance

    Periodic progress summary (annual reports, ABLLS, standardized tests, etc.)

    Transfer and transitional procedures

Training

For each training: title, intended audience, instructor, location, times, prerequisites, description, instructional goals, methods, syllabi, presentation slides, video, handouts, books and reading materials, required coursework and assignments, passing criteria.

- New employee orientation
- New parent orientation
- New student orientation
- Program policies and procedures (all staff)
- Introduction to autism and developmental disabilities
- Teaching in discrete trials
    - Attention and engagement
    - Materials and setting
    - Response prompts
    - Skill selection and presentation
    - Errorless teaching
    - Error correction
    - Reinforcement
    - Data Collection
- Incidental teaching
- Generalization
- Teaching in groups
- Inclusion
- Curriculum design for students with autism
- Language acquisition in students with autism
- Reading concepts, research, methods, and materials
- Mathematics concepts, research, methods, and materials
- Handwriting concepts, research, methods, and materials
- Assistive technology
- Supervision of instructional personnel
- Supervision program for the National Certification Exam for Board Certified Associate Behavior Analyst
- Parent training

- Behavioral programming
- Ethical guidelines for implementation of educational and behavioral treatment
- Rights of persons with disabilities—Federal and State Laws
- Physical management training

Supervision

- Observation and feedback
- Review of written products: evaluations, observations, functional analyses, behavior programs, progress reports
- Case discussion
- Ethics discussions

Communication

- Daily/weekly communication with parents
- Team meetings
- IEP related meetings
- Administrative meetings
- Student program reviews
- Guidelines for email communication
- Written reports and programs

Clinical Activity Log

Week: _____ Clinician: _____

Record activity and duration

Categories		MON	TUES	WED	THURS	FRI
PWR	Program Writing/Revision					
PRTM	Program Review/Team Meetings					
PO	Program Observations					
TG	Training Given					
TR	Training Received					
CSG	Clinical Supervision Given					
CSR	Clinical Supervision Received					
SIEP	Student IEP Meetings					
ACD	Agency Curriculum Development					
ACC	Agency Clinical Coordination					
NSE	New Student Evaluation					

Check One:

☐ Retrospective Report (list sources)
☐ Contemporary Report

Total Hours Worked: _____

Students on Caseload: _____

Organization Name
Consultation Plan

The following plan is an agreement between [Organization Name] and the contracting party named below. The purpose of the plan is to explicitly and objectively state the goals and objectives of consultation in order to facilitate achievement of the desired outcomes.

Program: _____   Consultant: _____

Address: _____   Date Written: _____

Consultation Model (Circle one):
☐ Expanded Support ☐ ABA Classroom Support ☐ Regular Classroom Support
☐ Resource Room Support

Program Description:

(Briefly describe program. Include number of students, staffing, and program environment)

_____

_____

_____

_____

Summary of Goals: (Briefly outline each goal and attach a goal sheet)

Goal 1:		Person(s) Responsible:	
Goal 2:		Person(s) Responsible:	
Goal 3:		Person(s) Responsible:	
Goal 4:		Person(s) Responsible:	
Goal 5:		Person(s) Responsible:	

Organization Name
Consultation Plan – Goal Sheet

Goal #:

Focus (check those that apply):

☐ Training ☐ Student Consultation and Planning ☐ Curriculum Development ☐ Administrative Support

☐ Clinical Supervision ☐ Parent Training & Support ☐ Other _____

Describe desired outcome of consultation in observable and measurable terms:

_____
_____
_____
_____

Start date _____ End date: _____

Person(s) responsible: _____ _____ _____ _____

Assigned resources (staff, materials, etc) _____ _____ _____ _____

Review dates (at least quarterly): _____ _____ _____ _____

Reviewers _____ _____ _____ _____

Clinical Supervisor assigned and phone:

Reviewed on _____
Reviewed on _____
Reviewed on _____
Reviewed on _____

Inclusion Plan

Student: _____ Date _____

Program _____

This inclusion plan has been developed for the year _____ to _____

Team members for this plan have been designated as follows:

Team Member:	Title:

Team Meeting Dates for Review have been scheduled as follows:

_____

_____

Circle one: Paraprofessional Support has/has not been assigned. Schedule:

Major accommodations or modifications (e.g. wheel-chair accessible, communication device) (See individual activity plans for additional details):

_____

_____

Behavior Intervention Plan Attached? ¨ Yes ¨ No ¨ In development

Individual Activity Plans attached for the following activities:

_____

_____

Inclusion Individual Activity Plan

Student _____   Year _____

Activity _____   Location _____

Times _____   Activity Leader _____

IEP Goal Reference:

Goals and Task Analysis for Activity

_____
_____
_____
_____

Procedure

_____
_____
_____
_____

Special Modifications

_____
_____

Baseline Date and Status

_____
_____

Paraprofessional Assigned? ¨ Yes ¨ No   Describe duties:

_____
_____
_____

Project Management Grid

Program Name/Location: **Teacher(s) and Contact Info:** **Consultation Plan Phase:**

Student Name	Current Curriculum Phase	Inclusion Plan Phase	Comments

Staff Name	Assignment	Training Phase	Comments

Consultation Plan Phases:
1. Initial draft of consultation plan developed based on input from district/agency
2. Consultation staff and teacher brainstorm overall schedule and goals for program development and add to consultation plan
3. Consultation Plan draft presented to school/district administration for approval
4. Consultation plan implemented
5. Schedule of review initiated

Curriculum Plan Phases:
1. Baseline assessment completed (both direct and indirect assessments)
2. Draft curriculum developed with team for entire day
3. Materials procured
4. Learning Sets, Curriculum List, and Data Sheets created
5. New curriculum demonstrated and implementers trained
6. Implementation observed, reviewed, and revised as necessary
7. Periodic Program Reviews Scheduled

Inclusion Plan Phases:
1. Team members identified
2. Inclusion teachers contacted
3. Appropriate inclusion experiences identified by team
4. Program plans for inclusion experiences presented to team and finalized
5. Verbal training for inclusion experiences completed for all implementers
6. Ongoing observation and feedback for inclusion experiences initiated
7. Periodic evaluations/reviews with inclusion team initiated

Training Phases:
1. Orientation Training CD completed
2. Basic verbal training completed (10 hours)
3. Quizzes successfully passed
4. Student curriculum demonstrated by teacher/consultant
5. Implementation of curriculum observed and feedback given
6. Performance criterion for implementation of curriculum met for discrete trials component
7. Performance criterion for implementation of curriculum met for incidental teaching
8. Performance criterion for implementation of curriculum met for group instruction

Program Audit

Program Name: _____   **Date of Evaluation:** _____

Evaluator: _____

Part 1: Review of Records, Resources, and Procedures

Record Keeping and Documentation

Description of Item	Date, Method of Review, and Results
Individual files exist for each student and are immediately accessible to authorized program personnel	
Files contain:	
Contact Information	
Important Medical Information	
Baseline Skills Assessment of appropriate curriculum items that is based on repeated direct measurement	
Copies of all relevant reports from outside consultants and professionals	
Photo and Video Release Permissions if applicable	
Behavior Programs/ authorization for restrictive procedures (if applicable)	
Copies of meeting minutes, letters, and memos concerning student	
Copies of completed (mastered) programs with associated data sheets, stimulus lists, and graphs	
Copies of outdated curriculum with date of revision	

Student Curriculum and Programs

Description of Item	Date, Method of Review, and Results
Individualized student curriculum is comprehensive in scope, appropriate to the age and needs of the student, and reflects continuity with the baseline evaluation.	

The Student's Individualized Curriculum:	
Covers all relevant domains	
Includes behavior program or procedures (if applicable)	
Covers home and community setting support and generalization of skills	
Specifies a variety of teaching settings and includes programs for incidental teaching and inclusion	
Contains comprehensive language program and includes natural environment training as well as work on individual skills in isolation	
The Student's Overall Program:	
Runs for at least 30 hours per week, including summer, without extended periods of vacation or breaks (as required by student need)	
Reviews progress on programs frequently, based on objective measures	
Revises programs in a timely manner if expected progress is not attained	
Is created by an educational team including the parents, teaching personnel, consultant(s), and supporting services such as speech therapy, physical therapy, etc. There is also provision made for participation from the home school district, or parents' advisors/ representatives as required.	

Program Book

Description of Item	Date, Method of Review, and Results
Separate program book exists for school and home programs (if applicable)	
Sections exist for all curriculum areas	

Description of Item	Date, Method of Review, and Results
Program write-ups contain clear descriptions of all procedures, methods, and target behaviors	
Data sheets and stimulus lists exist for all programs and are located with the program write-up	
Mand List, Reinforcer List, and Student Information Sheet exist and are located at the front of the program book	
Student schedule is complete and located in appropriate section of program book	
Student's individualized curriculum exists and is located in a separate section	
Meeting minutes are filed in a separate section of the program book	

Staff and Parent Training

Description of Item	Date, Method of Review, and Results
Training procedures for teaching personnel are described in writing	
Teaching personnel receive training in basic procedures before working with student	
Written training procedures are comprehensive and adequate including trainings in administrative policies, basic methods of applied behavior analysis, basic discrete trial instruction, incidental teaching, language instruction, understanding autism, and the specific program implementation methodologies used by the program.	
Written training procedures exist for training teaching personnel to implement a student's individual curriculum including understanding the program book, student schedule, stimulus lists, data sheets, graphs, mand lists, reinforcer lists, and to understand and participate in the various program review activities (clinics and other meetings).	
Training sessions are documented	
There is written evidence of ongoing professional training for certified teachers in the areas of applied behavior analysis	

Description of Item	
There is written evidence of ongoing professional participation and training for consultants	
Written training procedures exist for training parents and other relatives of students in procedures and programs to support the student at home and in the community.	
Procedures exist to orient new parents to the program and program methodology	
There is evidence of regular and effective communication (both formal and informal) between the parents and the program (and school district, if applicable)	
There is evidence that training is offered to relatives on a regular basis according to the needs and schedule of the relatives	
There is evidence of an ongoing outreach to inform and educate the neighboring community about effective autism treatment	

Staff Qualifications, Supervision, and Administrative Support

Description of Item	Date, Method of Review, and Results
Instructional Assistants (paraprofessionals) have appropriate experience and training before working with student	
Supervising teacher has experience, education, and professional credentials and certification in areas appropriate to the functioning level, diagnosis, and age of the students	
Supervising teacher has training in all procedures used in the program	
Supervising teacher is familiar with curriculum sequence and scope, as well as mastery criteria for each program	
Supervising teacher is trained in effective supervision techniques and personnel management	
Ratio of students to supervising teacher does not exceed reasonable limits for extended periods of time	

Supervising teacher is scheduled to be on premises for the majority of time	
Consultant(s) and other program supervisors meet the qualifications for Board Certified Behavior Analyst set by the Behavior Analyst Certification Board, Inc.	
Consultant(s) and other program supervisors meet qualifications for ABA consultants in autism set by the Special Interest Group of the Association for Behavior Analysis (1998)	
Formal program review by consultants occurs at least biweekly for each student	
Consultants are easily accessible by phone or other means when they are not present at the program	
Supervising teachers meet individually with paraprofessionals at least biweekly	
Paraprofessionals receive regular objective feedback on their performance, based on direct observation	
All personnel receive written performance reviews at least semi-annually.	
Adequate personnel resources are provided for administrative tasks such as hiring, accounting, and secretarial duties so that programmatic personnel spend time on tasks directly related to accomplishing student goals	
Provision is made for adequately staffing vacancies, illness, vacations, and leaves so that the minimum disruption in programming occurs for the student.	
Input on program goals and services is solicited from community members, parents, and other constituencies	

Environment, Materials, and Equipment

Description of Item	Date, Method of Review, and Results
Environment is large enough to accommodate number of students and adults	

Environment contains sufficient areas for play and other common activities like snack, lunch, and group activities	
Each student has individual space for programs	
Individual student spaces are relatively free from distractions (visual or auditory)	
Individual spaces are not open to view by public	
Environment contains sufficient common space to promote student interaction	
Common areas are readily accessible to student	
Student is regularly allowed access to common space while other students are present	
Environment is free from dirt, unpleasant odors, noise, dangerous equipment, and extremes of temperature	
Electrical outlets are made safe, according to needs of student	
Lighting of area is adequate	
Bathrooms are easily accessible and facilities are easily usable by children (height of sinks, size of toilets, etc.)	
Cleaning supplies are available as needed	
Food storage and preparation is safe.	
Environment contains areas for individual storage of student items	
Students have regular access to outdoors when weather permits	
Outdoor areas are safe and free from dangerous equipment, insects, or animal feces.	

Outdoor areas are well defined and away from vehicles	
Outdoor areas do not permit elopement of students into traffic or other dangerous areas	
Outdoor areas contain sufficient space for all children present to freely engage in gross motor activities	
Outdoor equipment is well maintained and appropriate to the age and developmental level of the children present	
Program possesses equipment and materials to implement all phases of the students' curriculum, including play activities and reinforcement.	
Office and conference areas are separate from programmatic areas	
Area is available for students who are upset to be away from others	
Storage space is sufficient to allow organized access and to keep materials not in use out of the way.	
Materials are clean and disinfected periodically	

Part 2: Case Review

Description of Item	Method of Review
Evaluator completes Instructor Evaluation Checklist on at least two separate occasions for two different students.	Instructor Evaluation Checklist
Student Name: _____ Date and time: _____ Attach completed Instructor Evaluation Checklist	
Student Name: _____ Date and time: _____ Attach completed Instructor Evaluation Checklist	

MSWO Preference Assessment Data Sheet

Student: _____ Instructor: _____ Date: _____

Positions

Trials 1 __ __ __ __ __ __ __ __ __ __

       2 __ __ __ __ __ __ __ __ __

       3 __ __ __ __ __ __ __ __

       4 __ __ __ __ __ __ __

       5 __ __ __ __ __ __

       6 __ __ __ __ __

       7 __ __ __ __

       8 __ __ __

       9 __ __

      10 __

Item Name: Trial Selected:

A _____   A _____

B _____   B _____

C _____   C _____

D _____   D _____

E _____   E _____

F _____   F _____

G _____   G _____

H _____   H _____

I _____   I _____

J _____   J _____

Instructor Observation and Feedback Form

Instructor:_____   Observer:_____   Date:_____

Time of Observation:_____   Setting:_____   Student:_____

Scoring

C- performance occurred *consistently* throughout the session
I- performance occurred *intermittently* throughout the session
DNO- performance <u>did not occur</u> or occurred infrequently throughout the session
NA- not applicable

Target	Score	Additional Comments
MATERIALS AND SETTING		
Materials were ready and organized prior to start of the session		
Work area was clear of unnecessary distractions		
Seating and table position was optimized		
Drill schedule was visible and utilized throughout the session		
Demonstrated appropriate level of enthusiasm, playfulness and physical interactions.		
ATTENDING AND ENGAGEMENT STRATEGIES		
Instructor utilized and modified pacing according to student needs		
Instructor followed attention hierarchy		
Instructor engaged the student before giving instruction		
Instructor built momentum in the beginning of the trial		
SKILL PROGRAM IMPLEMENTATION		
Instructor followed correct step by step instructions		
Instructor required the correct student target performance		
Stimulus list was correctly followed		
Instructor gave the correct SD		
Mastered stimuli/drills were integrated into the session as appropriate		
Data was correctly taken		

Instructor: _____ Date: _____ Observer: _____

Page 2

Target	Score	Additional Comments
USE OF PROMPTS		
Prompts were used to prevent errors as needed		
Type of prompt was appropriate		
Frequency and duration of prompts were appropriate		
Student required to perform successive approximation of target behavior as independently as possible		
Prompts faded within the set of trials when possible		
ERROR CORRECTION		
Error correction procedure was implemented correctly and consistently		
Required independent response prior to reinforcement following error correction procedure		
Required performance was simplified when errors persisted		
REINFORCEMENT STRATEGY		
Reinforcement was effective/appropriate for the student		
Reinforcers were delivered at appropriate times		
Token board used correctly when specified		
Reinforcers were readily accessible		
Duration, location and frequency were appropriate to work accomplished		
Student choice and preference were integrated into reinforcement strategy		
BEHAVIOR		
Procedures are related to functional assessment of behavior as outlined in BIP		
Instructor reinforced functional alternatives		
Appropriate data related to behavior recorded		
TRANSISTIONS		
Instructor structured, engaged and reinforced transitions as appropriate		

Instructor Observation and Feedback Form

Feedback Summary

Instructor: _____ **Date:** _____ **Observer:** _____

Additional Comments:

Strengths:

Target Skills for Development:

Next Steps:

Date of Next Observation and Focus:

Please sign and date to indicate this observation was reviewed:

_____   _____
Instructor Signature   **Date**

_____   _____
Teacher/Observer Signature   **Date**

Instructor Comments

Instructor Observation and Feedback Form: Observer Worksheet

Instructor: _____   Date: _____   Observer: _____

Time	Details (Skills program name, etc.)	Trial Presented (make a check mark for each trial presented	Additional Comments

References and Bibliography

Ahearn, W. H., Clark, K. M., Gardenier, N. C., Chung, B. I., & Dube, W. V. (2003). Persistence of Stereotypic Behavior: Examining the Effects of External Reinforcers. *Journal of Applied Behavior Analysis,* **36**, 439—448.

Altman, K., Hobbs, S., Roberts, M., & Haavik, S. (1981). Control of Disruptive Behavior by Manipulation of Reinforcement Density and Item Difficulty Subsequent to Errors. *Applied Research in Mental Retardation,* **1**, 193—208.

American Psychological Association. (2009). *Publication Manual of the American Psychological Association, 6th Edition.* Washington, DC: American Psychological Association.

Archer, A. L., & Hughs, C. A. (2011). *Explicit Instruction, Effective and Efficient Teaching.* New York, NY: The Guilford Press.

Athens, E. S., & Vollmer, T. R. (2010). An Investigation of Differential Reinforcement of Alternative Behavior Without Extinction. *Journal of Applied Behavior Analysis,* **43**, 569—589.

Atwater, J. B., & Morris, E. K. (1988). Teachers' Instructions and Children's Compliance in Preschool Classrooms: A Descriptive Analysis. *Journal of Applied Behavior Analysis,* **21**, 157—167.

Autism Special Interest Group of the Association for Behavior Analysis International. (2007). Consumer Guidelines for Identifying, Selection, and Evaluating Behavior Analysts Working with Individuals with Autism Spectrum Disorders.

Azrin, N. H. & Foxx, R. M. (1974). *Toilet Training in Less Than a Day.* New York, NY: Simon and Schuster.

Baer, D. M., Wolf, M. M., & Risley, T. R. (1968). Some Current Dimensions of Applied Behavior Analysis. *Journal of Applied Behavior Analysis* **1**, 91—97.

Baird, G., Cass, H., & Slonims, V. (2003). Diagnosis of Autism. *BMJ Publishing Group Ltd.,* **327**, 488—493.

Barbetta, P. M., Heron, T. E., & Heward, W. L. (1993). Effects of Active Student Response During Error Correction on the Acquisition, Maintenance, and Generalization of Sight Words By Students With Developmental Disabilities. *Journal of Applied Behavior Analysis,* **26**, 111—119.

Barbetta, P. M., Heward, W. L., & Bradley, D. M. (1993). Relative Effects of Whole-Word and Phonetic-Prompt Error Correction On the Acquisition and Maintenance of Sight Words by Students with Developmental Disabilities. *Journal of Applied Behavior Analysis,* **26**, 99—110.

Barbetta, P. M., Heward, W. L., Bradley, D. M., & Miller, A. D. (1994). Effects of Immediate and Delayed Error Correction on the Acquisition and Maintenance of Sight Words by Students with Developmental Disabilities. *Journal of Applied Behavior Analysis,* **27**, 177—178.

Barlow, D. H. & Hayes, S. C. (1979). Alternating Treatments Design: One Strategy for Comparing the Effects of Two Treatments in a Single Subject. *Journal of Applied Behavior Analysis,* **12**, 199—210.

Barton, E. S. (1970). Inappropriate Speech in a Severely Retarded Child: A Case Study in Language Conditioning and Generalization. *Journal of Applied Behavior Analysis,* **3,** 299—307.

Behavior Analyst Certification Board. (2012). Behavior Analyst Task List, Fourth Edition. Tallahassee, FL. retrieved from http://www.bacb.com/Downloadfiles/TaskList/BACB_Fourth_Edition Task_List.pdf on June 22, 2013.

Belfiore, P. J., Skinner, C. H., & Ferkis, M. A. (1995). Effects of Response and Trial Repetition on Sight-Word Training for Students with Learning Disabilities. *Journal of Applied Behavior Analysis,* **28,** 347—348.

Belfiore, P., Lee, D. L., Vargas, A. U., & Skinner, C.H. (1997). Effects of High-Preference Single-Digit Mathematics Problem Completion on Multiple-Digit Mathematics Problem Performance. *Journal of Applied Behavior Analysis,* **30,** 327—330.

Bennett, C. W. (1974). Articulation Training of Two Hearing-Impaired Girls. *Journal of Applied Behavior Analysis,* **7,** 439—445.

Blackwell, A. J., & McLaughlin, T. F. (2005). Using Guided Notes, Choral Responding, and Response Cards to Increase Student Performance. *The International Journal of Special Education,* **20,** 1—5.

Bouxsein, K. J., Tiger, J. H., & Fisher, W. W. (2008). A Comparison of General and Specific Instructions to Promote Task Engagement and Completion by a Young Man with Asperger Syndrome. *Journal of Applied Behavior Analysis,* **41,** 113—116.

Bullock, C., & Normand, M. P. (2006). The Effects of a High-Probability Instruction Sequence and Response-Independent Reinforcer Delivery on Child Compliance. *Journal of Applied Behavior Analysis,* **39,** 495—499.

Calderhead, W. J., Filter, K. J., & Albin, R. W. (2006). An Investigation of Incremental Effects of Interspersing Math Items on Task-Related Behavior. *Journal of Behavioral Education,* **15,** 53—67.

Cammilleri, A. P., Tiger, J. H., & Hanley, G. P. (2008). Developing Stimulus Control Of Young Children's Requests To Teachers: Classwide Application Of Multiple Schedules. *Journal of Applied Behavior Analysis,* **41,** 299—303.

Carbone, V. J. (2012). Increasing Speech Sound Production of Children with Autism. *Presented at 33rd Annual Conference of the Berkshire Association for Behavior Analysis, University of Massachusetts, Amherst, MA, Oct. 11, 2012.*

Carbone, V. J., Hagerty, M. M., & Sweeney-Kerwin, E. J. (2007). A Description of Performance Management & Data Based Decision Making Within a Center Based Program for Children with Autism. *NYS Association for Behavior Analysis, 17th Annual Conference, Verona, N.Y. November 1 & 2, 2007.*

Carbone, V. J., Morgenstern, B., Zecchin-Tirri, G., & Kolberg, L. (2007). The Role of the Reflexive Conditioned Motivating Operation (CMO-R) During Discrete Trial Instruction of Children with Autism. *Journal of Early and Intensive Behavior Intervention,* **4,** 658-680.

Carnine, J. S. (1984). A Review of *Theory of Instruction* by Seigfried Engelmann and Douglas Carnine. *The Behavior Analyst,* **7,** 205—210.

Carr, E. G. (1994). Emerging Themes in the Functional Analysis of Problem Behavior. *Journal of Applied Behavior Analysis,* **27,** 393—399.

Carr, J. E., Nicolson, A. C., & Higbee, T. S. (2000). Evaluation of a Brief Multiple-Stimulus Preference Assessment in a Naturalistic Context. *Journal of Applied Behavior Analysis,* **33,** 353—357.

Causin, K., Albert, K., Carbone, V. J., Sweeney-Kerwin, E., Carbone Clinic. (October 11-12, 2012). The Role of Joint Control In Teaching Complex Listener Behavior to Children with Autism. 33rd Annual Conference of the Berkshire Association for Behavior Analysis. Campus Center, University of Massachusetts-Amherst, Amherst, MA.

Charlop, M. H., Kurtz, P. F., & Milstein, J. P. (1992). Too Much Reinforcement, Too Little Behavior: Assessing Task Interspersal Procedures in Conjunction With Different Reinforcement Schedules With Autistic Children. *Journal of Applied Behavior Analysis,* **25,** 795—808.

Cohen, Steven L. (1998). Behavioral Momentum: The Effects of the Temporal Separation of Rates of Reinforcement. *Journal of the Experimental Analysis of Behavior,* **69,** 29—47.

Connecticut State Department of Education (2008). Using Scientific Research-Based Interventions: Improving Education for All Students.

Cooper, J. O., Heron, T. E., & Heward, W. L. (2007). *Applied Behavior Analysis, Second Edition.* Upper Saddle River, NJ: Pearson Education, Inc.

Cowley, B. J., Green, G., & Braunling-McMorrow, D. (1992). Using Stimulus Equivalence Procedures to Teach Name-Face Matching to Adults with Brain Injuries. *Journal of Applied Behavior Analysis,* **25,** 461—475.

Critchfield, T. S., & Perone, M. (1990). Verbal Self-Reports of Delayed Matching to Sample by Humans. *Journal of the Experimental Analysis of Behavior,* **53,** 321—344.

Crosbie, J., & Kelly, G. (1994). Effects of Imposed Postfeedback Delays in Programmed Instruction. *Journal of Applied Behavior Analysis,* **27**, 483—491.

Cummings, A. R., & Carr, J. E. (2009). Evaluating Progress in Behavioral Programs For Children With Autism Spectrum Disorders Via Continuous and Discontinuous Measurement. *Journal of Applied Behavior Analysis,* **42,** 57—71.

Cuvo, A. J., Ashley, K. M., Marso, K. J., Zhang, B. L., & Fry, T. A. (1995). Effect of Response Practice Variables on Learning Spelling of Sight Vocabulary. *Journal of Applied Behavior Analysis,* **28**, 155-173.

Daly, E. J. III, Wells, N. J., Swanger-Gagne M.S., Carr, J. E., Kunz, G. M., & Taylor, A. M. (2009). Evaluation of the Multiple-Stimulus Without Replacement Preference Assessment Method Using Activities As Stimuli. *Journal of Applied Behavior Analysis,* **42,** 563—574.

Davis, C. A., Brady, M. P., Hamilton, R., McEvoy, M. A., & Williams, R. E. (1994). Effects of High-Probability Requests on the Social Interactions of Young Children With Severe Disabilities. *Journal of Applied Behavior Analysis,* **27,** 619—637.

Davis, C. A., Brady, M. P., Williams, R. E., & Hamilton, R. (1992). Effects of High-Probability Requests on the Acquisition and Generalization of Responses to Requests in Young Children with Behavior Disorders. *Journal of Applied Behavior Analysis,* **25,** 905—916.

De La Piedad, X., Field, D., & Rachlin, H. (2006). The Influence of Prior Choices on Current Choice. *Journal of the Experimental Analysis of Behavior,* **85,** 3—21.

Deitz, S. M., Fredrick, L. D., Quinn, P. C., & Brasher, L. D. (1986). Comparing the Effects of Two Correction Procedures on Human Acquisition of Sequential Behavior Patterns. *Journal of the Experimental Analysis of Behavior,* **46,** 1—14.

DeLeon, I. G., & Iwata, B. A. (1996). Evaluation of a Multiple-Stimulus Presentation Format For Assessing Reinforcer Preferences. *Journal of Applied Behavior Analysis,* **29,** 519—533.

Deno, S. L. (2003). Developments in Curriculum-Based Measurement. *The Journal of Special Education,* **37,** 184—192.

Deno, S. L. & Mirkin, P. K. (1977). Data-Based Program Modification: A Manual. Reston VA: Council for Exceptional Children.

Deno, S.L. & Fuchs, L. S. (1987). Developing Curriculum-Based Measurement Systems for Data-Based Special Education Problem Solving. Focus on Exceptional Children, **19,** 1 - 15.

Deno, S.L. (1985). Curriculum-Based Measurement: The Emerging Alternative. Exceptional Children, **52,** 219-232.

Department of Defense. (July, 2007). Report and Plan on Services to Military Dependent Children with Autism.

Devany, J. M., Hayes, S. C., & Nelson, R. O. (1986). Equivalence Class Formation in Language-Able and Language-Disabled Children. *Journal of the Experimental Analysis of Behavior,* **46,** 243—257.

DiGennaro, F. D., & Martens, B. K. (2007). A Comparison of Performance Feedback Procedures on Teachers' Treatment Implementation Integrity and Students' Inappropriate Behavior in Special Education Classrooms. *Journal of Applied Behavior Analysis,* **40,** 447—461.

Dinsmoor, J. A. (2004). The Etymology of Basic Concepts in the Experimental Analysis of Behavior. *Journal of the Experimental Analysis of Behavior,* **82,** 311—316.

Doughty, A. H., & Lattal, K. A. (2001). Resistance to Change of Operant Variation and Repetition. *Journal of the Experimental Analysis of Behavior,* **76,** 195—215.

Drevno, G. E., Kimball, J. W., Possi, M. K., Heward, W. L., Garner III, R. G., & Barbetta, P. M. (1994). Effects of Active Student Response During Error Correction on the Acquisition, Maintenance, and Generalization of Science Vocabulary by Elementary Students: A Systematic Replication. *Journal of Applied Behavior Science,* **27,** 179—180.

Dube, W. & McIlvane, W. J. (2001). Behavioral Momentum in Computer-Presented Discriminations in Individual With Severe Mental Retardation. *Journal of the Experimental Analysis of Behavior,* **75,** 15—23.

Dube, W. V., Ahearn, W. H., Lionello-DeNolf, K., & McIlvane, W. J. (2009). Behavioral Momentum: Translational Research in Intellectual and Developmental Disabilities. *Behav Anal Today.* 2009, **10**, 238–253.

Dube, W. V., MacDonald, R. P. F., Mansfield, R. C., Holcomb, W. L., & Ahearn, W. H. (2004). Toward a Behavioral Analysis of Joint Attention. *The Behavior Analyst,* **27,** 197—207.

Dube, W. V., McDonald, S. J., McIlvane, W. J., & Mackay, H. A. (1991). Constructed-Response Matching and Spelling Construction. *Journal of Applied Behavior Analysis,* **24,** 305—317.

Ducharme, J. M., & Worling, D. E. (1994). Behavioral Momentum and Stimulus Fading in the Acquisition and Maintenance of Child Compliance in the Home. *Journal of Applied Behavior Analysis,* **27,** 639—647.

Esch, B. E., Carr, J. E., & Grow, L. L. (2009). Evaluation of an Enhanced Stimulus-Stimulus Pairing Procedure to Increase Early Vocalizations of Children With Autism. *Journal of Applied Behavior Analysis,* **42,** 225—241.

Fabrizio, M. A., & Pahl, S. (2007). An Experimental Analysis of Two Error Correction Procedures Used to Improve the Textural Behavior of a Student with Autism. *The Behavior Analyst Today,* **8,** 260—272.

Ferster, C. B. & Skinner, B. F. (1957). Schedules of Reinforcement. Englewood Cliffs, NJ: Prentice-Hall

Fovel, J. T. (2002). *The ABA Program Companion, Organizing Quality Programs for Children with Autism and PDD.* New York, NY: DRL Books, Inc.

Fovel, J. T., Robertson, M, Carr, S., Lilburn, L, & Donowitz, G (2010). Multi-Discipline Collaboration in ABA Programs based in a Public School Setting. Workshop presented to the CT Association for Behavior Analysis, Cromwell, CT, March 26, 2010.

Fuchs, L. S., Deno, S. L., & Mirkin, P. K. (1984). The Effects of Frequent Curriculum-Based Measurement and Evaluation on Pedagogy, Student Achievement, and Student Awareness of Learning. *American Educational Research Association,* **21,** 449—460.

Gagnon, E. (2001). Power cards: using special interests to motivate children and youth with Asperger syndrome and autism. Shawnee Mission, KS: Autism Asperger Publishing Co.

Gatch, M. B., & Osborne, J. G. (1989). Transfer of Contextual Stimulus Function Via Equivalence Class Development. *Journal of the Experimental Analysis of Behavior,* **51,** 369—378.

Gettinger, M. (1993). Effects of Invented Spelling and Direct Instruction on Spelling Performance of Second-Grade Boys. *Journal of Applied Behavior Analysis,* **26,** 281—291.

Glover, A. C., Roane, H. S., Kadey, H. J., & Grow, L. L. (2008). Preference for Reinforcers Under Progressive-And Fixed-Ratio Schedules: A Comparison of Single and Concurrent Arrangements. *Journal of Applied Behavior Analysis,* **41,** 163—176.

Gray, C. (2000) *The New Social Story Book*: Illustrated Edition. Arlington, TX: Future Horizons, Inc.

Grow, L. L., Carr, J. E., Kodak, T. M., Jostad, C. M., & Kisamore, A. N. (2011). A Comparison of Methods for Teaching Receptive Labeling to Children With Autism Spectrum Disorders. *Journal of Applied Behavior Analysis,* **44,** 475—498.

Hagopian, Long, & Rush. (2004). Preference Assessment Procedures for Individuals With Developmental Disabilities. *Behavior Modification,* **28,** 668-677.

Halle, J. W., & Holt, B. (1991). Assessing Stimulus Control In The Natural Settings: An Analysis of Stimuli That Acquire Control During Training. *Journal of Applied Behavior Analysis,* **24,** 579—589.

Harper, D. N. (1996). Response-Independent Food Delivery and Behavioral Resistance to Change. *Journal of the Experimental Analysis of Behavior,* **65,** 549—560.

Harper, D. N., & McLean A. P. (1992). Resistance to Change and the Law of Effect. *Journal of the Experimental Analysis of Behavior,* **57,** 317—337.

Herrnstein, R. J. (1961). Relative and Absolute Strength of Response as a Function of Frequency of Reinforcement. *Journal of the Experimental Analysis of Behavior,* **4,** 267—272.

Heward, W. L. (2008). A Place at the Education Reform Table: Why Behavior Analysis Needs to Be There, Why It's Not as Welcome as It Should Be, and Some Actions that Can Make Our Science More Relevant. *Behavior Analysis in Education,* **31,** Number 3.

Hineline, P. N. (2005). The Aesthetics of Behavioral Arrangements. *The Behavior Analyst,* **28,** 15—28.

Hoch, H., Taylor, B., & Rodriguez, A. (2009). Teaching Teenagers with Autism to Answer Cell Phones and Seek Assistance When Lost. *Behavior Analysis In Practice,* **21,** 14—20.

Holland, J. G., Solomon, C., Doran, J. & Frezza, D. A. (1976). *The Analysis of Behavior in Planning Instruction.* Reading, MA: Addison-Wesley Publishing Co., Inc.

Horner, R. H., & Day, H. M. (1991). The Effects of Response Efficiency on Functionally Equivalent Competing Behaviors. *Journal of Applied Behavior Analysis,* **24,** 719—732.

Horner, R. H., Day, H. M., Sprague, J. R., O'Brien, M., & Heathfield, L.T. (1991). Interspersed Requests: A Nonaversive Procedure for Reducing Aggression and Self-Injury During Instruction. *Journal of Applied Behavior Analysis,* **24,** 265—278.

Hosp, M. K., Hosp, J. L., & Howell, K. W. (2007). *The ABCs of CBM, A Practical Guide to Curriculum-Based Measurement.* New York, NY: The Guilford Press.

Houlihan, D., Jacobson, L., & Brandon, P. K. (1994). Replication of a High-Probability Request Sequence With Varied Interprompt Times In a Preschool Setting. *Journal of Applied Behavior Analysis,* **27,** 737—738.

Howard, J. S., Sparkman, C. R., Green, G., & Stanislaw, Harold. (2005). A Comparison of Intensive Behavior Analytic and Eclectic Treatments for Young Children With Autism. *Research in Developmental Disabilities,* **26,** 359—383.

Ingvarsson, E. T., & Hollobaugh, T. (2010). Acquisition of Intraverbal Behavior: Teaching Children With Autism To Mand For Answers To Questions. Journal of Applied Behavior Analysis, **43,** 1—17.

Iwata, B. A. (1987). Negative Reinforcement in Applied Behavior Analysis: An Emerging Technology. *Journal of Applied Behavior Analysis,* **20,** 361—378.

Iwata, B. A., Pace, G., Dorsey, M. F., Zarcone, J. R., Vollmer, T. R., Smith, R. G., Rodgers, T. A., Lerman, D. C., Shore, B. A., Mazaleski, J. L., Goh, H., Cowdery, G. E., Kalsher, M. J., McCosh, K. C., & Willis, K. D. (1994). The Functions of Self-Injurious Behavior: An Experimental-Epidemiological Analysis. *Journal of Applied Behavior Analysis,* **27,** 215—240.

Johnson, K. R., & Layng, T. V. J. (1996). On Terms and Procedures: Fluency. *The Behavior Analyst,* **19,** 281—288.

Karsten, A. M., & Carr, J. E. (2009). The Effects of Differential Reinforcement of Unprompted Responding on the Skill Acquisition of Children With Autism. *Journal of Applied Behavior Analysis,* **42,** 327—334.

Keilitz, I., Tucker, D. J., & Horner R. D. (1973). Increasing Mentally Retarded Adolescents' Verbalizations About Current Events. Journal of Applied Behavior Analysis, **6,** 621—630.

Keller, F. S. (1968). "Goodbye teacher...". *Journal of Applied Behavior Analysis*, **1,** 79—89.

Kennedy, C. H. (1994). Manipulating Antecedent Conditions to Alter the Stimulus Control of Problem Behavior. *Journal of Applied Behavior Analysis,* **27,** 161—170.

Kennedy, C. H., Itkonen, T., & Lindquist, K. (1995). Comparing Interspersed Requests and Social Comments as Antecedents for Increasing Student Compliance. *Journal of Applied Behavior Analysis,* **28,** 97—98.

Killeen, P. R., Posadas-Sanchez, D., Johansen, E. B., & Thrailkill, E. A. (2009). Progressive Ration Schedules of Reinforcement. *J Exp Psychol Anim Behav Process*, **35,** 35–50. doi:10.1037/a0012497.

Killu, K., Sainato, D. M., Davis, C. A., Ospelt, H., & Paul, J. N. (1998). Effects of High-Probability Request Sequences on Preschoolers' Compliance and Disruptive Behavior. *Journal of Behavioral Education,* **8,** 347—368.

Klatt, K. P., & Morris, E. K. (2001). The Premack Principle, Response Deprivation, and Establishing Operations. *The Behavior Analyst.* **24,** 173—180.

Koegel, L. K., Singh, A. K., & Koegel, R. L. (2010). Improving Motivation for Academics in Children With Autism. *Journal of Autism Developmental Disorders. 2010 September;* **40,** 1057—1066. Published online 2010 March 10. doi: 10.1007/s10803-010-0962-6.

Konarski, E. A. Jr., Johnson, M. R., Crowell, C. R., & Whitman, T. L. (1980). Response Deprivation and Reinforcement in Applied Settings: A Preliminary Analysis. *Journal of Applied Behavior Analysis,* **13,** 595—609.

Krageloh, C. U., Elliffe, D. M., & Davison, M. (2006). Contingency Discriminability and Peak Shift in Concurrent Schedules. *Journal of the Experimental Analysis of Behavior,* **86,** 11—30.

Kubina, R. M., & Yurich, K. K. L (2012). *The Precision Teaching Book.* Lemont, PA: Greatness Achieved.

Lattal, K. A., & Neef, N. A. (1996). Recent Reinforcement-Schedule Research and Applied Behavior Analysis. *Journal of Applied Behavior Analysis,* **29,** 213—230.

Lavie, T., & Sturmey, P. (2002). Training Staff To Conduct A Paired-Stimulus Preference Assessment. *Journal of Applied Behavior Analysis,* **35,** 209—211.

Lazar, R. M., Davis-Lang, D., & Sanchez, L. (1984). The Formation of Visual Stimulus Equivalences in Children. *Journal of the Experimental Analysis of Behavior,* **41,** 251—266.

Leaf, J. B., Oppenheim-Leaf, M. L., Dotson, W. H., Johnson, V. A., Courtemanche, A. B., Sheldon, J. B., & Sherman, J. A. (2011). Effects of N0-No Prompting on Teaching Expressive Labeling of Facial Expressions to Children with and without a Pervasive Developmental Disorder. *Education and Training in Autism and Developmental Disabilities,* **46,** 186—203.

Leaf, J. B., Sheldon, J. B., & Sherman, J. A. (2010). Comparison of Simultaneous Prompting and No-No Prompting in Two-Choice Discrimination Learning With Children With Autism. *Journal of Applied Behavior Analysis,* **43,** 215—228.

Leaf, R., & McEachin, J., Editors. (1999). *A Work in Progress, Behavior Management Strategies and a Curriculum for Intensive Behavioral Treatment of Autism.* New York, NY: DRL Books, Inc.

Leaf, R., McEachin, J., & Taubman, M. (2008) *Sense and Nonsense in the Behavioral Treatment of Autism, It Has To Be Said.* New York, NY: DRL Books Inc.

LeBlanc, L. A., Esch, J., Sidener, T. M., & Firth, A. M. (2006). Behavioral Language Interventions for Children With Autism: Comparing Applied Behavior and Naturalistic Teaching Approaches. *The Analysis of Verbal Behavior,* **22,** 49—60.

LeBlanc, L. A., Gravina, N., & Carr, J. E. (2009) Training Issues Unique to Autism Spectrum Disorders. In J. L. Matson (ed.), Applied Behavior Analysis for Children with Autism Spectrum Disorders. New York, NY: Springer-Verlag, LLC.

LeLaurin, K., & Risley, T. R. (1972). The Organization of Day-Care Environments: "Zone" Versus "Man-To-Man" Staff Assignments. *Journal of Applied Behavior Analysis,* **5,** 225—232.

Libby, M., Weiss, J. S., Bancroft, S., & Ahearn W. (2008). A Comparison of Most-to-Least and Least-to-Most Prompting on the Acquisition of Solitary Play Skills. *Behavioral Analysis in Practice,* **1,** 37—43.

Lindsley, O. R. (1996). Is Fluency Free-Operant Response-Response Chaining? *The Behavior Analyst,* **19,** 211—224.

Lionello-DeNolf, K. M., Dube, W., & McIlvane, W. (2010). Evaluation of Resistance to Change Under Different Disrupter Conditions in Children with Autism and Severe Intellectual Disability. *Journal of the Experimental Analysis of Behavior,* **93,** 369—383.

Lovaas, O. I. (1981). *Teaching Developmentally Disabled Children, The ME Book.* Austin, TX: PRO-ED, Inc.

Lovaas, O. I. (1993). The Development of a Treatment-Research Project for Developmentally Disabled and Autistic Children. *Journal of Applied Behavior Analysis,* **26,** 617—630.

Lovaas, O. I. (1987). Behavioral treatment and normal educational and intellectual functioning in young autistic children. *Journal of Consulting and Clinical Psychology*, **55,** 3-9.

Love, J. R., Carr, J. E., Almason, S. M, & Petursdottir, A. I. (2009). Early and Intensive Behavioral Intervention for Autism: A Survey of Clinical Practices. *Research in Autism Spectrum Disorders,* **3,** 421—428.

Luckevich, D. (2008). Verbal Behavior Targets – A Tool to Teach Mands, Tacts and Intraverbals. New York, NY: DRL Books.

Ludvig, E. A., Conover, K., & Shizgal, P. (2007). The Effects of Reinforcer Magnitude on Timing in Rats. *Journal of the Experimental Analysis of Behavior,* **87,** 201—218.

Luiselli, J. K. (2006). *Antecedent Assessment & Intervention.* Baltimore, Maryland: Paul H. Brookes Publishing Co.

Maag, J. W., Reid, R., & DiGangi, S. A. (1993). Differential Effects of Self-Monitoring Attention, Accuracy, and Productivity. *Journal of Applied Behavior Analysis,* **26,** 329—344.

Mace, F. C. (1994). Basic Research Needed for Stimulating the Development of Behavioral Technologies. *Journal of the Experimental Analysis of Behavior,* **61,** 529-550.

Mace, F. C., & Belfiore, P. (1990). Behavioral Momentum in the Treatment of Escape-Motivated Stereotypy. *Journal of Applied Behavior Analysis,* **23,** 507—514.

Mace, F. C., Hock, M. L., Lalli, J. S., West, B. J., Belfiore, P., Pinter, E., & Brown, D. K. (1988). Behavioral Momentum in the Treatment of Noncompliance. *Journal of Applied Behavior Analysis,* **21,** 123—141.

Mace, F. C., Lalli, J. S., Shea, M. C., & Nevin, J. A. (1992). Behavioral Momentum in College Basketball. *Journal of Applied Behavior Analysis,* **25,** 657—663.

Mace, F. C., Mauro, B. C., Boyajian, A. E., & Eckert, T. L. (1997). Effects of Reinforcer Quality on Behavioral Momentum: Coordinated Applied and Basic Research. *Journal of Applied Behavior Analysis,* **30,** 1—20.

Mace, F. Charles. (1996). In Pursuit of General Behavioral Relations. *Journal of Applied Behavior Analysis,* **29,** 557-563.

Mager, R. F. (1997). *Measuring Instructional Results or Got a Match? How to find out if your instructional objectives have been achieved.* Atlanta, GA: CEP Press (The Center for Effective Performance, Inc.)

Martens, B. K., Lochner, D. G., & Kelly, S. Q. (1992). The Effects of Variable-Interval Reinforcement on Academic Engagement: A Demonstration of Matching Theory. *Journal of Applied Behavior Analysis,* **25,** 143—151.

Matson, J. L., Benavidez, D. A., Compton, L. S., Paclawskyj, T., & Baglio, C. (1996). Behavioral treatment of autistic persons: A review of research from 1980 to the present. Research in Developmental Disabilities, **17,** 433-465.

Maurice, C. (1993). *Let Me Hear Your Voice, A Family's Triumph Over Autism.* New York, NY: Ballantine Books, a Division of Random House, Inc.

McClannahan, L. E., & Krantz, P. J. (1993). On Systems Analysis in Autism Intervention Programs. *Journal of Applied Behavior Analysis,* **26,** 589—596.

McIlvane, W. J., Kledaras, J. B., Munson, L. C., King, K. A., De Rose, J. C., & Stoddard, L. T. (1987). Controlling Relations in Conditional Discrimination and Matching by Exclusion. *Journal of the Experimental Analysis of Behavior,* **48,** 187—208.

McIntyre, L. L., Gresham, F. M., DiGennaro, F. D., & Reed, Derek D. (2007). Treatment Integrity of School-Based Interventions with Children in the Journal of Applied Behavior Analysis 1991-2005. *Journal of Applied Behavior Analysis,* **40,** 659—672.

McLean, A. P., & Blampied, N. M. (1995). Resistance to Reinforcement Change in Multiple and Concurrent Schedules Assessed in Transition and at a Steady State. *Journal of the Experimental Analysis of Behavior,* **63,** 1—17.

McReynolds, L. V. (1969). Application Of Timeout From Positive Reinforcement For Increasing The Efficiency Of Speech Training. *Journal of Applied Behavior Analysis,* **2,** 199—205.

Moore, R. & Goldiamond, I. (1964). Errorless Establishment of a Visual Discrimination Using Fading Procedures. *Journal of the Experimental Analysis of Behavior.* **7,** 269—272.

Mosk, M. D., & Bucher, B. (1984). Prompting and Stimulus Shaping Procedures for Teaching Visual-Motor Skills to Retarded Children. *Journal of Applied Behavior Analysis,* **17,** 23—34.

Murphy, C., Barnes-Holmes, D., & Barnes-Holmes, Y. (2005). Derived Manding In Children With Autism: Synthesizing Skinner's Verbal Behavior With Rational Frame Theory. *Journal of Applied Behavior Analysis,* **38,** 445—462.

Najdowski, A. C., Chilingaryan, V., Bergstrom, R., Granpeesheh, D., Balasanyan, S., Aguilar, B., & Tarbox, J. (2009). Comparison of Data-Collection Methods in a Behavioral Intervention Program for Children with Pervasive Developmental Disorders: A Replication. *Journal of Applied Behavior Analysis,* **42,** 827—832.

Narayan, J. S., Heward, W. L., Gardner, R. III, Courson, F. H., & Omness, C. K. (1990). Using Response Cards to Increase Student Participation in an Elementary Classroom. *Journal of Applied Behavior Analysis,* **23,** 483—490.

Neef, N. A., Iwata, B. A., & Page, T. J. (1980). The Effects of Interspersal Training Versus High-Density Reinforcement on Spelling Acquisition and Retention. *Journal of Applied Behavior Analysis,* **13,** 153—158.

Nevin, J. A. (1992). An Integrative Model for the Study of Behavioral Momentum. *Journal of the Experimental Analysis of Behavior,* **57,** 301—316.

Nevin, J. A. (1995). Behavioral Economics and Behavioral Momentum. *Journal of the Experimental Analysis of Behavior,* **64,** 385—395.

Nevin, J. A. (2008). Stimuli, Reinforcers, and Private Events. *The Behavior Analyst,* **31,** 113—126.

Nevin, J. A. (2009). Stimuli, Reinforcers and the Persistence of Behavior. *J Exp Psychol Anim Behav Process,* **35,** 35—50.

Nevin, J. A., Grace, R. C., Holland, S., & McLean, A. P. (2001). Variable-Ratio Versus Variable-Interval Schedules: Response Rate, Resistance to Change, and Preference. *Journal of the Experimental Analysis of Behavior,* **76,** 43—74.

Nevin, J. A., Mandell, C., & Atak, J. R. (1983). The Analysis of Behavioral Momentum. *Journal of the Experimental Analysis of Behavior.* **39,** 49—59.

New York State Department of Education (2001). *Autism Program Quality Indicators*, Retrieved from http://www.p12.nysed.gov/specialed/autism/apqi.htm on June 22, 2013.

New York State Department of Health Early Intervention Program (1999). Clinical Practice Guideline Quick Reference Guide: Autism/Pervasive Developmental Disorders - Assessment and Intervention for Young Children (Age 0-3 Years). Health Education Services, P.O. Box 7126, Albany, NY 12224 (1999 Publication No. 4216).

Norris, J. (1997). *Crafts for Young Children.* Monterey, CA: Evan-Moor Educational Publishers. www.evan-moor.com.

O'Brien, F., & Azrin, N. H. (1972). Developing Proper Mealtime Behaviors of the Institutionalized Retarded. *Journal of Applied Behavior Analysis,* **5**, 389—399.

O'Daly, M., Angulo, S., Gipson, C., & Fantino, E. (2006). Influence of Temporal Context on Value in the Multiple-Chains and Successive-Encounters Procedures. *Journal of the Experimental Analysis of Behavior,* **85**, 309—328.

Ollendick, T. H., Matson, J. L., Esveldt-Dawson, K., & Shapiro, E. S. (1980). Increasing Spelling Achievement: An Analysis of Treatment Procedures Utilizing An Alternating Treatments Design. *Journal of Applied Behavior Analysis*, **13**, 645—654.

Pace, G. M., Iwata, B. A., Cowdery, G. E., Andree, P.J., & McIntyre, T. (1993). Stimulus (Instructional) Fading During Extinction of Self-Injurious Escape Behavior. *Journal of Applied Behavior Analysis,* **26**, 205—212.

Paclawskyj, T. R., Matson, J. L., Rush, K. S., Smalls, Y., & Vollmer, T. R. (2001). Assessment of the Convergent Validity of the Questions About Behavioral Function Scale With Analogue Functional Analysis and the Motivation Assessment Scale. *Journal of Intellectual Disability Research*, **45**, 484—494.

Paramore, N. W., & Higbee, T. S. (2005). An Evaluation of a Brief Multiple-Stimulus Preference Assessment With Adolescents With Emotional-Behavioral Disorders In An Educational Setting. *Journal of Applied Behavior Analysis,* **38**, 399—403.

Patel, M. R. & Piazza, C. C. (2002). An Evaluation of Food Type and Texture in the Treatment of a Feeding Problem. *Journal of Applied Behavior Analysis*, **35**, 183—186.

Pennypacker, H. S., Gutierrez, A., & Lindsley, O. R. (2003). *Handbook of the Standard Celeration Chart (Deluxe Ed.).* Cambridge, MA: Cambridge Center for Behavioral Studies.

Podlesnik, C. A., & Shahan, T. A. (2009). Behavioral Momentum and Relapse of Extinguished Operant Responding. *Learn Behav.* 2009 November ; 37(4): 357—364. doi:10.3758/LB.37.4.357.

Podlesnik, C. A., & Shahan, T. A. (2009). Reinforcer Satiation and Resistance to Change of Responding Maintained by Qualitatively Different Reinforcers. *Behav Processes,* **81**, 126-132. doi: 10.1016/j.beproc.2008.12.002.

Podlesnik, C. A., Jimenez-Gomez, C., Ward, R. D., & Shahan, T. A. (2006). Resistance to Change of Responding Maintained By Unsignaled Delays to Reinforcement: A Response-Bout Analysis. *Journal of the Experimental Analysis of Behavior,* **85**, 329—347.

Podlesnik, C. A., Jimenez-Gomez, C., Ward, R. D., & Shahan, T. A. (2009). Resistance to Change and Frequency of Response-Dependent Stimuli Uncorrelated With Reinforcement. *Journal of the Experimental Analysis of Behavior,* **92,** 199-214.

Premack, D. (1959). Toward Empirical Behavioral Laws: I. Positive reinforcement. *Psychological Review,* **66,** 219—233.

Reed, D. D. & Kaplan, B. A. (2011). The Matching Law: A Tutorial for Practitioners. *Behavior Analysis in Practice,* **4,** 15—24.

Reid, D. H., & Green C. W. (2005). *Preference-Based Teaching.* Morganton, NC: Habilitative Management Consultants, Inc.

Riley-Tillman, T. C., & Burns, M. K. (2009). *Evaluating Educational Interventions, Single-Case Design for Measuring Response to Intervention.* New York, NY: The Guilford Press.

Roane, H. S., Kelley, M. E., Trosclair, N. M., & Hauer, L. S. (2004). Behavioral Momentum in Sports: A Partial Replication With Women's Basketball. *Journal of Applied Behavior Analysis,* **37,** 385—390.

Roane, H. S., Vollmer, T. R., Ringdahl, J. E., & Marcus, B. A. (1998). Evaluation of a Brief-Stimulus Preference Assessment. *Journal of Applied Behavior Analysis,* **31,** 605—620.

Rodgers, T. A., & Iwata, B. A. (1991). An Analysis of Error-Correction Procedures During Discrimination Training. *Journal of Applied Behavior Analysis,* **24,** 775-781.

Rogers, S. J., & Vismara, L. A. (2008). Evidence-Based Comprehensive Treatments for Early Autism. *NIH: J Clin Child Adolesc Psychol.,* **37,** 8—38. doi:10.1080/15374410701817808.

Rortvedt, A. K., & Miltenberger, R. G. (1994). Analysis of a High-Probability Instructional Sequence and Time-Out in the Treatment of Child Noncompliance. *Journal of Applied Behavior Analysis,* **27,** 327—330.

Ross, M. (1995). *Sandbox Scientist, Real Science Activities for Little Kids.* Chicago, IL: Chicago Review Press, Inc.

Roxburgh, C. A., & Carbone, V. J. (2013). The Effect of Varying Teacher Presentation Rates on Responding During Discrete Trial Training for Two Children With Autism. *Behavior Modification, DOI:10:1177/0145445512463046 SAGE,* **XX**, 1-26.

Saunders, K. J., & Spradlin, J. E. (1993). Conditional Discrimination in Mentally Retarded Subjects: Programming Acquisition and Learning Set. *Journal of the Experimental Analysis of Behavior,* **60,** 571—585.

Saunders, R. R., Wachter, J., & Spradlin, J. E. (1988). Establishing Auditory Stimulus Control Over An Eight-Member Equivalence Class Via Conditional Discrimination Procedures. *Journal of the Experimental Analysis of Behavior,* **49,** 95—115.

Schuster, J. W., Gast, D. L., Wolery, M. & Guiltinan, S. (1988). The Effectiveness of a Constant Time-Delay Procedure to Teach Chained Responses to Adolescents With Mental Retardation. *Journal of Applied Behavior Analysis,* **21,** 169—178.

Shahan, T. A. & Podlesnik, C. A. (2008). Quantitative Analyses of Observing and Attending. *Behavioral Processes,* **78**, 145-157.

Shahan, T. A. (2010). Conditioned Reinforcement and Response Strength. *Journal of the Experimental Analysis of Behavior,* **93**, 269—289.

Shahan, T. A., & Podlesnik, C. A. (2008). Conditioned Reinforcement Value and Resistance to Change. *Journal of the Experimental Analysis of Behavior,* **89**, 263—298.

Sidman, M. (1989). *Coercion And Its Fallout.* Boston, MA: Authors Cooperative, Inc., Publishers.

Sidman, M. & Stoddard, L. T. (1966). Programming Perception and Learning for Retarded Children. In N.R. Ellis (ed.), *International Review of Research in Mental Retardation.* Vol. **2**, 151-208. New York: Academic Press.

Sidman, M., & Stoddard, L. T. (1967). The Effectiveness of Fading in Programming a Simultaneous Form of Discrimination for Retarded Children. *Journal of the Experimental Analysis of Behavior,* **10**, 3—15.

Skinner, B. F. (1938). *The Behavior of Organisms: An Experimental Analysis.* Cambridge, MA: B.F. Skinner Foundation.

Skinner, B. F. (1992). *Verbal Behavior.* Acton, MA: Copley Publishing Group.

Skinner, B. F. (1968). *The Technology of Teaching.* Acton, MA: Copley Publishing Group.

St. Peter Pipkin, C., & Vollmer, T. R. (2009). Applied Implications of Reinforcement History Effects. *Journal of Applied Behavior Analysis,* **42**, 83—103.

Stahmer, A. C., Collings, N. M., & Palinkas, L. A. (2005). Early Intervention Practices for Children with Autism. *NIH Public Access: Focus Autism Other Developmental Disabilities,* **20**, 66—79.

Stella, M. E., & Etzel, B. (1983). Effects of Criterion-Level Probing on Demonstrating Newly Acquired Discriminative Behavior. *Journal of the Experimental Analysis of Behavior,* **39**, 479-498.

Stevens, K. B., Blackhurst, E., & Slaton D. B. (1991). Teaching Memorized Spelling With A Microcomputer: Time Delay and Computer-Assisted Instruction. *Journal of Applied Behavior Analysis,* **24**, 153—160.

Stoddard, L. T., & Sidman, M. (1967). The Effects of Errors on Children's Performance on a Circle-Ellipse Discrimination. *Journal of the Experimental Analysis of Behavior,* **10**, 261-270.

Stoddard, L. T., & Sidman, M. (1971). The Removal and Restoration of Stimulus Control. *Journal of the Experimental Analysis of Behavior,* **16**, 143—154.

Stokes, T. F., & Baer, D. M. (1977). An Implicit Technology of Generalization. *Journal of Applied Behavior Analysis,* **10**, 349—367.

Stromer, R., & Mackay, H. A. (1992). Spelling and Emergent Picture-Printed Word Relations Established With Delayed Identity Matching to Complex Samples. *Journal of Applied Behavior Analysis,* **25**, 893—904.

Stromer, R., Mackay, H. A., Howell, S. R., & McVay, A. A., Flusser, D. (1996). Teaching Computer-Based Spelling to Individuals With Developmental And Hearing Disabilities: Transfer of Stimulus Control To Writing Tasks. *Journal of Applied Behavior Analysis,* **29**, 25—42.

Sweeney-Kerwin, E. J., Carbone, V. J., O'Brien, L., Zecchin, G., & Janecky, M. N. Carbone Clinic. (2007). Transferring Control of the Mand to the Motivating Operation in Children With Autism. *The Analysis of Verbal Behavior,* **23**, 89—102.

Taylor, B. A., & Hock, H. (2008). Teaching Children With Autism To Respond To And Initiate Bids For Joint Attention. *Journal of Applied Behavior Analysis,* **41**, 377—391.

Terrace H. S. (1963). Errorless Transfer of a Discrimination Across Two Continua. *Journal of the Experimental Analysis of Behavior.* **6**, 223—232.

Terrace, H. S. (1963). Discrimination Learning With and Without "Errors". *Journal of the Experimental Analysis of Behavior.* **6**, 1—27.

Terrace, H. S., (1974). On the Nature of Non-Responding in Discrimination Learning With and Without Errors. *Journal of the Experimental Analysis of Behavior,* **22**, 151—159.

Touchette, P. E. (1968). The Effects of Graduated Stimulus Change on the Acquisition of a Simple Discrimination in Severely Retarded Boys. *Journal of the Experimental Analysis of Behavior,* **11**, 39—48.

Touchette, P. E. (1971). Transfer of stimulus control: measuring the moment of transfer. *Journal of the Experimental Analysis of Behavior.* **15**, 347—354.

Touchette, P. E., & Howard, J. S. (1984). Errorless Learning: Reinforcement Contingencies and Stimulus Control Transfer In Delayed Prompting. *Journal of Applied Behavior Analysis,* **17**, 175—188.

Turan, M. T., Croteau, N., & Moroz, L. (2010). Evidence-based error correction procedures. Presentation to the Association for Behavior Analysis International, San Antonio, TX, May, 2010.

Van Houten, R., & Rolider, A. (1989). An Analysis of Several Variables Influencing the Efficacy of Flash Card Instruction. *Journal of Applied Behavior Analysis,* **22**, 111—118.

VanDerHeyden, A. M., & Burns, M. K. (2010). *Essentials of Response to Intervention.* Hoboken, New Jersey: John Wiley & Sons, Inc.

Vismara, L. A., & Rogers, S. J. (2008). The Early Start Denver Model: A Case Study of an Innovative Practice. *Journal of Early Intervention,* **31**, 91—108.

Vladescu, J. C., & Kodak, T. (2010). A Review of Recent Studies on Differential Reinforcement During Skill Acquisition in Early Intervention. *Journal of Applied Behavior Analysis,* **43**, 351—355.

Vladescu, J. C., & Kodak, T. (2010). A Review of Recent Studies on Differential Reinforcement During Skill Acquisition in Early Intervention. *Journal of Applied Behavior Analysis,* **43**, 351—355.

Volkert, V. M., Lerman, D. C., Trosclair, N., Addison, L., & Kodak, T. (2008). An Exploratory Analysis of Task-Interspersal Procedures While Teaching Object Labels to Children With Autism. *Journal of Applied Behavior Analysis,* **41**, 335—350.

Wacker, D., Berg, W., McMahon, C., Templeman, M., McKinney, J., Swarts. V., Visser, M.,& Marquardt, P. (1988). An Evaluation of Labeling-Then-Doing With Moderately Handicapped Persons: Acquisition and Generalization With Complex Tasks. *Journal of Applied Behavior Analysis,* **4,** 369—380.

Ward, R. D., Johnson, R. N., & Odum, A. L. (2009). Effects of Prefeeding, Extinction, and Distraction During Sample and Comparison Presentation on Sensitivity to Reinforcer Frequency in Matching to Sample. NIH Behav Processes, **81**, 65—73.

Williams, J. L. (1973). *Operant Learning: Procedures For Changing Behavior.* Monterey, CA: Brooks/Cole Publishing Company.

Worsdell, A. S., Iwata, B. A., Dozier, C. L., Johnson, A. D., Neidert, P. L., & Thomason, J. L. (2005). Analysis of Response Repetition as an Error-Correction Strategy During Sight-Word Reading. *Journal of Applied Behavioral Analysis,* **38,** 511—527.

Ysseldyke, J. E., Thurlow, M., Graden, J., Wesson, C., Algozzine, B., & Deno, S. (1983). Generalizations from five years of research on assessment and decision making: The University of Minnesota Institute. *Exceptional Education Quarterly,* **4**, 75—93.

Zarcone, J. R., Iwata, B. A., Hughes, C. E., & Vollmer, T. R. (1993). Momentum Versus Extinction Effects in the Treatment of Self-Injurious Escape Behavior. *Journal of Applied Behavior Analysis,* **26**, 135—136.

Zarcone, J. R., Iwata, B. A., Mazaleski, J. L., & Smith, R. G. (1994). Momentum and Extinction Effects on Self-Injurious Escape Behavior and Noncompliance. *Journal of Applied Behavior Analysis,* **27**, 649—658.